THE

WORKS

Of the LEARNED

BENJAMIN WHICHCOTE, D. D.

Rector of St. LAWRENCE JEWRY,
LONDON.

VOLUME I.

ABERDEEN:

Printed by J. CHALMERS, for ALBᵣᵣⁱ
THOMSON Bookseller, and sold at
the *Broadgate.*

MDCCLI.

Some Account of the

L I F E

O F

Dr. Benjamin Whichcote.

DR. *BENJAMIN WHICHCOTE* was
descended of an antient and good family, and
was the sixth son of his father, being born in *Shrop-
shire*, *March* the 11th 1609. He was educated at
Emanuel College, in the university, where he was
chosen fellow, and was an excellent tutor and instructor of youth, and bred up many persons of quality, and others who afterwards proved useful and e-
minent ; as many perhaps as any tutor of his time.
About the age of four or five and thirty, he was made
provost of *King's College*, where he was a most vigi-
lant and prudent governor, a great encourager of
learning and good order ; and by his careful and
wise management of the estate of the college,
brought it in to a very flourishing condition, and left
it so. " It cannot, says Dr. *Tillotson*, be denied (nor
" am I much concerned to dissemble it) that here
" he possessed another man's place, who by the i-
" niquity of the times was wrongfully ejected.; I
" mean Dr. *Collins*, the famous and learned divini-
" ty-professor ot that university ; during whose life
" (and he lived many years after) by the free con-
" sent of the college there were two shares out of
" the common dividend allotted to the provost, one
" whereof was constantly paid to Dr. *Collins*, as if
" he had been still provost. To this Dr. *Whichcote*

" I did

" did not only give his confent (without which the
" thing could not have been done) but was very for-
" ward for the doing of it, though hereby he did
" not only confiderably leffen his own profit, but
" likewife incur no fmall cenfure and hazard as the
" times then were. And left this had not been kind-
" nefs enough to that worthy perfon, whofe place
" he poffeffed, in his laft will, he left his fon, Sir
" *John Collins*, a legacy of one hundred pounds.
" And as he was not wanting either in refpect or
" real kindnefs to the rightful owner ; fo neither
" did he ftoop to do any thing unworthy, to obtain
" that place, for he never took the covenant. And
" not only fo, but, by the particular friendfhip and
" intereft which he had in fome of the chief vifi-.
" tors, he prevailed to have the greateft part of the
" fellows of that college exempted from that im-
" pofition, and preferved them in their places by
" that means. And to the fellows that were ejec-
" ted by the vifitors, he likewife freely confented,
" that their full dividend for that year fhould be
" paid them ; even after they were ejected. Among
" thefe was the reverend and ingenious Dr. *Charles*
" *Mafon*, upon whom, after he was ejected, the col-
" lege did confer a good living which then fell in
" their gift, with the confent of the provoft, who
" knowing him to be a worthy man, was contented
" to run the hazard of the difpleafure of thofe times.
" So that I hope none will be hard upon him, that
" he was contented upon fuch terms to be in a ca-
" pacity to do good in bad times." Befides his care
of the college, he had a very great and good influence upon the univerfity in general. Every Sunday
in the afternoon, for almoft twenty years together,
he preached in *Trinity Church*, where he had a great
number, not only of the young fcholars, but of thofe
of greater ftanding and beft repute for learning in
the

the univerſity, his conſtant and attentive auditors ;
and in thoſe wild and unſettled times contributed
more to the forming of the ſtudents of that univerſity to a ſober ſenſe of religion, than any man in
that age. In 1658 he wrote a copy of Latin verſes
upon the death of *Oliver Cromwell*. It is printed in
*muſarum Cantabrigienſium luctus & gratulatio : ille in
funere Oliveri Angliæ Scotiæ & Hiberniæ protectoris ;
hæc de Richardi ſucceſſione feliciſſimâ ad eundem. Cambridge*, 1658, in 4to. Dr. *Whichcote*'s verſes are as
follow.

Non male mutati mores & lenior ætas ;
Olim vexârunt animas formidine pœnæ
Mentes torſerunt caupones relligionis,
Quos Chriſtus ducit, Romanus apoſtata cogit :
Flectit amore Deus, ſed papa timore coercet :
Inſtruit ille animum, & placido lenimine mentem
Suaviter emollit, meroque favore relaxat ;
Deſtruit hic corpus miſerum, carnemque flagellis
Affligit, propriis quo poſſit ſubdere votis.
Quæ prohibent removet, raptuſque furore gehennæ
Allegans cœlos, ad Tartara dira remittit.
Vis, dolus & fraudes ſunt inſtrumenta maligni
Paſtoris, ſatanæque artes, quas pura repellit
Relligio, nec cœleſtes ſinit eſſe ſcœleſtos.
Magna fides penetrat cor, ſpiritualibus armis
Aggreditur victrix, totum peragratque per orbem,
Plena ſui ſubnixa Deo, carnalia ſpernens,
Sobrius auſculta veterum quid pagina narrat :
Fata trahunt homines cruciatibus ingenioſos,
Decumbunt tremuli non ſiccâ morte tyranni,
Arte ſua pereant ſemper (juſtiſſima lex eſt)
Artifices nequam, quos inclementia pulſat.
At pater hic patriæ, non eſt tormenta minatus,
Annos uſque expirat, et alta in pace quieſcit.
Filius aſcendit ſimilis gratuſque Britannis,

Quæ-

Quæque Deum fapiunt fcit pectora flectere lente.
Nam ratione animum generofum ducere fuave eft ;
At mentem ingenuam trahere ingratum atque moleftum.

After he left *Cambridge*, he came to *London*, and
was chofen minifter of *Black Friars*, where he continued till the fire of *London* in 1665, and then reti-
red to a donative which he had at *Milton* near *Cambridge*, where he preached conftantly, and relieved
the poor, and had their children taught to read at
his own charge, and made up differences among the
neighbours. Here he ftaid till the promotion of
Dr. *John Wilkins* to the bifhoprick of *Chefter* in
1668, when he was by his intereft and recommendation, prefented to the rectory of St. *Laurence Jewry*. But during the building of that church, upon
invitation of the court of Aldermen, in the mayora-
lity of Sir *William Turner*, he preached before that
honourable auditory at *Guild-hall Chapel* every
Sunday in the afternoon with great acceptance and
approbation, for about the fpace of feven years.
When his church was built, he beftowed his pains
there twice a week, where he had the general love
and refpect of his parifh, and a very confiderable
and judicious auditory, though not very numerous,
by reafon of the weaknefs of his voice in his declin-
ing age. A little before *Eafter* in the year 1683,
he went down to *Cambridge*, whereupon taking a
great cold, he fell into a diftemper, which in a few
days put a period to his life. He died with uncom-
mon fentiments of piety and devotion. He expreffed great diflike of the principles of feparation, and
faid, that he was the more defirous to receive the
facrament, that he might declare his full commu-
nion with the church of Chrift all the world over.
He difclaimed popery, and as things of near affinity with it, or rather parts of it, all fuperftition and
ufur-

usurpation upon the consciences of men. He died in the house of his ancient and learned friend Dr. *Cudworth*, master of *Chrift's College*, in *May* 1683, and was interred in the church of St. *Laurence Jewry*, his funeral sermon being preached by Dr. *John Tillotson*, in which his character is drawn with great justice. "I shall not, says he, insist upon his exem-
"plary piety and devotion towards God, of which his
"whole life was one continued testimony. Nor will
"I praise his profound learning, for which he was
"justly had in so great reputation. The moral im-
"provements of his mind, a godlike temper and dif-
"pofition, (as he was wont to call it) he chiefly va-
"lued and aspired after; that universal charity and
"goodness, which he did continually preach and
"practise. His conversation was exceeding kind and
"affable, grave and winning, prudent and profita-
"ble. He was slow to declare his judgment and mo-
"dest in delivering it. Never passionate, never pe-
"remptory : so far from imposing upon others that
"he was rather apt to yield. And though he had a
"most profound and well poised judgment, yet he
"was of all men I ever knew, the most patient to
"hear others differ from him, and the most easy to
"be convinced when good reason was offered ;
"and which is seldom seen, more apt to be favour-
"able to another man's reason than his own. Studi-
"ous and inquisitive men commonly at such an age
"(at forty or fifty at the utmost) have fixed and
"settled their judgments in most points, and as it
"were, made their last understanding ; supposing
"that they have thought, or read, or heard, what
"can be said on all sides of things, and after that they
"grow positive, and impatient of contradiction,
"thinking it a disparagement to them to alter their
"judgment. But our deceased friend was so wise,
"as to be willing to learn to the last, knowing that
"no

" no man can grow wifer without fome change of
" his mind, without gaining fome knowledge which
" he had not, or correcting fome error, which he
" had before. He had attained fo perfect a mafte-
" ry of his paffions, that for the latter and greateft
" part of his life he was hardly ever feen to be
" tranfported with anger, and as he was extremely
" careful not to provoke any man, fo not to be pro-
" voked by any ; ufing to fay, if I provoke a man,
" he is the worfe for my company ; and if I fuffer
" myfelf to be provoked by him I fhall be the worfe
" for his. He very feldom reproved any perfon in
" company otherwife than by filence or fome fign
" of uneafinefs, or fome very foft and gentle word ;
" which yet from the refpect men generally bore
" to him, did often prove effectual. For he under-
" ftood human nature very well, and how to apply
" himfelf to it in the moft eafy and effectual ways.
" He was a great encourager and kind director of
" young divines, and one of the moft candid hear-
" ers of fermons, I think, that ever was ; fo that
" though all men did mightily reverence his judg-
" ment, yet no man had reafon to fear his cenfure.
" He never fpake well of himfelf, nor ill of others,
" making good that faying of *Panfa* in *Tully, Ne-*
" *minem alterius, qui fuæ confideret virtuti, invidere ;*
" that no man is apt to envy the worth and vir-
" tues of another, that hath any of his own to truft
" to. In a word, he had all thofe virtues, and in a
" high degree, which an excellent temper, great
" condefcenfion, long care and watchfulnefs over
" himfelf, together with the affiftance of God's
" grace (which he continually implored and migh-
" tily relied upon) are apt to produce. Particular-
" ly he excelled in the virtues of converfation, hu-
" manity and gentlenefs, and humility, a prudent
" and peaceable, and reconciling temper. As he
                                                " had

" had a plentiful estate, so he was of a very chari-
" table disposition : which yet was not so well
" known to many, because in the disposal of his
" charity, he very much affected secrecy. He fre-
" quently bestowed his alms on poor housekeepers,
" disabled by age or sickness to support themselves,
" thinking those to be the most proper objects of it.
" He was rather frugal in expence upon himself,
" that so he might have wherewithal to relieve the
" necessities of others. And not only charitable in
" his life, but in a very beautiful manner at his
" death, bequeathing in pious and charitable lega-
" cies to the value of a thousand pounds : to the
" library of the university of *Cambridge* fifty pounds,
" and of *King's* college, one hundred pounds, and of
" *Emanuel College*, twenty pounds, to which college
" he had been a considerable benefactor before, hav-
" ing founded three several scholarships there to the
" value of a thousand pounds, out of a charity with
" the disposal whereof he was entrusted, and which
" not without great difficulty and pains he at last
" received. To the poor of the several places where
" his estate lay, and where he had been minister,
" he gave above one hundred pounds. Among those
" who had been his servants, or who were so at his
" death, he disposed in annuities and legacies in mo-
" ney, to the value of above three hundred pounds.
" To other charitable uses, and among his poor
" relations, above three hundred pounds. To eve-
" ry one of his tennants, he left a legacy according
" to the proportion of the estate they held, by way
" of remembrance of him ; and to one of them,
" who was gone much behind, he remitted in his
" will seventy pounds. And as became his great
" goodness he was ever a remarkably kind landlord,
" forgiving his tennants, and always making abate-
" ments to them for hard years, or any other acci-
                                        " dental

" dental losses that happened to them. He made
" likewise a wise provision in his will to prevent law-
" suits among legatees, by appointing two or three
" persons of the greatest prudence and authority a-
" mong his relations, final arbitrators of all diffe-
" rences that should arise."

His select sermons were printed at *London*, 1698, in 8vo, with a preface by the late *Earl of Shaftsbury*, author of the CHARACTERISTICKS, which collection was since republished at *Edinburgh*, in the year 1742 in 12mo, with an excellent recommendatory epistle, by the revd. and learned Dr. *William Wishart* principal of the college of *Edinburgh*. Four other volumes of his discourses were published by Dr. *John Jeffery*, Archdeacon of *Norwich*, at *London*, 1702, in 8vo.

We shall conclude this short account of our author with the character which bishop *Burnet*, that excellent prelate, gives of him. Speaking of those divines who were generally called *Latitudinarians*, he says, " Dr. *Whichcote* was a man of a rare tem-
" per, very mild and obliging. He had great credit
" with some that had been eminent in the late times
" but made all the use he could of it, to protect
" good men of all persuasions. He was much for
" liberty of conscience. And being disgusted with
" the dry systematical way of those times, he studied
" to raise those who conversed with him, to a noble
" set of thoughts, and to consider religion as a seed
" of a DEIFORM nature : (to use one of his own
" phrases) in order to this, he set young students,
" much on reading the ancient philosophers, chiefly
" *Plato*, *Tully* and *Plotin*; and on considering the
" christian religion, as a doctrine sent from God,
" both to elevate and sweeten human nature, in
" which he was a great example, as well as a wise
" and kind instructor."

CON-

CONTENTS

VOL. I.

CONTENTS.

DIS-

DISCOURSE I.

The SHORTNESS of HUMAN CHARITY.

JONAH iv. 1, 2.

But it displeased Jonah exceedingly, and he was very angry. And he prayed unto the Lord, and said, I pray thee, O Lord, was not this my saying, when I was yet in my country? therefore, I fled before unto Tarshish; for I knew that thou art a gracious God, and merciful, slow to anger, and of great kindness, and repentest thee of the evil.

'**B**UT it displeased Jonah *exceedingly, and he was very angry.* And what is the matter, that a good man, an extraordinary person, a prophet, yea, of all the prophets, a type of Christ, in whom our Saviour doth instance: that he is so much offended, and that he is so very angry? We may imagine, doubtless, some very great cause, something mightily amiss, and out of order: no less certainly, than one of these three things.

1. Certainly, here is some great *dishonour to God.* Here is some, sure, that declare for atheism, profaneness and irreligion, that hath so provoked the spirit of the good man. As we find good *Hezekiah,* he rent his clothes, and fell into a grievous passion upon *Rabshakeh's* blasphemy, and reviling the God

of

of heaven, and comparing him with idol gods. *Have any of the gods of the nations,* faith he, *delivered his land out of my hands, that the Lord should deliver Jerufalem out of my hand,* Ifa. xxxvi. 18, 19, &c.

Or certainly, here is fome uncircumcifed *Philiftine* that is rifen up to defy the hoft of *Ifrael,* which was fuch a provocation to *David,* that, upon it, he put his life into his hand, and went out againft him, as you read, 1 *Sam.* xvii. 39, 40.

Or certainly, here is fome *Baal's* worfhip maintained and applauded ; which was a provocation to *Elijah's* fpirit, that he commanded them to be taken and flain, every man of them, 1 *Kings* xviii. 40.

Or certainly, one would think that here was fuch a thing as *falfe worfhip*; which was fuch a provocation to *Mofes,* that made him throw down the tables which were in his hands, in which were writ the commandments of God, and to break them to pieces, as you find it, *Exod.* xxxii. 19. Or,

2. Some great *enormity* or *departure* from the immutable and unchangeable law of everlafting righteoufnefs, goodnefs and truth ; that law of heaven, which is according to the very nature of God himfelf. As *Nathan* reprefented to *David,* a cafe, wherein a rich man fpared his own flocks and herds, which were very many, and took the poor man's ewe-lamb, which he had nourifhed up, as you may read, 2 *Sam.* xii. 1, 2. Prodigious cruelty and unmercifulnefs ! yea, fo great unrighteoufnefs, that at the very reprefentation thereof to *David,* tho' a perfon guilty, and he himfelf reprefented

by

by this fhadow, as having highly offended God ;
yet his anger was greatly kindled againft the man,
infomuch that he faith to *Nathan, The man that hath
done this thing, fhall furely die.*

Or elfe, certainly here is fome fuch thing as the
Ifraelites meditated againft the *Benjamites,* when
they lay in wait to deftroy them, *Jofhua* ii. 2. becaufe they had fet up a new temple, and provoked
the Lord by their folly.

Or fomething like what St. *John* faw in his vifi-
on, *Rev.* xvii. 2. *A fpiritual whore, making drunk all
the potentates of the earth, with the wine of her forni-
cations ;* true caufes indeed, of indignation, and of
juft exafperation. Or,

3. If neither of thefe two, at leaft there is fome
dreadful *denunciation of judgment,* and fome terrible
threatnings, at which the very nature of man doth
ftartle and tremble, as you have our Saviour fpeaking, *Mat.* xxiv. concerning the deftruction of *Jerufalem,* that there fhould *not be one ftone left upon another, which fhould not be thrown down.*

Or, fuch commiffion as was granted to *Saul* to deftroy *Amalek,* and not to leave either man or beaft a-
live. And fo certainly one would think that the
prophet is moved by human pity and compaffion, as
Zipporah was at the circumcifion of the child, *Exod.*
iv. 25.

Or certainly, here is fuch cruelty as is practifed
upon the cities of *Ammon,* 2 *Sam.* xii. 31. where
we read, that *David brought forth the people that
were therein, and put them under faws and harrows of
iron, and axes of iron, and made them pafs through the*

A 2

brick-

brick-kiln, &c. One would not think nor imagine
lefs to be the caufe that *Jonah* was fo highly difpleafed, and greatly angry.

But here is the wonder ; nothing that is any *juft*
caufe ; indeed there is no caufe at all of any true
offence, or real provocation : 'tis a fhame to fay
what is the caufe. The good man is difpleafed
with God himfelf, and he is offended at the divine
goodnefs and compaffion, and that God hath refpect to the repentance of finners ; for fo I find it,
at the end of the foregoing chapter ; *and God faw*
their works, that they turned from their evil way, and
God repented of the evil that he had faid that he would
do unto them, and he did it not, Jonah iii. 10. And
immediately it follows, that when *Jonah* underftood
this, he was highly difpleafed and greatly angry.
But ftrange it is, that he fhould be angry at this ;
for this is a thing contrary to the fenfe of the *lower*
and *upper world.*

1. Contrary to the fenfe of the *lower world* ; for
we find that the fhepherd rejoiceth when he hath
found his loft fheep, *Luke* xv. 5. and verfe 9, the
woman rejoiceth when fhe hath found her loft piece
of filver ; and the father rejoiceth when his prodigal fon returneth home again, verfe 20.

2. Contrary to the fenfe of the *upper world* ; for
we read, that the angels of heaven, they rejoice at
the converfion and repentance of one finner, verfe
10.

But we have now found the man, of whom it is
fpoken in the gofpel, that *his eye was evil, becaufe God*
was good, Mat. xx. 15. He doth prefer his own
conceited

conceited credit and esteem, before the lives and
beings of sixscore thousand persons ; for so God
himself hath given us the number of them, verse 11.
of this chapter : and I will say *conceited credit*, because God himself hath given us to understand, that
all his denunciations against sinners are to be understood with a clause of reservation ; and he doth always except this case, *if the sinner repent*. Though
his denunciations seem to be positive and peremptory, yet they always include this condition, unless the
sinner do repent, as I will shew you by three scriptures
for the present, among many, *Jer*. xviii. 8. where
God saith thus, *That if he doth declare against a nation
or people ; if that nation or people against whom he hath
denounced evil, turn from the evil of their ways, he
will repent of the evil he thought to do unto them*; and,
Ezek. xviii. 21. *If the wicked turn from his evil way,
and set himself to observe my statutes, and do that
which is right in my sight, all his wickedness shall not
be remembred against him*. Again, *Ezek*. xxxiii. 14.
When I say to the wicked, thou shalt surely die ; *if he
turn from his wickedness, and do that which is lawful
and right, he shall not die*. Though God had said it
before, that the *wicked should surely die* : but thus he
would have it be understood, that if he forsake his i-
niquity, he *shall surely live* ; and verse 19. you have
the same words. These scriptures I have brought
you for the encouragement of men to repent, and
to leave off to sin, and to return to their duty, and
to convert to God, be their case never so forlorn
and desperate. For what can more encourage him,
than that judgment shall be suspended, and the re-

penting

penting finner received unto mercy and favour.
You fee God doth make this declaration, even after his denunciation of judgment ; if the cafe of repentance come between, then God is not bound to
proceed. And for your fatisfaction further, I leave
this notion with you. There is a mighty difference
between God's declaring himfelf in a way of *promife*
and in a way of *threatning :* if he declares by way
of promife, he is obliged to make it good, for by
this he gives a *right* to the thing promifed ; and
men may claim as good title from God's promife,
though of grace and favour ; for God is faithful,
and he will perform what he hath promifed : but if
he *threaten*, here is no right acquired ; for who will
demand of God that he will fulfill his threatning ?
But to proceed.

That which makes the wonder the greater ; *Jonah*, whom we find in this diftemper, is of all the
prophets the *type of Chrift* ; our Saviour inftanceth
in him, *There fhall be no fign given, but the fign of the
prophet* Jonah, *Mat.* xii. 40. I am fure, in this
temper and difpofition of his, he is no type of Chrift ;
for our Saviour doth declare, that the Son of man
came, *to feek and fave that which was loft*, Luke xix.
20. And he *wept over* Jerufalém, when he did but
confider the deftruction that was approaching : but
this temper of *Jonah's* admits of no apology. This
felfifhnefs that is in *Jonah*, and his preferring his
own conceited credit before the fafety of multitudes ;
I fay, this admits of no apology. You may fee it in
five particulars.

1. That

1. That nothing is more *unreasonable in it self.* Should not finite and fallible creatures, (as the best of men are) having erred and mistaken, if they return to sober judgment, right apprehensions, see their error, and disclaim what they have done amiss, humble themselves, ask God forgiveness, and submit to him, and deprecate his displeasure; should not such find mercy with infinite goodness? there is nothing more reasonable.

2. *Nothing is worse for* Jonah *himself, and the whole world besides him.* For, what should become of us all, if there were no place for repentance? and for *Jonah* himself, how shall he be pardoned for his present distemper, if God should not allow place for repentance?

3. *Nothing is more unnatural, in respect of his office;* for by his office, he was a prophet; and, was it not his work to promote repentance and reformation among sinners? and should this be without effect? But,

4. *Nothing worse can be put upon God,* than to be represented implacable and irreconcileable. Will he have God full of anger, and retain it for ever? Would he have God forget to be merciful?

5. And lastly, This would *render men hopeless and desperate in the world.* 'Tis pity, *Jonah's* notion should be true. What, no place for repentance, and repentance without effect? what, all one with the impenitent and penitent? this is the case; but this is not the first distemper that we find *Jonah* in.

For, if we look to *Jonah*, chap. 1.

1. We

1. We shall find *Jonah* in great refractoriness and disobedience ; God sends him to *Nineveh*, and he goes to *Tarshish*, Jonah i. 3.

2. We shall find him *stupid* and *senseless*, and more blockish than the idolatrous mariners ; and of them, they use to say, *None nearer death, none farther from God.* These stupid persons learned this in the storm, to apply to their gods ; and *they* came and awakened him with indignation, and said unto him, *What meanest thou, O sleeper ? arise and call upon thy God ; art thou not sensible of the danger that thou art in ?* Jonah i. 5, 6.

3. We find him in a case of desperate *insolency* ; for when the mariners found out that he was to blame, (for he could not avoid telling them) they incline to compassionate him, and rowed hard to bring the ship to land, but he bid them *throw him into the sea*, verse 12, 13. ; for we have no reason to think that this came from the greatness of his faith ; for we do not read any word of his application to God, or of his prayer, till he came into the whale's belly.

Take notice here by the way, that *Jonah* is not wrought upon by storms and tempests, but he is affected with the sense of God's preservation. 'Tis ingenuity, goodness, and kindness that works upon men, that effects their repentance, and brings them home to God ; and this is his course generally. *Despisest thou the riches of his goodness, not knowing that the goodness of God leadeth thee to repentance,* Rom. ii. 4.

But

But for all this, we find *Jonah* in a bad temper, *Jonah* iv. 9. where God asks him, *if he did well to be angry*; and he said, *I do well to be angry, even unto death.* Here you see he was refractory, peevish, and in a disingenuous temper. But

4. We find him in a state that is *unnatural, barbarous* and *inhumane*; for he desired the destruction of sixscore thousand persons, body and soul, to secure his credit, and reputation of being a true prophet; as you may see by God's reasoning with him, *Jonah* iv. 11.

5. All these his distempers are *aggravated* by his late *deliverance* in the belly of a whale.

6. He is not *overcome* by the declaration of the *reason of things*; no, not out of the mouth of God himself. For, God reasons with him by a gourd, which he had caused to come up as a shelter for him; but he caused a worm to smite it, so that it withered. But *Jonah* had pity on the gourd, and he was angry for what had happened to it; and God made advantage of this, and improved it for his information: *Hadst thou compassion on the gourd, for which thou didst not labour, but it rose up of itself in a night,* on a sudden, and a thing of no long continuance , *and should not I have compassion of such a multitude of people?* Jonah iv. 10, 14.

And *lastly*, The story leaves him without any account of *returning to himself,* and to a due temper; upon which I shall observe this; that *in high iniquities and great enormities, we should not be too forward to pass a sentence of absolution upon high and great offenders.* Not that I will deny them the *benefit* of

repentance,

repentance, but I would not have them have the credit of it in this state ; for it may prove but hurtful to the community, and contrary to the example of scripture : for so we find concerning *Solomon,* notwithstanding so great things are spoken of him before his idolatry, yet afterwards there is no mention of him ; so that we are left without any declaration of his state God-ward. And *David,* after his great sin, there is never absolute testimony given of his integrity, but with reservation. It is to the hurt of mankind, that great and enormous offenders should have the sentence of absolution passed upon them. I do not deprive any of the benefit of repentance for the safety of their soul ; but let us not talk so much of it, as to give them the credit of it ; for this would be to credit their state, which we should not do, neither do we follow the example of scripture therein.

Now, to make some *observations* upon what we have been speaking.

1. Let us learn from what we have heard of *Jonah,* to consider, in how sad and forlorn a condition we are, if God be not with us. Let every man use *Jonah* as a glass for him to see his own foulness in : and let us examine and see what hath been past, and if in some time of our life, we have not been in such a distemper as *Jonah* here was.

2. Observe how *sin multiplies,* and grows upon us, if once we fall into a distemper. Here is disobedience, and peevishness and wrathfulness, and displeasure against God ; and barbarous cruelty, and inhumanity, and casting off the bowels of compassion.

3. Take

3. Take notice from hence, of the *great danger of selfishness,* and stiffly adhering to a man's own sense. If once we relax our selves from the rules and laws of action, and then humour ourselves, see how we may be misguided.

4. Let this be for *caution* and *admonition* ; which is a very unhappy observation, That persons acquainted with religion, if once out of the way of reason and conscience, they prove rather more exorbitant than others ; as we have sad instances of it in scripture. When *David* had once broken loose, we then find him idle, and from idleness to wantonness, from wantonness to adultery, and from adultery, to murder : we also find him, 2 *Sam.* xii. 31. practising cruelty, beyond the bounds of reason, contrary to the doctrine of religion and human nature ; for had it not been enough to have subdued the *Ammonites,* but he must cause them to pass under *saws and harrows of iron, and to go through the brick-kiln* ; things which were never commanded him to do ; and a man should never prosecute revenge to the utmost. Thus we find *David* to do, after he had contracted the guilt of those former sins : and 2 *Sam.* xix. 29. we find him most rash in his judgment ; for a false accusation of *Mephibosheth,* he gives his land to his servant, and upon complaint made unto him, he saith, *Trouble me no more in this matter* ; *I have said, thou and* Ziba *divide the land.* Even so, when *Peter* had once broken loose and denied his master, he soon after adds imprecations and cursings. I do not now instance in these failings of good men, but for our advantage ; for the apostle hath told us that

all

all things that stand upon record in scripture, are *for our admonition, upon whom the ends of the world are come,* 1 Cor. x. 11. Hence we are taught what great care a man ought to take, to preserve his innocence and integrity, for these are a safeguard and protection to him ; these give him security, and preserve him in safety. A man doth defy sin at the first, but when he is out of the use of his principles, which are wont to stay and govern him, he is as a weak man without a staff. Principles of religion and conscience, they are a bar against iniquity, whereby it receives a check, a stop, and controul : but if a man discharge himself once of the reason of his mind, or the rule of conscience, we do not know how far he may miscarry. If once the principles of religion and conscience give way, and we voluntarily or negligently incur a forfeiture of our innocency and integrity, and by so doing, lose God's protection, we shall be exposed to all manner of evils ; for these are as a dam, which once being broken down, all evils will flow in upon us : for, *beginnings of sin, are like the lettings in of mighty waters,* which at the first might have been prevented, but if once it hath got over, twenty times as much will not stay it. So it is in sin ; while a man retains his innocence, there is a modesty and ingenuity upon his mind, and that will be his preservation ; but if once a man, either by gross neglect, or voluntarily doth consent to iniquity, and so betray himself, he doth incur a forfeiture of God's protection, and cast away that which is his greatest security and defence ; and this is the true account of that great impudence

and

and immodefty that many finners arrive unto. For our better fecurity, let us confider,

1. That it is much eafier to prevent, than to re-ftrain fin, and to recover a man's felf. 'Tis eafier a great deal, not to confent to fin, than to lay any limits upon one's felf.

2. Let us be very *wary* and *cautious* of approach-ing evil ; while we are upon our legs, and are ourfelves, let us be jealous and cautious of approach-ing evil.

3. Let us have no *felf-confidence* ; let us not ar-rogate to ourfelves, as if we were felf-fufficient, but know that our *fufficiency is of God,* whofe ftrength is fufficient for us in our weaknefs. And thefe are the advantages that I make of *Jonah's* diftemper.

Now to proceed. It is pity, that that fhould be true which *Jonah* would have, that a finner fhould in any ftate be uncapable of repentance, even after denunciation of judgment ; or that repentance fhould not at any time take effect ; and this *Jonah* would have had. It were a thoufand pities it fhould be fo, for it would prove the undoing of the world, and the worft news that could be brought from hea-ven unto men ; that there fhould be an incapacity of repentance in any ftate of fin whatfoever ; or that repentance, in any cafe, at any time, fhould prove fuccefslefs and ineffectual ; and yet, this is that which *Jonah* would have had. And he is a great deal the more to blame, becaufe he is wilful in his diftemper : for in the text we find, that *Jo-nah* knew before hand, that if they did repent, God was fo gracious and merciful, that he would

revoke

. 2. That we offer to God in facrifice, *prayer-mat-
ter*. Let us look to the temper of our fpirits, and
the government of our minds, and our due intention. You fee truth for the matter, may be falfe for
for the manner. He brings this for an argument,
that *God was merciful*; this was true for the matter,
but a ftrange argument for that which *Jonah* would
plead for by it. The devil fpoke truth in the fcripture fometimes, but always for ill purpofe. That
which *Jonah* would have had, would have undone
him, and all the world befides. Sometimes we wifh
and pray for our harm. Let us fubmit our prayer
to God ; 'tis fometimes better that God fhould not
anfwer us in what we pray for.

You fee upon reading thefe words, a man would
not imagine the cafe as we find it. For here we
have a perfon of eminent priviledge ; *Jonah*, who
lived before other of the prophets (the certain time
not certainly known) of all the prophets, a *type of
Chrift*. The prophet *Ifaiah* is called the evangeli-
tal prophet, for that he fpoke concerning the kingdom of Chrift very clearly : but *Jonah* had the advantage of being the type of Chrift. An extraordinary perfon, a prophet, a type of Chrift ; yet a man
exceeding difpleafed, and very angry, and that
without any caufe at all. For if you confider thefe
two things, you aggravate *Jonah*'s diftemper beyond
meafure.

1. The *perfon with whom* he is difpleafed.
2. The *caufe for which* he is difpleafed.
1. The *perfon with whom* he is difpleafed ; and
that

that is with God himſelf. He in whom all ſouls delight; he in the enjoyment of whom we have hearts-
eaſe and ſatisfaction, and whom to enjoy is happineſs and eternal life : the light of whoſe countenance
is better than life itſelf. Now *Jonah* is offended
with God himſelf.

2. The *cauſe* of his offence. He is offended with
God's goodneſs, he is offended with ſinners repentance; he is offended that repentance doth take effect. Was ever a man offended in this manner ?
behold here the infirmity of human nature ! let no
man be ſelf-confident or preſumptuous : let every
man's mind be cloathed with modeſty, and dwell in
humility. Let us all fear ourſelves, and live in the
ſenſe of our dependance upon God. What prodigious creatures we are, if we fall into diſtemper ?
how monſtrouſly may we miſunderſtand ourſelves ?
and this is not only manifeſt from the caſe of *Jonah,*
but is univerſally acknowledged. St. *James* ſpeaks
of *Elias,* that extraordinary perſon, *Jam.* v. 17. That
he was a man ſubject to like paſſions with other men.
And ſo, *Acts* xiv. 15. *Paul* and *Barnabas,* when in the
exerciſe of their commiſſion, ſo behaved themſelves,
that the people were ready to deify them : but they
acknowledged themſelves to be men of *like paſſions*
with them.

Since then all is not true reaſon that takes place
in the lives of the very beſt of us, it is to be wiſhed
that we would be no where peremptory, no where
ſelf-pleaſers, that we would not be dogmatical and
ſelf-aſſuming ; that we would not judge and cenſure
one another ; that all our paſſions would diſplay

themfelves in tendernefs and compaffion. In fo do-
ing we fhould reprefent God himfelf. Pfal. ciii. 8.
The Lord is merciful and gracious, flow to anger, &c.
Ifa. xlix. 15. *As a father pitieth his children, fo the
Lord pitieth them that fear him.*

See then that you keep out of paffion, if you would
not fhamefully mifcarry ; and if you be in a paffion,
never believe yourfelves, or be confident of any
thing you did, if not in calm reafon.   If in paffion,
review and examine ; and when calm, confider and
rectify that which you did amifs : you fee you have
reafon from the mifcarriage of *Jonah*.   'Tis ftrange
that a man fhould be angry and difpleafed with God ;
yet thus far did his paffion draw him.   Let us from
hence know how frail and fubject to infirmity we
are.   That ever it fhould come into the head of a
man to be aggrieved that there is place for repentance ! and that God fhould pardon upon repentance ! and that God fhould give over to punifh
when men repent ! one would think, we fhould be
merciful for our own fakes.   Was not *David* rafh
in judgment when *Nathan* reprefented in a parable
what he himfelf had done ? he paffed a fentence that
he would not have had executed.   That we may
not forfake our own mercies, and pafs judgment u-
pon ourfelves, let us be very cautious and deliberate, and eafy to make candid conftructions of other
mens actions.   Then how unreafonable is it to be
aggrieved at God's goodnefs, at finners repentance ?
*If a man be once out of the ufe of reafon, there is no
bounds to unreafonablenefs* ; once out of the way of
reafon, who knows what will be, or how far a man
will

will go ? how defperate a thing it is in *Jonah*, that
he would have this ftand upon record in holy fcripture, *that God did refufe to give finners repentance, and*
when they had repented, he did refufe to accept them ;
and yet this *Jonah* would have had upon record,
clean contrary to the dealings of God. For we find
when *Ahab* (who was a perfon that had fold himfelf to do wickednefs) did but repent and humble
himfelf, God promifeth, that *the evil fhould not come*
in his days ; but by *Jonah's* confent, God fhould not
give way to repentance.

But you will afk, wherefore do I blemifh the reputation of a prophet, of a type of Chrift ?

I anfwer, whatfoever is upon record in the fcripture, is for our admonition : we look upon him
now, how he acts in his diftemper, not to cry him
down, but, by his lofs, to give ourfelves advantage.

1. Let us in this inftance, fee our own weaknefs and infirmity, and be modeft and humble. Let
us not brag of our own reafon and wifdom. Let us
all know, *that we are fafe only in God's hands* ; and
that if we incur a forfeiture of God's protection, we
may extremely mifcarry ; as we may fee in this inftance of *Jonah*.

2. Let us *preferve our innocence*, and fear to fall
into paffion, beware of running into fuch heat and
diftemper of mind.

3. Take care of *felfifhnefs* and narrownefs of fpirit : the narrownefs of *Jonah's* mind, who fo much
valued his credit of being a true prophet, that the
fafety of fo many thoufands feemed nothing in his
eye ; though herein he contradicted the very nature

of

of God, and his own knowledge : for, faith he, *I
knew that thou wert gracious, &c.* And also, it was
contrary to the exprefs declarations that God had
made, that though he fhould denounce againft finners, and commiffionate a prophet to declare the
particular judgment ; yet he is not bound to bring
the judgment upon that place or perfons againft
whom he had denounced them, if the cafe of repentance interveen.

DISCOURSE II.

The PERFECTION of the MERCY of God.

JOEL ii. 13.

*For he is gracious and merciful, flow to anger, and of
great kindnefs, and repenteth him of the evil.*

ALTHOUGH I have changed my text, I
have not left my argument ; and I have done
it for this end : in *Jonah* we find the felf fame
words, but to a very unnatural ufe ; by thefe words
Jonah would juftify himfelf. I therefore purpofely
left that prophet, becaufe I would not further inquire into his diftemper ; though it is of great ufe,
that *Jonah* reports thus of God, who would not
have it fo. The advantages that I have made, are
thefe.

1. That

1. That by taking notice of the miscarriage of so eminent a person, that he should so fail and miscarry, we may thereby see the frailty of human nature; and this should teach us to be modest and humble, and to live in a daily sense of our dependence upon God. *Moses,* the meekest man upon earth, stands upon record, that he spake unadvisedly with his lips.

2. *Jonah's* distemper represents to you the danger of passion; how *Jonah* misbehaves himself to God, how injurious and uncharitable to man, when in a passion! It is not safe for any man to believe himself, or to trust himself, if in a heat. Beware then of running into heat and distemper of mind.

The *third* advantage that I make is, to recommend the spirit of the gospel; it is always to be found in a spirit of love. Our Saviour, living and dying, was always in a spirit of love; and the first martyr St. *Stephen,* he exactly writes after his copy, *Acts* vii. 60. *And he cried with a loud voice, Lord, lay not this sin to their charge.* Wherein he doth much exceed the testimony in the Old Testament, by *Zachariah,* who saith, *The Lord require it at their hands.* I cannot say, but *Zachariah's* prayer was just; but St. *Stephen's* was gracious. These things are upon record for our instruction; therefore we are to take notice of them to make us wary, lest we ourselves be overtaken; and to make us tender-spirited, out of the sense of our own fallibility.

This for a reason why I take notice of *Jonah's* misbehaviour.

I now follow this prophet, *For he is gracious and merciful* &c. B 3 When

When God paſſed by *Moſes*, he made this declaration of himſelf, *Exod.* xxxiv. 6. *The Lord, the
Lord God, merciful and gracious, long-ſuffering, abundant in goodneſs and truth,* &c. And in *Pſal.* lxxxvi.
5. *Thou Lord art good, and ready to forgive.* And in
Pſal. cxii. 4. *He is gracious, and full of compaſſion.*
In theſe places of ſcripture, you have either all theſe
words, or as much ſaid of God ; and indeed, nothing is more true of God, than that he is the *firſt
and chiefeſt good* ; his prime perfection is goodneſs,
and our trueſt notion of him is, that he is *almighty
goodneſs.*

For what I have further to ſay, I ſhall obſerve
this method.

I. I ſhall ſpeak in point of *Vindication,* and give
ſatisfaction to objections that ariſe againſt this great
truth.

II. I ſhall make *Explication* of the ſeveral phraſes
in the text.

III. Proceed to *Confirmation* of it by ſatisfactory
argument.

IV. To matter of *Caution.*

V. And laſtly, make ſome *Application.*

I. For *Vindication.* There are *three objections* to
be removed, and then the heart of man cannot object any thing againſt this repreſentation of the divine goodneſs.

1. The ſeveral *inſtances* of *ſeverity* repreſented to
us in ſcripture, and in other ſtories.

2. Some ſcriptures repreſent God very *terrible.*

3. The

3. The necessity of *justice*; for, as some imagine, it is indispensible, and of absolute necessity that sin be punished.

1. For the several *instances* of God's *severity* in the scripture, which seem contrary to this goodness and great kindness of God to man. We have the instance of the deluge, wherein all mankind (except some few) were swept away with the flood, *Gen.* vi. The instance of the seven nations which God commanded to be destroyed, *Deut.* vii. 23, 24. The *Israelites*, when brought out of *Egypt,* led up and down the wilderness, and at last consumed. *Nadab* and *Abihu*, for their inadvertency, in offering strange fire, were consumed by fire, *Lev.* x. 1. 2. *Uzzah*, in his good will, meddling with the ark without God's express command, smitten dead; 1. *Chron.* xiii. 9, 10. Five hundred of the *Beth-shemites*, that rejoiced at the return of the ark from the *Philistines*, slain suddenly for looking into it, 1. *Sam.* vi. 19. The instance of the desolation of the *Jewish nation*, Mat. xxiv. *Ananias* and *Sapphira*, who were great benefactors to the church, reserving part of what they sold to the use of the church, were punished with sudden death, *Acts* v. 1. &c. *Herod* who took the applause of the people to himself, died a most dreadful death, *Acts* xii. 23. And the dreadful destruction of *Sodom* and *Gomorrah*, Gen. xix. 24. To which I answer in several propositions.

1. It is enough to be gracious, not to be wanting in necessaries, for any ones good : and he that doth so, may abound in his courtesies as he himself pleaseth. When necessaries for our good are afforded, and by any neglected, the blame lies upon them. 2.

2. Sometimes the fins of nations and of perfons are come to their height, and God forced to punifh.

3. The judgments of God in this life are *exemplary* and *difciplinary*, Luke xiii. 3, 5. and 1. *Cor.* x, 6. 11. And better a mifchief fhould fall on particular perfons, than that a general inconvenience fhould follow.

4. God fometimes lets us feel fomething of hell, here, to prevent it hereafter. Chaftifements are exercifes of virtue not effects of vengeance *Heb.* xii. 10. 11.

5. There may be a particular account given in feveral cafes.

I will fingle out the hardeft. As to *Nadab* and *Abihu, Uzzah*, and the *Bethfhemites*, *Ananias* and *Sapphira*; to thefe, particular reafons may be given.

When *Nadab* and *Abihu* finned, the *Mofaical* inftitution was but newly fet up and when *Ananias* and *Sapphira* finned, the gofpel inftitution was new. Now when a new law is fet up, there is fevere inflicting of punifhment in cafe of tranfgreffion. For if authority fhould fuffer it to go unpunifhed, it would be underftood and thought an allowance of it; and therefore did God fo feverely punifh thefe *firft tranfgreffions* of his new inftitutions. Then, as for *Uzzah* and the *Bethfhemites*, we muft confider, that God had feverely plagued the *Philiftines* (when the ark was in their hands) with emerods in their fecret parts; and they not acquainted with the religion of the ark; therefore furely He would not pafs by and overlook *Uzzah* and the *Bethfhemites* who did know it. It cannot be imagined, that God would allow a rafhnefs and abfurdity in them, having fo feverely punifhed the *Philiftines* before.   6. Though

6. Though we do not know what time or leisure God will allow to sinners to repent, yet we certainly know God will grant forgiveness to penitents ; which is enough to declare God gracious and merciful.

7. If it be not the case of repentance, there is no other way for God's forgiveness ; for this is the tenor of the Grace of God, *Acts* xi. 18. *Repentance unto life.* Acts v. 31. *Him hath God exalted with his right hand, to be a prince and a Saviour, to give repentance to Israel, and forgiveness of sins.* Luke xxiv. 47. *And that repentance. and remission of sins should be preached in his name.* I cannot expect the subsequent act of forgiveness, where there is not the antecedent act of repentance, and conversion, and reformation. For what we have done amiss, and do not recal by repentance, we are thought to stand to.

8. We cannot competently judge concerning the proceedings of God to his creatures, when taken in iniquity ; because we are not privy to the spirit in which men sin. This for answer to the first objection.

The *second objection* is relating to such scriptures as represent God severe, by giving up to a reprobate sense, stupidity and hardness of heart, &c. Psal. lxix. 23. *Let their eyes be darkned, that they may not see, and bow down their back always.* And *Rom.* xi. 10. To give an account of these places in short, see but against what persons these are spoken ; persons that were contumacious, and resolved to go on in an evil way : and where there is this case of wilful sinning pursued with impenitency and contumacy ; in this case I must say two things. 1. This

1. This cafe hath no promife. And

. 2. It is not fit for the exercife of grace and mercy.

 1. It hath no promife of God.   For the grace of the gofpel runs in this ftrain ; *repentance unto life, repentance and remiffion of fins,* Acts xi. 18.   Never remiffion promifed without repentance ; and this is the tenor of the grace of the gofpel, *Luke* xxiv. 24.

. 2. This cafe is not fit for the exercife of grace and mercy ; for this cafe is not compaffionable ; for this finner would not have God to difturb him ; he would be let alone ; he makes no application to God at all ; he doth not defire to be beholden to him.   Now God cannot be faid to be wanting, though in this cafe he leaves men to their own hearts lufts, becaufe it is to them according to their own hearts defire.   For thefe finners defire not the knowledge of God's ways ; they choofe the pleafures of fin, whatever follows upon it.

But if any fhall fay, or think, God may if he pleafe, by an irrefiftable power prevent all fin and mifery : I anfwer, is it reafonable, that God having made intelligent and voluntary agents fhould force them, and make them do either this or that ; fo or fo ; whether they will or no ? fee what will follow.

1*ft.* There would be no exercife of virtue, for all virtue is in choice. 2*dly.* No happinefs, for we fhould be under force and conftraint.   3*dly.* Of what ufe would our natural faculties then be ? 4*thly.* It would alter the very ftate of God's creation.   It could be no probation ftate ; and it is the contrivance of wifdom, firft that we fhould work, and then have a reward.   5*thly.* God hath made us of natures to be

other

otherwife dealt withal. God draws with the cords of a man, *viz.* perfuafion and inftruction ; and if God draws, it is expected we fhould follow him. God works with us, and it follows that we fhould work out the affairs of our falvation with care and diligence. This gives you an account of fome fcriptures, whereat fome may ftumble. As that of God's hardning *Pharaoh*'s heart ; *Pharaoh* goes on wilfully and impenitently to fin againft God, and refolves to be ftubborn ; and God withdraws upon provocations ; and with-holds his grace, and lets him alone ; and this is called the hardning of *Pharaoh*'s heart. When men affect to be arbitrary and law-lefs, God leaves them to their own hearts lufts, and gives them over to vile affections. And this is the cafe accounted for in *Ifa.* vi. 9, 10. *Go and tell this people, hear ye indeed but underftand not, and fee ye indeed but perceive not. Make the heart of this people fat, and their ears heavy, and fhut their eyes, left they fee with their eyes, and hear with their ears, and underftand with their hearts, and convert, and be healed.* And this is referred to, fix times in the new tefta-ment, *viz. Matt.* xiii. 14. and *Mark* v. 12. and *Luke* viii. 10. and *John* xii. 40. and *Acts* xxviii. 26. and *Rom.* xi. 8. Not that this is fpoken prophetically, but fpoken by the prophet firft, and by the evangelifts and the apoftle afterward, referring to the prophet in the like cafes. For this is only what is confequent upon men's difobedience ; nothing was antecedent-ly intended by God. But to juftify God in this cafe two things I lay down. 1*ft.* None are wicked through any neglect of God ; but by their own wil-

fulnefs

fulnefs. *2dly.* None are miferable by God's contrivance, but by their own wickednefs. So that God
is free from the blood of all men; our deſtruction is of
ourſelves, but our ſalvation is of God. So that thoſe
ſcriptures that repreſent God terrible, are in the caſe
of man's conſenting to wilful ſin, and continuing impenitent. God in this caſe, upon provocation, gives
men up to their own hearts luſts.

For the *third objection.* The neceſſity of juſtice
in caſe of ſin. This will be reſolved by a true explication of juſtice. *God's juſtice is the ſame with his
integrity and uprightneſs.* Now theſe conſiſt with the
reaſon of the thing, and the right of the caſe : theſe
are the perfections of his nature ; from which no
action of God varies. But without prejudice to theſe,
ſcripture attributes to God kindneſs and ſeverity ;
Rom. xi. 22. And theſe are limited and determined by his will ; in reſpect whereof 'tis ſaid, *He will
have mercy on whom he will have mercy : and he doth exerciſe loving-kindneſs and judgment and righteouſneſs in
the earth,* Ex. xxxiii. 19. Jer. ix. 24. Loving-kindneſs
that is of grace, the other two are of juſtice. But in
regard of the loving-kindneſs of God, *he is maſter of
his own right* ; and he doth as he pleaſeth ; for his
grace is free, and his will is the law to him ; and it
is apparent that he hath done differently ; as in the
caſe of men and angels, *John* iii. 16. *Godſo loved
the world, that he gave his only begotten ſon, that whoſoever believeth in him ſhould not periſh, but have ever-
laſting life.* And then for the angels, it is ſaid, 2
Pet. ii. 4. *God ſpared not the angels that ſinned, but
caſt them down to hell, and delivered them into chains*

of

of darkness, to be reserved unto judgment. In the one case is his loving-kindness, and in the other his severity. He exerciseth judgment according to the law of his nature he exerciseth loving kindness according to the law of his will. Now to bring this home to the case. I say, if God punish sin where sin is committed, it is just ; God may justly do it, for sin deserves punishment. But we cannot say it is necessary that God should punish sin ; for if you say that, you take away God's liberty, you destroy all acts of grace, you leave no room for repentance. *Just if it be done, but not just to be done* ; for then it cannot be undone, but God must be unjust ; and then God cannot pardon. If we affirm the latter, we may make a law for God. God may if he please remit and abate of his own right ; for every one that is an owner may dispose of his own if he will. They who receive not these things, I dare say, they are wanting to a solid foundation of their own faith. *It is justice in God to do men good, and it is goodness in God to punish sin if unrepented,* saith Origen.

II. The next thing in the method of the discourse is *explication* of the several *phrases* in the text. In the text you have *five* several words ; not that they denote several perfections in God, but express divine goodness suitable to our case and condition ; the same in God, but distinguished by the quality of the case.

1*st.* He is *gracious* ; which imports three things. 1*st.* So as to do good freely, without constraint. 2*dly.* Because he doth good, above the measure of right and just. 3*dly.* Because he doth good, without antecedent desert, or after recompence.

2*dly,*

2dly. He is *merciful* ; take that also in three particulars. *1st.* So as to compassionate his creatures in misery. *2dly.* So as to help them, in respect of their infirmities. *3dly.* So as to pardon their iniquities.

3dly. He is *slow to anger* ; and that also in three particulars. *1st.* So as not to take advantage against his creatures. *2dly.* So as to overlook provocation. *3dly.* So as to allow space for repentance.

4thly. He is *of great kindness* ; take that also in three particulars. *1st.* What he doth, he doth in pure good will, and for our good. *2dly.* Not in expectation of being benefited by us. *3dly.* It is infinite, not according to the proportion or disposition of the receiver.

5thly. He *repenteth him of the evil* ; take that in four particulars. *1st.* So as either it comes not at all : or, *2dly.* It proves not what we fear and imagine. Or, *3dly.* It stays but a while if it do come. Or, *4thly.* He turns it into good. I give you but hints, and leave the rest to your meditation.

III. The third thing in the method of the discourse is *confirmation* of the truth of the proposition in the text. There are four names and titles given to God that make this out.

1st. His *creation* in infinite goodness, wisdom and power.   This speaks God to be full of goodness ; for communication speaks goodness in the principle. The variety, order, and fitness of things to their ends, declare the wisdom of God. And to bring things together so remotely distant, *non ens* to *ens,* declares his power. .

2dly. Conservation, protection, and *government,* declare

clare God to be good, and full of loving-kindnefs ; in which refpect God works and we work ; for we are all *workers together with God.*

3*dly. Reftoration* and *recovery* out of the ftate of fin and mifery, fpeaks God's goodnefs. When we were undone, when we had marred and fpoiled ourfelves, God finds out a way for our recovery.

4*thly.* Future *confirmation* and fettlement in glory and happinefs, the miracle of God's goodnefs, wifdom and power. Thefe four things abundantly declare God good and gracious.

IV. The fourth thing in the method of the difcourfe, is matter of *caution,* in two particulars.

1*ft.* Not to *abufe* this declaration of divine goodnefs, either by holding truth in unrighteoufnefs, or turning the grace of God into wantonnefs. *Having therefore thefe promifes (dearly beloved) let us cleanfe ourfelves from all filthinefs of the flefh and fpirit,* 2 Cor. vii. 1. Should we abufe his goodnefs, it were to produce an effect contrary to the principle.

2*dly.* Let there be no *hafty* or *rafh judgment.* If any thing feem harfh in the difpenfation of providence, we may underftand it in a little time ; therefore he that believes fhould not make hafte. We are in the hands of a good God ; whatfoever the appearance is, undoubtedly this reprefentation of God is true, *viz. That he is gracious and merciful, flow to anger, and of great kindnefs, and repenteth him of the evil.* And although we cannot underftand prefently, in the particulars, what God doth ; yet it is undoubtedly true, that it is a mild and gentle fpirit, and loving to mankind, that governs the world.

V. The

V. The fifth thing in the method of this difcourfe is *application.*

1*ft.* Here is matter of *information.* Then have we a true judgment of God, when we think of his great-nefs in conjunction with his goodnefs. Never divide his almightinefs from his goodnefs. It is very true, *no true majefty without goodnefs* : yea I dare fay it, it is the greateft act of power to commiferate and par-don ; for other acts of power fubdue things without, but he that doth commiferate and pardon, fubdues himfelf, which is the greateft victory. General good will, and univerfal love, and charity, are the greateft, both perfections and acts of power. To be rea-dy to forgive, and to be eafy to be reconciled, are things that are grafted, not in the wildernefs of the world, but in the moft noble and generous natures. They are under the fulleft communication of God that give themfelves up to acts of clemency and compaffion, and are forward to relieve, and to do good, to pardon and to forgive. Thefe are the per-fons that are endued with divine power. If goodnefs and righteoufnefs were not in an unfeparable con-junction with almighty power, the whole creation were in danger and hazard ; and could not be fafe, nor have any fecurity.

2*dly.* Here is matter of *imitation.* Let us imi-tate and refemble God. Afford thy fellow-creature that meafure that God doth thee ; the contrary is an argument of thy not partaking of the divine na-ture. *He that hateth his brother abides in death.* And how fay'ft thou, that *thou loveft God whom thou haft not feen, and loveft not thy brother whom thou feeft ?*.
They

They who are indeed acquainted with God, and naturalized to him, they live in a spirit of hearty love and univerfal good will, 1 *John* iv. 16. *God is love, and he that dwells in love, dwelleth in God, and God in him.* The firft thing in religion, is to have right notions and apprehenfions of God, what is true concerning God ; *for we never fhall be right in our felves, if we have wrong thoughts of God.* Therefore this is firft in religion, to know what is true in God, and the next is to partake thereof ; *i. e.* for us, in our meafure and degree, to be what Gcd is in fulnefs, height and excellency, wherein Gcd is imitable and communicable. *Eph.* v. 1. 2. *Pet.* i. 4.

3*dly.* Here is matter of *confolation* to all that are willing to do well, and would be good. They are in the hands of a good God ; fo that they may be encouraged, and their hands ftrengthened in their duty. They have an account to give to an equal Lord ; they ferve a loving mafter. Who would not be engaged to fuch an one, *who is gracious and merciful, flow to anger, and of great kindnefs, and repenteth him of the evil ?* This is our great encouragement, that faithfully ferve God, that if there be a hearty good will on our part, and an honeft endeavour to pleafe God ; fo ample and abundant is the grace of God, that it will fupply all that is defective, either affording more ftrength, or by candid conftruction, or free pardon of all our miftakes. If not by giving more ftrength, yet by candid conftruction of what is weakly done, but well meant ; or by free pardon. *God is far better than we can conceive of him.* For 1*ft,* He is infinite in all his perfections ;

and we are but finite in all our apprehenfions, and conceptions of him. And 2*dly*. We are able through grace to avoid evil, and do good. And 3*dly*. Our imperfections are eafily pardoned ; *for God pitieth us, as a father pitieth his children. He knoweth our frame, and confidereth we are but duft,* Pfal. ciii. 14. Now this fhould quicken and enliven us chearfully to obey God, and heartily to love him. I dare fay, he doth not know God at all, as he is ; nor is he in a good ftate of religion, who doth not find in himfelf at times, ravifhings with the fweet and lovely confiderations of the divine perfections, *viz.* his benignity expreffed to all his creatures, and his benefits conferred upon mankind. He that hath not a fenfe and confideration of thefe, and on whofe mind thefe have made no impreffion, he is devoid of all true knowledge of God, and I dare fay, he is not in a ftate of true religion.

But what I now fpeak of, is not to impenitent and contumacious finners ; none of this reacheth them. To them there is no promife, as I told you before ; their cafe is not compaffionable. If we ufe our principles of reafon, we cannot put it upon God, to act contrary to the quality and perfection of his nature. The very goodnefs of God doth oblige him to punifh impenitent and contumacious finners ; and to controul and difcourage fin ; for if goodnefs be the perfection of the divine nature, then it is fuitable to him, to promote goodnefs in his creation.

Thus have I run over thefe things only fummarily, wherein I have done you this courtefy, I have given you matter for your meditation.

DIS-

DISCOURSE III.

The Difference of TIMES, with respect to RELIGION.

PSALM XCV. 7.

To day if ye will hear his voice, harden not your hearts.

TO give myself advantage, and to command your attention; in the first place I will take notice how this place of scripture is referred to, and quoted in the new testament.

If you look into *Heb.* iii. 7. You will find these words brought in, *as saith the Holy Ghost, to day if ye will hear his voice.* What therefore is said as consonant to them, you are to look upon, to receive and entertain as the word of God, and as dictated by the Holy Spirit. For the words themselves, there is much matter in them, and they are of great weight and importance. But I will only declare to you in several particulars, *That upon a spiritual account, there is great difference in time* ; for *this* is suggested, as that wherein the *force* of the exhortation doth lie, *To day,* &c. And to make this out, I will shew you,

I. That *sooner and later* are not alike in respect of *eternity* ; and that the main work we have to do in time, is to prepare for eternity.

II. I

II. I will ſhew, that *times of ignorance* and of *know-ledge* are not alike.

III. That *before* and *after voluntary commiſſion of known iniquity*, are not alike.

IV. That *before* and *after contracted naughty habits*, are not alike.

V. That the time of *God's gracious and particular viſitation*, and the time when God *withdraws* his gracious preſence and aſſiſtance, are not alike.

VI. The flouriſhing time of our *health* and *ſtrength*, and the hour of *ſickneſs, weakneſs*, and approach of *death*, are not alike.

VII. Now and hereafter, preſent and future, *this world*, and *the world to come*, are not alike.

And by that time I have given you an account of theſe particulars, and made it evident to you, that *all times are not alike*, for the purpoſes of eternity, and the concernments of our ſouls ; it will appear highly adviſeable (conſidering the advantages of life, health and ſtrength, and the reference of time to eternity) for us all to lead ſuch lives, upon which we may ſafely die ; and to employ ourſelves in ſuch actions as are accountable when we come to leave the world, ſince our welfare to eternity depends upon it. We are, I ſay, highly concerned, ſo to order our converſations in the world, ſo to govern our ſpirits, and lead ſuch lives, as when we ſhall come to leave the world, we may reflect with ſatisfaction upon what we have done, as good *Hezekiah* did, 1 *Kings* xx. 3, 4. when the meſſage came to him that he ſhould die and not live, he

turned

turned his face to the wall, and said, *I beseech thee,
O Lord, to remember now how I have walked before
thee in truth and with a perfect heart, and have done
that which is good in thy sight.* If we do not consider
this, we shall be wanting to the true interest of our
immortal souls. We often read in scripture, of
hardness of heart; which is nothing but want of consideration : for *Mark* vi. 52. we read, that *they considered not the miracle of the loaves, for their heart was
hardned*: and *Exod.* vii. 23. we read that *Pharaoh*
did not set his heart to consider things. But brief-
ly to speak to these particulars.

I. *Sooner* and *later* are not alike upon a spiritual account. For the time of life is the day of exercise and
time of work for God, and for the publick : for God
and the publick have a due of service from us all ; for
we came not into the world to gratify sense, and to
serve our lusts, but to serve God and the publick, not
to promote our own ends and little designs, but the
common good, and as we would not neglect our duty,
so we must not mispend our time. We are to be doing
our duty to God, ourselves and others, as soon as we
come to the use of reason and understanding ; for
motion of religion doth begin with reason ; and so
soon as a man is able to make use of reason and judgment, he ought to put himself upon motion of religion, for we are as capable of religion, as we are of
reason ; and indeed no man can use his reason as
he ought but religion will be predominant with him,
and over-rule all his motions. *Solomon* saith, *Prov.*
xvi. 3. *That the hoary head is a crown of glory* ; but
how ? *if it be found in the way of righteousness* ; that
is,

is, if a man hath ufed himfelf all his days, from the time he came to the ufe of reafon, to the time of old age, in ways of religion, his *grey hairs will be a crown of glory to him.* 'Tis of great advantage to begin well, for fo faith *Solomon*, Prov. xxii. 6. *Train up a child in the way that he fhould go, and when he is old, he will not depart from it.* 'Tis true indeed that fome do degenerate ; for thefe *proverbs* are not to be taken ftrictly, but only to fignify what is moft common and likely, and what is to be expected ; and *this* is of that nature ; and doth fhew a man to be the greater finner if he depart from a good way that he was early brought into.   For we eafily do what we have been bred unto, and ufed to do. It is true, that ferious repentance, wherefoever it is, doth alter the cafe ; but then you muft know, that late repentance is feldom true ; and this I am very fure of, that there is little or no proof of late repentance, becaufe there is not opportunity to act.   And they do mightily abufe themfelves, that put off their repentance with hopes of being like the *penitent thief*, who begun ill, but ended well.   But pray confider, that this was an extraordinary cafe, a miraculous work of God's grace ; and fuch as we cannot expect the like again, till the Saviour of the world fhall come again, and fuffer.   And the apoftle tells us, that there can be no more facrifice for fin than that which hath been already offered.   Others there are that do abufe that paffage in the xx. of *Mat.* where we read, that *the Lord of the vineyard went forth to hire labourers into his vineyard, and took fome at the laft hour of the day.*   But here I will obferve four things.
1. That

1. That they which were hired late, ftood all that time in the market-place in *expeffation*.

2. They were no fooner hired, and appointed, but they went into the *vineyard*.

3. They had *no plea* at all for the wages of a day. For it was faid unto them, *I will give you what is right*. Not the wages of a day : that was left wholly to the Lord's good pleafure.

4. It was *beyond their expeffation*, or at leaft beyond the common ground of expeftation. And we find their fellow-labourers were not fatisfied in it, that *they* fhould have the recompence of a days work when they had not done the work of a day. Therefore let us not be fo much miftaken, as to think we may defer the work of repentance, and making provifion for eternity, till the laft. They which do fo, little underftand what fanftification imports ; what reconciliation with the nature, mind, and will of God, and the law of heaven, doth fignify. No lefs than this can we underftand by it, to glorify God by a holy and unblameable converfation, and to do good, and ferve God in our generations. For *heaven is more a ftate and temper, than a place*. That for the firft : *fooner* and *later* are not alike.

II. Times of *ignorance* and of *knowledge*, are not alike : for, the time of ignorance, that is as *the night, in which no man can work*, John iv. 4. And the apoftle tells us, *Afts* xvii. 30. That, *thefe times of ignorance God winked at*. And that *if they had been blind, they fhould have had no fin*, John ix. 41. which you are not to underftand abfolutely, that thofe that are ignorant and ftupid are not guilty ; but that they are

are not fo great finners as thofe which pretend to
know. And therefore it is faid, that *their fin remaineth*, that is, it doth remain with all manner of aggravation.   For you cannot fay more or worfe of a-
ny man, than that he doth evil knowingly, and a-
gainft his confcience. It is univerfally acknowledged, that ignorance doth greatly excufe, and therefore we have charity for idiots ; and where men have
never heard and are without the pale of the church,
we leave them to God's mercy, and exclude them
not.   But it is quite otherwife where men are *a law
to themfelves*, as the apoftle fpeaks, *Rom.* ii. 14.

There are three things in which every man that
is born into the world, and hath the ufe of reafon,
is a law unto himfelf ; and if he do not obferve that
law in thofe particulars, he will be felf-condemned
and neither himfelf nor any other man can juftify
him.

1. As to the point of *fobriety* and *temperance*. That
we do moderate our appetites, and not abufe ourfelves, through exceffive and inordinate ufe of the
things of this life.

2. A man is a law to himfelf as to *juftice* and
righteoufnefs.   And he will be felf-condemned if he
do not ufe fairnefs and equal dealing with other men:
fuch as he would himfelf receive from others, he is
obliged to give.   If a man fail in thefe particulars,
he goes againft the law that is connatural to him,
and would be felf-condemned though he had no o-
ther revelation from God, and had never heard of
the bible.

3. A man is a *law to himfelf* in refpect of that
fear

fear and *reverence* which he owes to *God*. For a man knows nothing more certainly, than that he was not original to his own being, and that he did not make himself ; but that he was brought into be-ing by some agent, that was more able, wise, and powerful than himself. For he that knows how un-able he is to continue himself in being, cannot but know that he did not bring himself into being but that he owes his being to another ; and that he ought to fear, reverence, and adore him from whom he receiv-ed it, and if he do it not , he must condemn himself. Therefore I am sure there is no man shall be condem-ned by God, that is not first condemned by himself, in some or other of these particulars that I have named. In some other, and *lesser matters*, there may be invincible ignorance, and this may excuse in those particulars; but in the great matters of religion and conscience, there is no invincible ignorance. If men are at any loss as to these things I have named ; their igno-rance is affected, and 'tis through gross self-neglect, and practice contrary to knowledge. And in these cases their guilt is aggravated, and their case is not compassionable. And that for the second. Times of *ignorance*, and the times of *knowledge* are not a-like.

III. Before and after *voluntary commission of sin*, is not alike, upon a spiritual account. It is not imagi-nable the loss that a man sustains by consenting to iniquity ; how much he spoils his principle, mars his spirit, and spoils his parts. This you have ac-knowledged in the counsel of *Achitophel*, which he gives to *Absalom*, which is called the *good counsel* of

Achitophel

Achitophel, 2 *Sam.* xvii. 14.   Not that it was good
in itſelf, for it was as wicked counſel as ever was
given : for he adviſeth *Abſalom* to do a vile fact
to confirm himſelf in his rebellion againſt his father,
and to remove the boundaries of good and evil ; than
which there is not a more deſperate undertaking.
For a man under pretence of power to controul the
rule of right, the meaſures of heaven, is to divert
things from their natures, and to change their natural courſe ; which is as monſtrous in morals as in
naturals. The mind uncorrupted is a tender thing,
and ſuffers moſt by violence, and unnatural uſe. The
ſcripture ſpeaks of hardneſs of heart, as a moſt monſtrous ſtate, *Jer.* xiii. 23. *Can the ethiopian change
his skin, or the leopard his ſpots?* Theſe things are naturally impoſſible.   No more can one that hath a-
buſed himſelf, and made havock of conſcience, by
accuſtoming himſelf to do evil, learn to do well, without the eſpecial grace and favour of God.   The
coming in of ſin is like the coming in of water : it
may be ſtopped by a little turf at the firſt ; but if
it once find a way over, it breaks down all before it.
It is much eaſier to retain innocence than to recover a
man's ſelf. If a man will venture to do that which is not
fit to be done, no body knows where he will end.
The practice of iniquity makes men ſhameleſs and
impudent ; the devil is eaſily let in, but hardly got
out.   Let us therefore take heed how we betray
ourſelves, and give way to iniquity.   Let us approve ourſelves to our *home-God.* Conſcience is always ready to ſpeak to us ; let our ear be always
ready to hear what it hath to ſay, and be very careful

ful never to depart from its counfel, in going againſt the fenfe of our own minds and judgment. When once a man hath confented to do that which is bafe and unworthy, as he hath made havock of his own confcience, fo he hath broken his credit, which is a further fecurity, and great prefervative againſt evil.

IV. Before and after contracted *evil habits*, by frequent uſe and repeated acts of evil, is not alike, as to the concerns of eternity. *Men are more what they are uſed to, than what they are born to*; for cuſtom is a fecond nature. Every man *hath himſelf as he uſeth himſelf*. When men loſe all government of themſelves, they foon contract hardneſs and an injudicious mind ; an undifcerning mind, or as it is rendred *Rom*. i. 28. A *reprobate mind* and *confcience*. The mind by abuſe of itſelf, or groſs ſelf-neglect, may come to be as ſalt that hath loſt its ſavour : ſo the mind loſes its power of judging and difcerning, and of reproving and controuling. The apoſtle ſpeaks of fome that had *their confciences ſeared as with a hot iron*, 1 Tim. iv. 2. by reafon whereof they loſe all ſenfe and judgment ; and then 'tis no wonder that nothing will work upon them, becauſe, as the apoſtle ſpeaks, *Eph.* iv. 19. *They are paſt feeling* ; which cafe is reprefented by the prophet, *Iſa.* vi. 9. *Make the heart of this people fat, and their ears heavy, that they may not hear.* And there is no place in all the ſcripture fo often referred to as this place ; it is referred to by all the evangeliſts, and in the acts of the apoſtles, and in the epiſtle to the *Romans*. And when this is the cafe, that men have groſly neglected or abuſed themſelves, and brought themſelves

by

by wicked practices into the love of sin and vice and dislike of goodness ; then it comes to pass with them, that *seeing, they see not, and do not perceive ; and hearing, they hear, and do not understand.* And this place is no less than six times referred to in the new testament, as giving an account of this place of the prophet. We many times wonder to see men act so contrary to all advice and counsel, to all sober judgment, and to plain scripture, against the true interests of their souls, and bodily health, to the consuming of their estates, ruin of their credits, to the undoing of their families ; and all this without any manner of profit or advantage ; so that a man may say to them as the apostle, *Gal.* iii. 1. *Who hath bewitched you ?* to see men run on so desperately, and to disclaim all rules of government, and to practise without any manner of consideration : not to be limited by right and justice, against all advice and counsel, against all threatnings too, having neither the fear of God, or regard to man : one would think they are besotted, and act like mad-men. But this is the account : they have brought themselves into an unnatural estate ; and are not now as God brought them into the world, nor like to continue so long here as they might have done. But as the wise man saith, *Ecc.* vii. 17. *Be not overmuch wicked, neither be thou foolish, why shouldest thou die before thy time ?* for want of self-government the wicked are like to die before their time, and often by their own hands too. How shall these men give an account of themselves, when they had a fairer allowance of time, and would not use it ? How odious are those
that

that lay violent hands upon themfelves ? the law doth not allow them the common place of burial. Now all intemperance is of the fame nature. Though men do not intend it, yet they take a courfe to fhorten their days, and their fin goes before hand unto judgment. A man would think that rational nature fhould not be fo depraved ; but that we have woful experience of it. Infomuch that the prophet, *Jer.* vi. 15. fays of fome, *were they afhamed when they had committed abomination ? nay, they were not afhamed, neither could they blufh.* All fhame is laid afide, and that which is the governor of man, conftituted by God, reafon and underftanding is dethroned, and brutifh fenfe fet up in its ftead, and men give up themfelves to paffion, malice, envy, fury, and revenge ; and are infolent, arrogant, haughty, and unreafonable; whereas God made no fuch, nor ever brought any fuch order into the world. Thefe men came into the world upon the fame terms with other men ; but they have made themfelves fuch by abufe of themfelves. And now they will tell you, they *cannot do otherwife* ; they *cannot* ; why ? becaufe they have contracted evil habits, by ill ufe, cuftom, and practice ; and are not willing to be at the pains to work them off ; which through the grace of God, and by a little violence to themfelves at the beginning, they might effect.

V. The times of God's *gracious vifitation* in mercy and kindnefs to men's fouls ; thefe are not like thofe times wherein *God fuffers men to walk after their own ways.* And to make this out I propofe three things.

1. That God is neither at firft nor laft, wanting

in

David ; when the fpirit of God was upon him, how doth he *defy the armies of the aliens* ; but at another time, *I fhall one day perifh by the hand of* Saul. A vaft difference there is, when we are under divine motion, and when not; and therefore every man ought when he is in a good difpofition, and well affected, to follow thofe impreffions, for then that will be done which at another time will not be done.

VI. There is a vaft difference between the flourifhing condition of *life, health,* and *ftrength* ; and the hour of *ficknefs, weaknefs* and *death.* In the former there is the vigour of nature ; in the latter 'tis enough for a man to bear his infirmities. The moft we can then expect to do, is to bear up againft the pangs of death, and difmal apprehenfions of it. And *he is mad that hath a days work to do when he is going to bed.* We fee what great mifchief came upon one's being late on his journey, *Judg.* xix. the *Levite* being overtaken in the night. We muft know that the work of converfion is a fober, ferious and deliberate work, and ought not to be deferred to ficknefs and the hour of death, which is an hour of hafte, hurry and confufion. It is the greateft bufinefs of life, and of concernment to eternity ; and fhall we prefer things that are trifles in comparifon, and beftow all our time, and thoughts and care upon them, and leave that which is fundamental to the ftate of eternity to the laft ? efpecially confidering,

Firft, That no man is fure of warning, or of a moderate, leifurely ficknefs. Some drop down all on the fudden, and never have the ufe of reafon to

fpeak

speak a word; as they that die of apoplexies, lethargies and the like. Many die before either they themselves, or they that are about them, are aware; but if they die not so soon, a man may be *non compos mentis*, through the height of his disease: and if not so, there is very great danger of despairing; if the foundation of hope be not laid before; for, take it for granted, *there are none so much in danger of despairing at the time of death, as they which have been most presumptuous in the course of their lives.*

Again, the enemy of our souls, who hath been so ready to deceive us in life will double his diligence at the hour of death. So that, if we are not *now* able to withstand his temptations, how shall we be able to do it, when we shall have less ability, and he come upon us with more force and violence.

Further, sometimes men expect assistance from friends; but they may be absent when we want them; or they may prove like *Job's* friends, miserable comforters. But if this should be otherwise, it is then too late to begin a new scene of life, and learn the knowledge of religion; for knowledge is leisurely gotten, and with difficulty; but however, *that* is no time for practice. If a man could be made fit for it, and taught in a moment, he hath no time to perform and exercise religion. The mind cannot be discharged of its ill habits in a moment, which have been settled by conversation, and the work of a man's life.

VII. And *lastly*; now, and *hereafter*, the present and the future, this world and the world to come, are not alike, for the concerns of our souls. For now

is the time of working out our falvation ; the next
world will be for reckoning, and in judgment : As
this life leaves us, eternity will find us. See therefore what great advantages we have in this day, and
let us make ufe of them.   We have the direction
of holy fcripture, which we may read as often as we
will : we have friends and guides for the inftruction
of our fouls ; we have all God's inftitutions and ap-
pointments, and the divine Spirit's affiftance, and the
gofpel promifes to affure us that our applications to
God fhall not be in vain, if they be fincere.   But
then for *hereafter* ; what word of promife in all the
bible, for any thing that is to be done by us here-
-after ? what fcripture doth fay, that that may be
done hereafter which is now neglected ? No ; we
read, *Prov.* i. 26. *That becaufe I called, and ye would
not anfwer, I will then laugh at your deftruction, and
mock when your fear cometh* : and *Luke* xvi. we read
of the rich glutton, that he is tormented ; and poor
Lazarus, that made an advantage of his poverty,
and did his work in this world, *he is comforted.* If
therefore we are real, fincere, and hearty in our religion, we fhall not put it off.   Matters of weight
and moment we do not put off at large, but we appoint a fit and convenient time ; and if the thing be
of concernment, we will appoint a time near and
certain ; for delays and put-offs are next to denials.
    From hence, I infer,
    1. That we are to *difcern* the time.
    2. That we are to *ufe* the time.   And
    3. That we are to *recover* the time which is loft
or mifpent.

                                                    1. That

1. That we are to *discern* the time. This was wanting in them, *Luke* xii. 56. *Ye hypocrites, ye can discern the face of the sky, and of the earth ; but how is it that ye do not discern this time ?* This, as it argues stupidity, so it is a forerunner of ruin, *Luke* xix. 44. *They shall lay thee even with the ground, and thy children within thee, and they shall not leave in thee one stone upon another, because thou knewest not the time of thy visitation.* This is an account of *Jerusalem's* doom. To know time and season in every profession and way of living, is a principal piece of skill. No good is to be done in any way, if this be not understood, *Ecclef.* iii. 11. *He hath made every thing beautiful in his time,* and ver. 1. *To every thing there is a season, and a time to every purpose under heaven ;* and *the misery of man is great,* because he does not discern this time, *Ecclef.* viii. 6. *Because to every purpose there is time and judgment, therefore the misery of man is great upon him.* For the purpose of religion, the time of youth, and nature's strength ; the time before men are acquainted with evil; the time of God's affistance, indulgence, grace, and favourable acceptance, are most proper : these make the time properly for working. Elder years are attended with weakness and infirmities, which greatly indispose for action, especially if we are to begin a new thing. This is rather a time of patience and passion, than of work.

2. That we *use* the time. That time is lost that is not used ; the virtue of it confists in the use of it. The true improvement of time, is in the recovery of our selves by reconciliation with God : our

minds

minds being renewed, our loffes fupplied, and our
perfons recommended. 'Tis an argument of the
fevereft reproach and challenge, that a man is at
years of underftanding, and yet his mind is not informed ; no rule of life and action confidered and
examined : this is to moralize *Solomon's* proverb,
Prov. xxiv. 30. *I went by the field of the flothful,* &c.
Every ones mind is his field, and the fluggard's
mind is overgrown with thiftles. A man may be
afhamed to have lived fo long in the world to fo
little purpofe ; when his time is gone, and his work
not done : wife for other things, only uninftructed,
or elfe carelefs in matters of the higheft concernment and greateft importance between God and
their confciences.

I may add, that time is burdenfome, if we have
not employment for it. We have a phrafe,
To drive away time ; alas for its confequence ; *ab
hoc momento pendet æternitas* ; there is a reference
of time to eternity. We fhould be fure to carry
on our main work with the time ; and if we be
fhort in circumftances, not to fail in fubftance :
let nothing lefs than this be the account of the improvement of time, that our minds are difcharged
of all unnatural difpofitions, whatfoever we have
acquired that jarrs with the principles of God's
creation in us ; that we have gotten the victory of
our paffions, taken ourfelves off from foolifh affections and fond imaginations, from being carried a-
way after the guife of this mad and finful world :
that our faculties be planted with divine graces,
fruits of the divine Spirit : that we be in conftitu-
                                                    tion

tion and temper, in converfation and practice, conformable to Chrift's doctrine, through Chrift deftroying in us the works of the devil, and communicating to us the divine nature: that our perfons be reconciled, pleafing, acceptable to God, through Chrift's mediation and interceffion. 'Tis a reproach to us to number ourfelves by years, fifty, feventy, eighty : thefe things being not done, in which the only true account of time is. Further I add by way of *caution*, notwithftanding the difference of time.

Firft, I tell no man (take him as I find him) that it is impoffible for him to repent ; for I know not the extent of God's grace.

Secondly, I fay to no man, that if he does repent, it will be too late to find mercy ; for I know not the length of God's patience, and repentance doth alter the cafe : but this I ferioufly advertife. If we will be true to our own fouls, and not *forfake our own mercies*, let us take the advantage of God's particular application to us ; then act, when God acts upon us. The facred fcriptures thus declare, *Prov.* i. 23. *Turn ye at my reproof; behold I will pour out my fpirit unto you.* Prov. viii. 17. *Whofo feeks me early, fhall find me.* Pfal. xxxii. 6. *For this fhall every one that is godly pray unto thee, in a time when thou mayeft be found,* Ifa. lv. 6. *Seek ye the Lord while he may be found, call upon him while he is near.* For this bufinefs of religion is no flight or perfunctory work ; 'tis expreffed in fcripture, by what imports a mighty change, being made *new creatures*, not by tranfubftantiating our natures, but by transforming our minds, and mending our tempers ; by being par-

D 3

takers

takers of the divine nature ; by being created after
God in righteousness and true holiness ; not by being Godhead with God, but by being *renewed in
the spirit of our minds.   By perfecting holiness in the
fear of God. By crucifying the old man and his deeds.
By purging ourselves from all filthiness of the flesh and
spirit. By putting off the body of sin* : And by *mortifying the flesh, with the affections and lusts.*

Can we reasonably think that such a work can
be done in a moment, or in the most inconvenient
circumstances of old age, and the decays of nature,
or on a death-bed ? for is not old age burden e-
nough, except it be attended with the sad remembrance of a careless life ?

3. *Recover* time lost, so far as is possible, with
double industry, care, and diligence, *Eph.* v. 16. u-
pon this encouragement, *habenti dabitur* ; to him
that hath shall be given, and *ab utente non auferetur*,
and from him that useth it shall not be taken away.
Think that for this purpose, God hath so long continued thee in being. 'Tis safe to make the best
interpretation of God's dealing with thee, which is
to encourage application to him ; for this is the
contrary to turning the grace of God into wantonness. The credit of a good beginning is lost, if we
persevere not in goodness. The disrepute occasioned from the vanity of the younger years, is abated
by the seriousness and stayedness of the age of understanding. Since we cannot absolve ourselves
from any ill use or abuse of time past, considering
the improveableness of time, and the reference
thereof to eternity : let us carefully redeem that
                                            which

which remains ; refcue it out of the huckfter's hands ; vindicate it to the nobleft purpofes, that the remainder of it through true improvement, may anfwer the account of the whole.

Nothing will lie heavier upon our minds, when we come to die, than that we have neglected the day of grace, been wanting to ourfelves in preparations for eternity, by bad ufe of time ; depraved our minds, fo as to go out of the world in far worfe ftate and condition than we entred into it.

The *perfuafives* hereunto are,

1. That here is *hearts-eafe* and fatisfaction in the motion of repentance ; in that we have revoked, and morally voided that which fhould not have been done. *The firft beft is not to have done ill ; the fecond, is to condemn it :* this is all we can do in the cafe, all elfe muft be left to God ; and this makes the cafe compaffionable ; and when the cafe is fuch, there is nothing to hinder God to fhew mercy.

2. *Entrance into eternity,* mainly depends upon the immediate difpofition of the mind ; wherefore we are to take all care to depart hence in renunciation of the guife of this mad world ; in reconciliation with the rule of righteoufnefs ; in agreeablenefs of temper with the heavenly ftate.

3. We have done a great deal of *harm* in the world, by bad example, ftrengthning the hands of the wicked : let us take it off by renunciation of it, by condemning ourfelves in it, by giving teftimony to truth and right ; this is the leaft that can be done in all reafon ; elfe we may be faid to be *alive to do mifchief in the world, when we are dead and gone.*

D I S.

DISCOURSE IV.

The J o y which the Righteous have in G o d.

Preached in the New Chapel, *December* 7. 1668.

Ps A L M. xxxiii. 1.
Rejoice in the Lord, O ye righteous, for praise is come-ly for the upright.

AND can we meet in this *new structure* and *fabrick*, raised out of its former ruins, and not perform the duty of the text ? If I be not mistaken, this is the first that is again employed in sacred use, since the dismal and fatal fire. Let those that are here present, give a good example to all that shall follow after ; and let us now, as the text calls upon us, rejoice and triumph in the divine goodness, for praise is comely for the good and upright man. The remarkable providences, and happier dispensations of God, call upon us to be glad in the Lord, and thankful for his benefits. God hath not only given us leave to rebuild our ruins, and repair our waste places, but he hath been with us, and given us encouragement to this good undertaking. We read that the *Jews* when they returned out of captivity, and had but rebuilt their walls, they had meetings of joy and triumph ; as you find it among

other

other places, *Ezra* iii. 11. and vi. 16. and *Nehem.* xii. 27. And this is not only pious, but a tranfcendant act of faith, and confidence in God; upon fuch occafions to blefs him, to rejoice in him, and to praife him. And they are of the bafeft, and moft fordid temper, that are not affected with the expref- fions of the divine goodnefs and kindnefs. And tru- ly if we do not do the former duty of the text, we fhall fail in the latter; if we be not glad and rejoice in the Lord, we fhall never be thankful nor blefs his holy name. For pray what thankfulnefs when the heart is poffeft with melancholy, and the fpirit full of heavinefs ? but befides this, it is the general direction of wifdom, to *acknowledge. God in all our ways*; therefore in things remarkable, fo much the more; and 'tis the effect of religion to do it ; for what is religion, but a participation, imitation, and refemblance of the divine goodnefs, both in the tem- per of the fubject, and in its expreffions of gratitude, ingenuity, acknowledgment, and the like. I know no other refult of religion but this. And furely were religion eftimated by *this*, we fhould endeavour af- ter it, and be all good friends, and he would be ac- counted the beft man, that is moft free and ingenu- ous in the fenfe of divine goodnefs. At leaft let us not neglect to make acknowledgments to God up- on thofe eminent advantages that the courfe of his providence doth afford; fuch as are eminent fuc- ceffes in our undertakings, and happy recoveries out of any trouble and calamity ; and giving us to fee light after darknefs. Such opportunities as thefe, pious fouls have been wont to clofe withal. And it

is

is noted of one, a very good perfon, a king of great
fame, as a thing that was very unnatural and unbecoming him, and very ill refented by God, that he
did *not render unto the Lord according to the great be-*
nefits that was beftowed upon him. Thus it is reported of *Hezekiah,* 2 *Chron.* xxxii. 21. *But his heart was*
lifted up. Now pride is oppofite to the acknowledgment of God, and giving thanks to him.   He that
hath his heart lifted up, will arrogate and affume to
himfelf, and this feems to have been his fault ; for
which wrath was upon him, and the *Ifrael* of God.
Now let fuch failings as thefe were, though in former ages, be for our admonition, as the apoftle tells
us, that *things before us were for our example, upon*
whom the ends of the world are come, 1 Cor. x. 11.
If God had not taken pleafure in us, and in this
great undertaking, to reftore and rebuild this ancient city, he might have obftructed and prohibited
the fame ; as *Jofhua* did curfe any one that under-
took rebuilding of *Jericho.* You fhall find the curfe,
Jofhua vi. 26. and in effect, 1 *Kings* xvi. 34. Therefore we have caufe, both to be fenfible of the divine
goodnefs, in that his good hand of providence hath
been over us, and given fuccefs to our endeavours ;
and fcattered our fears and fad apprehenfions, and
given us to fee fo much of reftoration as at this day,
and as this place gives teftimony of.

  In the text we have two things.

  I. The *duty* : and.

  II. The *reafon* of it.

I. The

I. The *duty* is expreſſed in two words, *rejoice in the Lord,* and *praiſe him* : and the *reaſon* in theſe words, *for it is comely ſo to do.*

Rejoice in the Lord. Then certainly religion is not ſuch a thing as 'tis repreſented to the world by many men. For it is looked upon as a doleful, troubleſome, melancholy thing ; hurtful to the body and diſquieting to the ſouls of men. But ſee whether this be true. Look upon religion in its actions and employment : and what are they ? *rejoice and give thanks.* Are not theſe actions that are grateful and delightful ? what doth tranſcend divine joy and ingenuous acknowledgments ? But then.

II. The *reaſon. It is comely.* Whatſoever is the true product of religion, is graceful, beautiful, and lovely. There is nothing in religion that is diſhonourable, ſelfiſh ; that is particular, and narrowſpirited. No, it is a principle of the greateſt noblenefs, and generouſnefs in the world. They are worldly ſpirits, that are low, narrow, and contracted : the truly religious are moſt noble and generous ; and are the freeſt from narrownefs, diſcontent and ſelfiſhnefs. There is the moſt ſolid peace, and moſt grounded ſatisfaction found in it. *Job.* x. 5. *The triumph of the wicked is ſhort, and the joy of the hypocrite is but for a moment.* But for the good man and the righteous, *Pſal.* iv. 7. *Thou haſt put more gladneſs into my heart, than when their corn, and wine, and oil encreaſed.* And *Iſa.* xiv. 16. *I will glory in the holy One of Iſrael.* And *Iſa.* lxi. 10. *I will greatly rejoice in the Lord, and my ſoul ſhall be joyful in my God.* Nay, in the greateſt ſtraits and exigency,

Hab.

Hab. iii. 17. *Though the fig-tree fhould not bloffom,
though there fhould be no fruit in the vine, and the labour of the olive fhould fail,* &c. *yet will I rejoice in
the Lord, and joy in the God of my falvation.*

I. *Rejoice in the Lord.*

1. For *himfelf* ; becaufe of his own goodnefs.

2. In *other things,* with refpect to him.   But

1. For *himfelf.* 1*ft.* God is the moft excellent
object in the world.   And 2*dly,* what he is in himfelf, he *is to the righteous,* who have intereft in him,
and who are in reconciliation with him.   'Tis vanity and emptinefs to glory in men, and ordinary
things, and where there is no property ; though
things are excellent, yet there is no glory in that
cafe.   Men are prone to envy ; therefore it is requifite to glorying, that men have property, that
men think upon God as their *own* ; for where men
have no property, they are apt to fay, *what am I the
better ?* The devilifh nature delights in God, the
lefs, becaufe of his goodnefs ; for the more good
God is, the further is he removed from their degenerate temper   'Tis our unfuitablenefs and un-
likenefs to God, that hinders our delight and fatisfaction in him.   'Tis a great faying, *Whofoever is
pleafed with God, pleafeth God.*   Whofoever, I fay,
is pleafed with that which God is pleafed with, is
pleafing unto God.   But they that are in an un-
fuitable temper and difpofition, (as the unregenerate man, and fenfual fpirit, as the atheiftical and
profane, and thofe that are malicious and devilifh):
they are in a fpirit oppofite to the Spirit of God,
and therefore they are offended with God, as well

as

as God is offended with them : but, *whofoever are* *pleafed with God, God is pleafed with them :* but to the wicked and unregenerate, God himfelf (as good as he is) he is a burden ; for it is the temper of wickedness to fay unto God, *Depart from us, for we do not defire the knowledge of thy ways,* Job xxi. 14. For it is univerfally true, that things are to perfons, according as they are in ftate, fpirit, and temper. Let men pretend love to the things of God never fo much, they will not relifh them, un- lefs they be born of God : 'tis they that are natu- ralized to heaven, that relifh and favour divine things. That which is born of the world, is enmi- ty againft God. But

2. Our rejoicing muft be with fome refpeft to God ; and though it be in *other things,* yet it muft be in the Lord : and this is done, when

1. We acknowlege God originally, as the *foun- tain* from whence all good things come, and the firft caufe of all good. When we are fenfible that we receive from him, and hold of him, and have what we enjoy, from his bounty.

2. When we account *God better than all* other enjoyments whatfoever, and have all things in fub- ordination to him.

3. When we look upon all our enjoyments as fruits of the divine goodnefs, and confider them as enjoyments,

Firft, To *endear God* to us, and

Secondly, Of *obliging us to God.* For you know, a courtefy is accounted as loft, if the party doth not gain the good-will and affeftion of the perfon, to

whom

whom he fhewed kindnefs. Even fo it is in refpect
of God ; if God be not endeared to us by his kindnefs, and we obliged to him for his goodnefs, all is
loft. But

4. We then may be faid to *rejoice in the Lord,*
when we make God the *final end,* and make all
things fubfervient to his glory ; and account ourfelves bound to difpofe of what he gives us according to his appointment, and for the ends of virtue.
And to this purpofe, that we may rejoice in the
good things, that through providence we do enjoy,
with fome refpect to God ; two things are neceflary.

1. It is neceflary to give God *place* in the world.

2. That we *take pleafure* in the works of his providence. For there is nothing that God doth, or
that he doth permit to be done, but it doth offer
to the intelligent mind, fome *notion from God,* and
caufe fome obfervance of God in the world ; and
doth give advantage to fome divine contemplation,
and fo doth put the foul upon fome action of acknowledgment and adoration of God.

To enforce this *joy in God* ; I fubjoin two things.

1. That joy is *neceffary* to the life of man. The
apoftle hath told us, that *worldly forrow caufeth death.*
Sorrow and fadnefs, melancholy and difcontent fpoils
the temper of a man's mind ; it vitiates the humours
of the body ; it prevents the divine, and hinders the
phyfician. For the *divine* deals by reafon ; but this
being obliterated, he can do nothing : for he applies himfelf to the mind and underftanding ; but
forrow and melancholy hinders the receiving of
true

true reafon, and then his work is at an end. And it alfo hinders the *phyfician* ; for if the mind be difcompofed by melancholy, it doth not afford due benevolence to the body. You have an inftance in *Nebuchadnezzar*, who was by melancholy transformed into a beaft : not that he was fo by external form, but he did fo efteem himfelf ; and things are as men conceive them. The four and melancholy, they are unthankful to God, and cruel to themfelves, and peevifh in their converfe ; fo that joy and rejoicing is *neceffary* in refpect to ourfelves. But

2. In *refpect to God* ; joy and rejoicing is fafe for us, and prefervative to us, as I fhall fhew you in fundry refpects.

1. If we have refpect to God in our joy, we can never *tranfgrefs*.

2. We cannot *exceed*, nor any ways mifbehave ourfelves : we cannot do ourfelves any harm. For we read of fome that have fuddenly died, by reafon of joy, at the tidings of good, as well as fudden bad news.

3. Our joy will then be *fincere* and *pure*, not frothy and fantaftical.

4. It will *offend none*, nor be irkfome to any.

5. It will always keep company with *gratitude* and *humility*. For obferve it in the text, they are made reciprocal, to rejoice in the Lord, and to give thanks unto him.

6. It will always leave us in a *good temper* ; which worldly joy will not do.

7. It is wholly separate from all *surfeiting*, drunkennefs and uncleannefs, and will free the soul from the *spiritual fins* of haughtinefs, infolency and felf-affuming. If our triumph be in the Lord, it feparates from fenfual things, and from the fpiritual fins of pride and arrogancy : therefore let there be always fomething that is fpiritual in the ground, reafon, or occafion, or motive of your joy ; fome notion of God's providence in all your mirth. Sadnefs and joy are things of the moft powerful influence in the life of man ; the former breaks his heart, and the latter many times greatly tranfports him. But now an eye to God in both, doth poife and balance them, and makes the foul fafe and fteady under them. And fo much for the former part of the text, *rejoice in the Lord.*

II. *For praife is comely for the upright.* 1*ft.* Thefe words you fee are exegetical to *rejoicing. Rejoice in the Lord,* for *praife is comely.* If praife and rejoicing were not the fame, there were no argument in the words, *for praife is comely.* And then, 2*dly. Uprightnefs* is exegetical *to righteoufnefs. Rejoice in the Lord, O ye righteous, for praife is comely for the upright.* By uprightnefs is here meant our fincerity and integrity, our honeft meaning and true intention ; which through God's gracious acceptance is our righteoufnefs. *We are, none of us, at all better than we mean :* our gracious God takes us by what we underftand, intend and mean. And the truth is here, there is no difpenfation for failure in intention. For mifapprehenfion, God doth grant allowance, and difpenfe with human frailties ; but for a failing of
intention

intention there is no difpenfation. Fail here, and
you are *hypocrites*, and falfe-hearted ; and therefore,
uprightnefs is our perfection, and our righteoufnefs.
For, either you intend well, or you do not ; if
you do, you are upright; if you do not, you are hypocrites. It goes mighty far in religion, that a man
doth fimply, honeftly, and in plainnefs of heart,
mean and intend God and goodnefs, righteoufnefs
and truth. He is upright that means well : though
he be in many particulars, miftaken and incumbred
with weakneffes, yet he is righteous in the fight of
God, through God's gracious acceptance. Therefore it becomes us to be highly charitable, one
towards another, fince God is fo gracious, and
fets fuch a value upon our good meanings and fincere intentions, as to account of this for righteoufnefs, either in practice or opinion. If a man, in
the integrity of his heart, doth honeftly mean God,
goodnefs, righteoufnefs and truth, God will receive
him. *Every man's mind is himfelf, and a man is what*
he means and intends ; and what a man means not,
that he is not, that he does not. And this I have faid,
becaufe in the text, there are two words made exegetical, *praife* and *rejoicing, righteoufnefs* and *up-*
rightnefs. Rejoice in the Lord, O ye righteous, for
praife is comely for the upright.

This remains to be fpoken to ; and 'tis a gallant
notion in this age that tends fo much to atheifm.

Praife is comely. This is fpoken by way of argument ; and 'tis no argument, if this be not true,
that *there is a reafon for what we do, from the things*
themfelves. I mean this, and if you grant but *this,*

that there is that which of itself is good and come-ly, juft and right, and there is that which of itfelf is finful and abominable ; we exclude atheifm out of the world : and this muft be acknowledged, o-therwife there is no argument in thefe words, *for praife is comely.* If all things are alike, and no dif-ference of things, one thing is no more comely than another. Now becaufe this is an excellent rule, and a way to exclude atheifm out of the world, I will fhew you that this notion is abundant in fcripture, *viz. That goodnefs and truth are firft in things* ; and though they are fo in mens apprehenfions *fecondari-ly,* yet they are fo *firft* in themfelves ; and that men live in a lie, and are in a lie, if their apprehenfions be not conformed to things in their reality and ex-iftence. Several fcriptures have this notice : *Phil.* iv. 8. runs upon it all along. *Whatfoever things are venerable, juft, honeft, praife-worthy,* &c. How infig-nificant were thefe fayings, if all things were alike as men would have them ? fo *Rom.* xiii. 13. *Walk decently or honeftly.* 1 Cor. vii. 35. 1 Cor. xiv. 40. *Let all things be done decently.* 1 Cor. xi. 13. *Is it come-ly, is it decent ?* Eccles. v. 18. Pfal. xcii. 1. *It is good to fing praife to the Lord.* Pfal. cxlvii. 1. *Praife is comely,* &c.

The reafon of things is, that law and truth which none muft tranfgrefs : I fay, the reafon of things is a law and truth which none, either by power or priviledge may tranfgrefs. And for this I will give you fuch arguments for convinction, that greater can-not be given : for I tell you, *'tis a law in heaven, and that which God takes notice of in all his difpenfati-*

ons

ons to his creatures. It is that which God will give an account of himself by, to the underftandings of his creatures. For this I will produce many fcriptures ; *righteoufnefs and judgment are the habitation of his throne,* Pfal. xcvii. 2. Can any man underftand this to be nothing but what is arbitrary ? *Job.* viii. 3. and xxxiv. 12. *Will he by power pervert that which is right ?* Rom. iii. 3. *Is there unrighteoufnefs with God ? God forbid.* How infignificant are all thefe expreffions, if all things be alike and arbitrary, if the difference of things be nothing elfe but fantaftical and conceited ? and yet this and much more muft the atheift fay, or elfe his opinion is worth nothing. For if there be a difference in things, he will be felf-condemned. We have *Abraham's* queftion, *Gen.* xviii. 25. *Shall not the judge of all the earth do right ?* thefe were certainly prefumptuous, arrogant, and bold fpeeches to be faid to God, if my notion were not true ; for thefe conclude will, and fhut it up, as having no rule in this law of right. So *Acts* xvii. 31. it is faid, *God shall judge the world in righteoufnefs.* If there be not difference in things, and a rule of right, thefe words fignify nothing. I could quote you hundreds of places for this ; *all the ways of God are ways of truth of righteoufnefs and of judgment.* Can any man imagine, that this fignifies no more, but that things are as *will* would have them. Therefore I tell you, (and it is that by which you and all the world fhall be judged) that thefe are not bare words and titles, not fhadows and imaginations. . There is that which is decent and fitting to be done ; or that which is equal ; that

E 2 which

which is fair ; that which is comely and feemly : *there is that which holds of itfelf*, and is decent, comely and fitting. *Truth and goodnefs are firſt in things, then in perfons* ; and 'tis our duty to obferve them, and our uprightnefs to comply with them. All things are not arbitrary and pofitive conftitution ; but there is that which is lovely and comely in itfelf ; and there is that which is impure and ugly in its own nature and quality ; and if any man meddles with it, let him be fure it will difparage him, and render him contemptible, vile, and bafe. There is alfo that which is generous, noble and worthy, and will gain repute and credit to him that ufes it. 'Tis not all one for an intelligent and voluntary agent, to do one thing or another ; for there are rules of right wherewith all intelligent agents muft comply, and they do righteoufly when they do, and finfully when they do not. There is fuch a turpitude in fome things, that there is no priviledge or protection ; nothing that can be alledged that will gain a man liberty to do them, for they have an intrinfick malignity and impurity ; and thefe things are a difparagement to any perfon whatfoever. And there are things that are juft and righteous, worthy and generous, that will recompence the perfon that is exercifed in them.

And then God made man with a judgment of difcerning, and 'tis expected that man fhould judge and difcern, and reafon concerning things. And this is not fo much our priviledge, as our charge and truft, to obferve the difference of things. The whole motion of the world below men, is nulled upon

pon a moral confideration ; and no morality to be found in any agent below man : the motions of all elfe, are no better than mechanick. Now this is the foundation of fcripture, exhortation, and admonition : we are to examine by reafon and by argument, becaufe God applies to reafon and judgment, and to underftanding, which is infeparable to choice and refolution.

In fhort, a man is accomplifhed by two things, 1*ft*. By being enlightned in his intellectual faculties. 2*dly*. By being directed in his morals to refufe evil, and to do good ; and to chufe and determine things according to the difference of them. The 1*ft*. is the perfection of a man's underftanding. The 2*d*. is the goodnefs of his mind, *Phil.* ii. 13. *Work out your falvation with fear, for it is God that worketh in you,* &c. This fuppofes a judgment of difcerning ; and then confequently, that God does expect, that a man, according to his apprehenfion and judgment, fhould chufe, refolve, and determine. Now where we are called upon to work in the affair of falvation ; fee how cautioufly the fcripture fpeaks of it, *Phil.* ii. 12. *Work out your own falvation, for it is God that worketh in you, both to will and to do of his own good pleafure.* From hence no body fhould be difcouraged from the fenfe of his own difability ; nor arrogate to himfelf, or be prefumptuous ; *for God worketh in him to will and to do of his good pleafure.* If this notion were but well obferved, a great part of fome controverfies, at this day, would be refolved ; for fcripture doth attribute to us that which God doth with us : that which we do

E 3

is

is attributed to God ; and that which God doth by
us, is both afcribed to God, and to us ; we work,
and God works ; we are awakened, directed, and
affifted by him, fo that I think there is too much
heat in many controverfies, and a right ftating them
would extinguifh them from being in the world.

We fee there is a direct and exact government in
heavenly bodies. When did ever the fun fail ? It
were prodigious if it fhould : and why fhould not
we,that are guided by principles of reafon and illumination, (which is a far greater communication
from God) why fhould we be fo irregular and inconfiftent, fince the lower creation is fo regular and
uniform ? For there is nothing of conflagration in
the heavenly motions, becaufe no oppofitions : and
if *we* were uniform to principles of reafon and right
underftanding, all motions with us would be fo,
and tend to mutual information and edification, but
not at all to provocation, or exafperation, one of a-
nother.

Pray let me leave this notion with you, that *there
is a differente in things* ; there is that which is comely, that which is regular, decent, and directed according to rule, and the ftanding principle of God's
creation. You fee how much time I have fpent in
the notion, or that which is the force of the argument ; we *are to rejoice and give thanks*, becaufe *it
is comely*. The reafon lies in the quality of the thing,
which doth fuppofe, that *there is a difference in things*;
by which the atheift is excluded out of the world,
and mens liberties reftrained to that which is right.
'Tis no rule to a man's actions, to do that which
he

he may maintain by power and priviledge ; but to
do that which is fit to be done, *juft* and *right* : to
comply in all things with the *reafon of things*, and
the rule of right, and in all things to be according to
the nature, mind and will of God, the law of juftice, the rule of right, the reafon of things. Thefe
are the laws, by which we are to act and govern
our lives ; and we are all born under the power of
them : and if this be not true, this argument of
the pfalmift is infignificant, *praife ye the Lord, for it
is comely.* The reafon of things therefore, is our
rule, both in religion and converfe, one with ano j
ther ; and though thefe are different forms of fpeech,
yet they are always in conjunction. The reafon of
the mind is by thefe to be directed ; and indeed, all
principles of religion are founded upon the fureft,
moft conftant, and higheft reafon in the world.
There is nothing fo intrinfically rational as religion is ;
nothing fo felf-evident, nothing that can fo juftify
itfelf, or that hath fuch pure reafon to commend itfelf, as religion hath ; for it gives an account of itfelf to our judgments and to our faculties ; and this,
God himfelf doth acknowledge, *Ifa.* v. 3. *Judge, I
pray you, between me and my vineyard.* So, 1 *Cor.*
xi. 13. *Judge in your felves, is it comely,* &c. He
brings that for an argument, the indecency of it.
But fo much for the notion, *That there is a difference in things ; that good and evil are firft in things ;
right and wrong firft in things themfelves.* This is not
arbitrary, nor imagined, nor determined by power
and priviledge, but there is good and evil, comely
and uncomely in things themfelves. A word of this
particular cafe, and I have done.   *Praife*

Praife is comely. It is nature's fenfe, 'tis the import of any man's reafon : every man's mind tells
him that *this is decent* ; and no man can have peace,
quiet and fatisfaction in the contrary ; unlefs he be
funk down into bafenefs, and degenerated into a
fordid temper, he will acknowledge the kindnefs of
his benefactor. Now, becaufe God doth infinitely
tranfcend all the benefactors in the world, if any
man doth not acknowledge his goodnefs, and praife
him for his benefits, he is funk down into bafenefs,
and fallen beneath his creation and nature.

God loves us, and therefore he doth us good : we
love God becaufe we are partakers of his benefits.
Now praife and thankfgiving is all the return that
our neceffity and beggary is capable of : and it is
very comely for us, that are fo much beholden to
the divine goodnefs, to make our due acknowledgments ; and therefore it is obferved that in ingratitude there is a connexion of all vice. All difinge-
nuity and bafenefs are concentred in the bowels of
ingratitude. He that will not be engaged by kindnefs, no *cords of man will hold him.* It is obferved
both by God and man, as degeneracy in its ultimate
iffue, the greateft depravation that nature is capable
of, to be infenfible of courtefies, and not to make
due acknowledgments. How often doth *David*
complain of thofe perfons, that were obliged to him
by kindnefs, that they turned his enemies, *Pfal.* xli.
and xlv. *he that fat at meat with me, hath lift up his
heel againft me.* How is he reprefented by him, as
a moft fordid wretched perfon, one that was degenerated to the fulleft degree ? and then God himfelf

felf complains, *Deut.* xxxii. 15. Jeſhurun *waxed fat
and kicked, he forfook God that made him, and lightly
eſteemed the rock of his ſalvation.* God and man complains of the ungrateful, becauſe all favours and cour-
teſies are loſt. Yea, 'tis well obſerved, that it is the
only way to make a deſperate enemy, to beſtow
kindneſs upon an unthankful perſon. And this is
too well known, that thoſe that have been made
friends by courteſy, proving falſe, have been the
greateſt betrayers. Therefore, of all perſons and
tempers, the inſenſible and ungrateful are the
worſt : yea, truly, theſe are the very peſts of the
world, the enemies of human nature ; they harden
mens hearts, who otherwiſe were free to do cour-
teſies, becauſe they do not know but that they may
make an enemy. I will make this out (*viz.* the
baſeneſs of ingratitude) in theſe *two* words.

. 1. Becauſe *nothing is more due to God than our
gratitude ;* for he *loadeth us with his benefits, and is
pleaſed to pleaſe us,* and doth many things to gratify
us.

2. By this we give *teſtimony of our minds to God ;*
for we have nothing at all to ſacrifice to God, but
the conſent of our minds ; an ingenuous acknowledgement. We have nothing to bring him, but
the conſent of our minds ; and this the grateful
perſon doth, and by this he ſignifies, that if it were
within his compaſs, he would requite the divine
goodneſs ; for 'tis not ſo much the gift, as the mind
of the giver. He that is unthankful, is moſt full of
himſelf, and apt to think that all the world was
made for him, and that all men are bound to be
                                                          his

his servants, and to attend his purpose, and that he may serve himself of all mens parts, powers, privileges and opportunities; but he himself is exempt from all men; so that he is an enemy to God and men.

DISCOURSE V.

The secret BLASTING of MEN.

PSALM xxxix. 11.

When thou with rebukes dost correct man for iniquity, thou makest his beauty to consume away like a moth; surely every man is vanity. Selah.

NOTHING is less true, nothing more unbecoming us, limited, finite, and fallible creatures, than the thought of independency and self-sufficiency. And indeed, the whole creation of God, in comparison with God himself, is less than the dust of the balance; and if you come to compare, will hold no weight. Nothing becomes us more, than to know what we are: nothing befits us better, than that we know our own state, and to be sensible of our own dependence and necessity, and to make due acknowledgement to God. If a man seriously weigh these words, he will always veil to God, humble himself, submit, and deprecate. So many things there are emphatical in these words, *When thou,* &c.

Sin,

Sin, on man's part, is that that makes him much
more liable and obnoxious to God, than he is in
refpect of his creature-ftate : *when thou with rebukes doft correct man for iniquity thou makeft his beauty,* that that he values himfelf by, that that is his
only thing, his top excellency, *to confume away like a
moth,* without any refiftance, without any ftop, in-
fenfibly : fo that he that doth contemplate what is
faid in the former part of the words, will prefently
acknowledge, that *every man, even in his beft eftate is
vanity, altogether vanity.*

Thefe words give an account of two things which
are the matter of the greateft wonder.

Firft, How it comes to pafs there are fo *many and
fo great evils* in the world.

Secondly, How fo many perfons come to wither
and fall away, and come to nothing in the world.
And thefe two are the greateft matters of *wonder* and
admiration among men.

Firft, How it comes to pafs that there are fo *many, and fo great evils* in the world : and the wonder is
this, that God governs the world, and God is known
by his goodnefs : what, thefe evils from the hand of
a good God ! how can this be ? the greateft queftions that have ever been in the world, have been
thefe two.

1. Whence *evils* come ? and

2. How it comes to pafs they were not *fubdued,*
as foon as they did appear; I believe it would puzzle
the head of any one in the world to anfwer them ;
if he do not learn an anfwer from fcripture. Now
this place refolves you ; you have here God chal-
lenging

lenging, controuling and rebuking it.   For if you find out the procuring *cause*, you find out all :   not he that doth the thing, but he that was the cause of the thing being done, doth the mischief.

Secondly, Then how comes it to pass that *so many wither* in the world, with all advantages, honour, titles, dignity and estate, that they never spent their thoughts about getting; and out-live it all. Whereas you have others born naked into the world ; and through the improvement of natures. powers, they rise to estates and revenues.   How comes this to pass ? in these words you have an account.   *When thou with rebukes dost correct a man for iniquity, thou makest his beauty to consume away like a moth.*

These two considerations are enough to engage your attention : every body hath their ears open to hear resolutions of wonders.

In the words you have *four things.*

I. What is *intimated*, and that is, that sin is the procuring cause of punishment. *When thou with rebukes dost correct man for sin*, &c.   Sin is the procuring cause of punishment.   It is sin that doth the world all the mischief that is in the world. A fault deserves punishment : the fault going before, doth naturally draw on with it punishment.

II. Take notice of what is *supposed*, that God doth regularly and usually chastise sinners. God doth, as a thing becoming him in the government of the world, he doth controul sinners, and chastise men for sin.   The word is very remarkable, *When thou with rebukes*, &c. which intimates something *in secret* : not only openly punished in the view of the
world ;

world ; but sinners feel checks' and reproofs from God, which unless they themselves tell, others are not aware of. An *internal* stroke ; for these rebukes are *secret* ; though they are certainly felt by those that are under them, by-standers take no cognizance of them. *The torments of a* man's own breast are beyond any evil that befalls the body : trouble in a man's mind, is beyond the pain of the stone or gout. For if a man's mind be whole, he can bear up against bodily infirmity. *But a wounded spirit who can bear?* Prov. xviii. 14.*

III. Take notice what is *proposed*; that these rebukes of God *blast* men : when thou with rebukes correctest man for sin, *thou makest his beauty to consume.* *His beauty*, that is, that which is most desirable, that which is most valuable; his health, his wealth, his friends, his internal peace, the parts of his mind : for these are a man's excellency, and all these are meant by his *beauty.* And if God blast a man, all these wither away, and come to nothing : thou makest his *beauty to consume away like a moth* : a moth is always fretting, not apt to be found out, not apt to be resisted, but brings all to confusion. These rebukes of God blast men.

IV. Take notice what is here *inferred : surely every man is vanity.* And no conclusion doth more plainly follow from any thing premised. For every man is *vanity* upon a double account.

1st, Because he is *fallible*, and so subject to miscarry ; else he would never be found in the ways of iniquity, and

* Si dii deæque omnes, &c. Tacitus in Tiberio.

2dly, Because

2dly, Becaufe he is fo controulable and *account-able* ; and under a power that he cannot refift.

Thus I have given you an account in thefe four particulars, of the matter that lies in the words. And really, the text offers to you things of *great moment*, and weighty confideration. I will fpeak fhortly to all *four :* and becaufe I will be brief, I will put the two firft together, and they will do well fo, *viz.*

I. That iniquity is the foundation of punifhment, and II. That it is regular, ufual and ordinary for God to controul and punifh finners. This is expected, and it becomes him, as he is the governor, and maintainer of righteoufnefs, and truth. And if you fpeak properly of punifhment, God doth only chaftife *finners,* fo, and no otherwife, *finners,* and none elfe. And then it is a great note, and will teach us to fpeak more accurately when we fpeak of *punifhment,* for if we fpeak properly God doth not punifh but in the cafe of fin. But becaufe ufe and practice hath amplified this word and in a more large fenfe of the word, we fay a man is punifhed, when any evil thing befals him, though he hath done nothing that may procure it ; I will therefore in a preparatory way offer *four cafes,* which we are not to call punifhment.

1. The effects of God's *abfolute fovereignty,* and power. We acknowledge, that God in the ufe of his fovereignty, may deal differently with feveral of his creatures : and yet, where he deals better, he doth not reward, and where he deals worfe, he doth not punifh. And if this were well underftood, thofe paffages in *Rom.* ix. would be better underftood : fuch as thefe, *Jacob have I loved, and Efau have I*
                                                        hated :

hated : it imports no more than that it was the pleasure of God, to take the younger brother *Jacob*, and
make him the progenitor of the promised *Messias*,
and not *Esau* : and this is the meaning of that scripture. *Hating* there, is *less loving* ; and our Saviour
so useth the word, *Luke* xiv. 26. when he bids us
hate our own life, and hate father and mother ; whereas we are enjoined to honour father and mother ;
and to preserve our lives ; and it is our duty ; for
if we may not kill another we may not kill ourselves;
and this is expounded in *Matt.* x. 37, 38. by
defending our life, that is, with denying Christ, *&c.*
So again, *hath not the potter power over his clay, &c.*
that is, he may make one, a vessel of higher use ;
another of inferior use : and this belongs to God's
undoubted priviledge, power and sovereignty ; to
raise one to a higher condition in the world, and
place another in an inferior condition ; to make one
high, another low ; one rich, another poor ; one a
master, another a servant. Now we are not to say
that God doth punish him that is in the worst condition ; here is no notion of punishment ; this is
neither the reward of any man's virtue, nor the punishment of any man's fault ; for punishment properly is where there is *pœna ratione vindictæ* ; but
these things are as God pleaseth. Now this I make
further appear, by interpreting St. *Paul* by himself, where he speaks of *vessels of honour, and vessels
of dishonour,* 2 Tim. ii. 20. His own words are,
*In a great house, there are not only vessels of gold and
silver, but also some of wood and of earth, and some to
honour, and some to dishonour.* The *vessel to honour,*

as

as the cup he drinks in ; the veſſel to *diſhonour,* as other utenſils. Now, who hath any ill deſign upon his neceſſary utenſils ? ſo that all theſe differences are within the latitude of God's ſovereignty, and ſpeak nothing, either of love or hatred.

2. That that is natural evil, ſometimes comes from God, barely for *trial,* and for *exerciſe :* and God doth not intend puniſhment at all, neither doth he look at any provocation, nor hath diſpleaſure at the perſon ; and this was plainly good *Job's* caſe. For in the beginning of the firſt chapter, *Job* hath God's recommendation to the full, and yet the devil hath *Job* in his power, and is only reſtrained as to his life. Therefore, *Job* was not puniſhed, but he was put upon the uſe and exerciſe, and trial of his patience, and ſeveral other virtues and graces ; and therefore, *Job* did well to diſpute againſt his friends ; for they run upon this notion, that if any man ſuffered evil, it muſt be puniſhment; and that *Job,* notwithſtanding his outward appearance, was either a hypocrite, or ſome way obnoxious : but he ſtands to it, and will maintain his uprightneſs. And in the xlii chap. there God juſtifies him, challenges his friends, and ſends them to *Job,* and he muſt ſacrifice for them. So that, notwithſtanding *Job* ſuffered ſo much evil, he was not an offender, nor puniſhed, but exerciſed : and God may tempt us in this kind, to try our affections to him, and whether we will ſtand to him, or no.

3. There are chaſtiſements, or harder conditions for the *increaſe* of virtue, the contempt of the world, the increaſe of modeſty and humility. We might

over-

over-value the world, and value ourfelves too much, if we were not fometimes taught, that thefe things are not to be taken into the account of our happinefs.

4. There is fometimes alfo evils for an *evil neighbour's fake* : a very good man, at whom God takes no offence, he may fuffer fome evil for his neighbour's fake ; as good *Jofiah* was overborn by the evil that was done in the days of *Manaffeh* ; and in this fenfe, is to be underftood that in *Ezek.* xxi. 3. *I will cut off from thee the righteous with the wicked.* And here is no punifhment neither ; for they that are not in the fault, may fuffer becaufe of the unhappinefs that comes upon their neighbours. And God knows how to make up this their lofs in time, and in eternity. In neither of thefe cafes, is God faid to punifh. Neither of thefe cafes come within the cafe of the text.

But now, thefe cafes being taken out, I come to give you an account of the truth of the propofition, *that fin is the caufe of punifhment,* and that in *five* particulars.

1. Many fins are the *natural caufes* of the evils that are confequent upon them : as intemperance of certain difeafes, diftempers, and dying before mens time. Some men drink themfelves into fevers, and fome into dropfies. Here fin is the *natural caufe* of evil. Men of intemperate and diffolute lives deftroy their bodily health ; dull and ftupify their reafon and underftanding ; and wafte their eftates. It is moft apparent that fome men have overthrown ftrong and healthy conftitutions ; and ftupified quick

VOL. I.   F   and

and nimble parts, by diforderly living. They might
have been much more in both, had they been fober ; had they not fpoiled themfelves by mif-govern-
ment, *Ecclef.* vii. 17. It is apparent that fome men
that never knew the getting of a penny, as they had
not wit to get an eftate, fo they have not had the
prudence to enjoy, fo as to keep an eftate ; but have
wafted it fafter than others got it.   Now in thefe
cafes no body can fay that God was fevere ; but
thefe men were mad, and played the fool. Let not
us therefore afcribe that to God, that is properly
confequent upon mens own excefs, temerity and
rafhnefs.

   2. Some iniquities are the *moral caufes* of evil ;
for this there are feveral inftances. *Herod* taking
God's glory to himfelf, was the moral caufe of his
dying of the loufy difeafe, *Acts* xii. 23. Becaufe he
did arrogate and affume to himfelf *that that was*
proper to God, God would not fuffer him to go
out of the world with the common honour of mankind. The *Ifraelites* calf-worfhip, (the firft inftance
of idolatry we read of) or worfhipping God by a
falfe medium, (which is idolatry, whatfoever the *Papifts* fay) was the true *moral caufe* of the flaughter of
fo many of them. *Sennatherib* blafphemes God,
and the hoft are all found dead corpfes that night,
2 *Kings* xix. 35.   The cafe of *Corah, Dathan* and
Abiram : God created a new thing in the world ;
the earth opens her mouth, and fwallows them up
alive, *Numb.* xiv.   *Nebuchadnezzar* vaunting himfelf of his majefty and his glory, prefently is made
lefs than a man, finks into melancholy ; and by his
                                                   own

own conceit, was difpoffeffed of his kingdom, and eat grafs with the ox, &c. Dan. iv. 24. if that be the explanation. *Ananias* and *Sapphira*, lying to the Holy Ghoft, are fmitten dead, one after another, *Acts* v. whereas they did a brave act, fold their eftate, and brought a moiety, which if they had brought it as a moiety, had been well enough ; but bringing half, as if that were all, they were flain (for lying to the Holy Ghoft) by the word of St. *Peter*'s mouth. Here is fin the *moral caufe*, that is, the matter of the provocation, the procuring caufe of punifhment.

3. Some evils are the proper *remedies* of certain fins ; as fcarcenefs, and famine, of *fulnefs of bread*, and excefs : throwing fome men out of place and power, the remedy to cure oppreffion and wrongdoing. The ftraitened condition of fome men that are lavifh, prodigal and expenfive ; the low eftate of fome that are proud and conceited ; this keeps them within fome meafure and bounds. This is the 3d cafe ; fome evils the proper *remedies* of certain fins.

4. Punifhments are requifite to maintain God's honour in the world. God would be forgotten to be the governor of the world : he would not be thought to be concerned, if he fhould wholly neglect to punifh, *Eccl.* viii. 11. *Becaufe fentence againft an evil work is not executed fpeedily, therefore the hearts of the fons of men are fully fet in them to do evil. Therefore* are *open fins* controuled, and *fecret fins* are punifhed, left God fhould be denied to be the *fearcher of hearts*. God might be forgotten to be the fu-

preme

preme moderator and governor of the world, if the world should not hear of him, when there be high exorbitancies.

5. The *variety of things*, and *changeable conditions* are as requisite to maintain virtue and holiness among mankind, as the winds, which occasion storms and tempests, which put the air and sea into motion; and so keep them from stench and putrefaction. In nature, we do observe that all things are continued, and preserved in their purity, by *motion*. And where there is not motion, there is putrefaction. Now since the *world rational* is as subject to corrupt as the *world natural* is, therefore it is fitting the world of mankind should be put upon motion and activity; as it is requisite for the *world natural* to be put upon motion, by the winds fanning the air, and putting the sea into motion, and thereby preserving them. This I observe, a great many scriptures impute creatures degeneracy to their living at ease, *Amos* vi. 1. *Jer.* xlviii. 11. *Zech.* i, 15. And *I am sore displeased with the heathen that are at ease,* &c. So *Luke* xii. 19. and *I will say to my soul, soul, thou hast much goods laid up for many years, take thy ease, eat, drink, and be merry.* Upon this account the lesser evils, such as are the evils of smart, are preventive of the greater evils; such as are rancor, malignity, and naughtiness of mind; and this tends to preservation. And here is the account of God's punishment; not that he loves punishment; but as becoming a governor, and maintaining right, and for the good of his creatures.

And

And thus have I given you a juft account of what
is in thefe words *intimated* and *fuppofed;* that fin is
the procuring caufe of punifhment ; and that God
doth regularly and ufually controul and punifh finr
ners. A word of *inference.*

1. It is good fervice to mankind to *reftrain* evils and
hinder them *James* iv. 1. This the magiftrate may do ;
this the preacher of righteoufnefs, it is proper for
him to do ; *this,* the holy liver, by his good example,
doth conftantly do. The great evils that do infect
and difturb the world, they have their being and
foundation in fin : and therefore whofoever prevents
iniquity and fin, he doth the work of a Saviour in
the world, and a preferver. The world would be
another thing, were it not for the iniquity that pre-
vails in it.

2. Then let us *net forfake our own mercy,* but favour ourfelves, not expofe ourfelves to ruin, by caufe-
lefs and unprofitable commiffion of fin. Here I
would take up St. *Peter's* counfel, and it's excellent
good in this cafe. *Matt.* xvi. 22. *Be it far from
thee,* &c. Do not yourfelves fo great harm, for
that that will not profit : do not do yourfelves mifchief upon fo eafy an account. Every thing of fin
is irrational and unprofitable, and a man offers violence to himfelf when he doth it, and doth himfelf
wrong. Therefore, favour yourfelves, do not do
yourfelves wrong, upon terms fo unreafonable, and
fo unprofitable.

3. Since iniquity doth fo much prevail in the
world, let *God* be *excufed* from our charge of his u-
furpation over his creation. Not he that brings on

the harm, but he that is the peccant party, doth the mischief. As in war, not he that raiseth the first army, but he that gives the first offence, is the cause of the war. Therefore let us not think that God doth usurp, or gratify any thing in himself, when he doth punish : no, the true and proper cause is the delinquent party ; he that gives the first offence.

4. When the judgments of God are upon us in pursuit of sin, let us then do as *Joshua* did, let us search out the provoking cause, to use *Daniel's* word, the *abomination of desolation*, that is, the abominable thing that doth provoke God to desolate. Let us remove that that is the cause, and doth contain the disease.

DISCOURSE VI.

The secret BLASTING of MEN.

PSALM XxxiX. II.

When thou with rebukes dost correct man for iniquity, thou makest his beauty to consume away like a moth ; surely, every man is vanity. Selah.

I Have already spoken to what in these words is intimated, that *iniquity is the procuring cause of punishment* ; and also to that that is here *supposed, that it is regular and ordinary, that God should give testimony against iniquity,* that he should challenge sinners. Of these two I have given an account. In the III. Place

III. Place I come to, that that is *propofed* in thefe
words, that is, *that thefe rebukes of God do blaft men,
and caufe them to wither. When thou with rebukes dijt
correct man for iniquity, thou makeft his beauty to confume away like a moth.* This is the *main point* of the
words, and that which I mainly thought upon, when
thefe words came firft into my mind.   When God
takes a finner in hand, and fets himfelf to reverfe
what the finner hath unduly done, he fails and comes
to nothing; he cannot bear up againft God. *Thou
makeft his beauty to confume away like a moth.* I might
enlarge thefe words to take in all the judgments of
God upon a finful world, which are as fo many tefti-
monies of God againft iniquity, fuch as are the con-
fufions that are made by war; fuch as are the de-
folations that are made among men by famine,
plague, and peftilence, and all other judgments,
wherein there is a common fuffering, which all men
acknowledge to be the hand of God; and in refpect
to thefe, *God is known by the judgments he doth execute.* But, not excluding thefe, I fhall only take notice of the words, as to what may pafs *immediately
between God and the finner in fecret,* and are not fo
vifible to the eyes of the by-ftanders, and that for
thefe confiderations. Confidering the *Hebrew* words
ufed in the text for *rebukes,* import fuch rebukes,
reproofs, as carry with them a notion, reafon, and argument of conviction, and felf-condemnation.* They fignifie *corripere, erudire;* to re-

* *Increpationes* hic reales intellige, h. e. pœnas, quæ
funt vice increpationum, & quafi advocati, feu inter-

prove, and teach by inflitution, rules, law, and difcipline : as *Gideon* is faid to have taught the men
of *Succoth*, with briars and thorns ; together with
his remembring them of their fcorn put upon him.
That is, when thou doft fecretly call him to account
and reprove him by reafon, by arguments of conviction, and by felf-condemnation ; *thou makeft his beauty*, &c. Here is another word confiderable ; the effects and iffue of thefe ftrokes do terminate upon
things that are *moft valuable*, precious, *and defirable*,†
by which a man doth prefer himfelf and efteem
himfelf ; fuch as his health and ftrength, his wealth,
his friends, the ufe of his parts, his wit and his brain
his reafon and underftanding, his internal joy, mental fatisfaction, and felf-enjoyment : thefe come to
nothing, when God rebukes ; thefe *confume and melt
away*, as the *word* fignifies. The iffue expreffed by
the verb, is no fudden, violent motion, but that
which we call a *dying life*, or a *lingring death*, as
the fcripture otherwhere ufeth it ; and as it is ufed
Jofhua v. 1. when the kings of the *Amorites*, and the
kings of the *Canaanites* heard that the waters of *Jor-
dan* were dried up before the children of *Ifrael*, their
hearts *melted away* : and *Pfal.* cvii. 26. their *foul
melted away*, becaufe of trouble.   So when God

pretes (ut Hebræi loquuntur,) inter Deum & homi-
nem.   V. fynop. crit.
    † Ejus defiderium.   Defiderabile ejus.   Quicquid
in eo eft defiderabile. *Things of value and efteem. Dan.*
x. 3. Panis defideriorum. *Pleafant bread, things neareft, and deareft, moft valuable, defirable by the perfons fuffering.*

comes

comes to call a great finner to an account, and to inquire of him ; he is fo far from giving any account or making any apology, that he *melts away,* finks under confufion, and falls under the charge of the Almighty ; fo that I would read the words thus, *when thou with fecret rebukes, doft charge a perfon for his fecret iniquities, thou makeft his beauty, the things that he values himfelf by, to confume away like a moth.*

God can immediately by his influence, fortify and encourage a man's mind ; or elfe throw him down into difcontent and frowardnefs. For the minds and fpirits of men lie open to God, as much as ought of the creation ; and there is the moft inward relation between the creator and the creature ; and wherein foever a man can keep out all created power (the world, the devil, yea the angels of glory) there he cannot keep out God : for God can call to advertency ; God can call off all other avocations, and then man muft mind what God will have him confider. When God will, the hearts of men will ferve them, and be more than themfelves ; and if God withdraws, they come to nothing. And indeed that that is truly and ftrictly man's weal or woe, depends upon that, which paffeth between God and a man's foul ; the terms that are between God and a man's felf. How contented are fome men in a condition that the world doth defpife ? and how much difcontent in others, that live in worldly fplendour ? Therefore the difference muft arife from the temper of mens minds, and the thoughts that men have of the terms that are between God and themfelves. 'Tis this notion that is in Gods an-

fwer

fwer to *Moses* praying for *his* fifter *Miriam*, Numb. xii. 14. *If her father had but fpit in her face, fhould fhe not have been afhamed feven days ?* How much more, when the difcountenancing is from the *Father of Spirits ?* In fpeaking to this point, I fhall confider two things.

Firft, Whereby chiefly God doth thus blaft men; *how* it is brought about, and whereby it comes to pafs.

Secondly, In what fpecial *cafes*, we may fear judgments in this fort : hearing from God in this worft fenfe.

For the *firft*, I fhall give an account in *fix* particulars.

1. Thefe fecret rebukes may lie in God's fuffering the *foundation of nature to fail, and fink*; fo that men do not continue in the true ufe of reafon and underftanding : where men wholly ceafe to be themfelves, as to the reafon of their minds ; or elfe what remains of mens reafon, is not for themfelves, but is turned againft them. As in the cafe of *Achitophel* and *Judas*, they were fo difpofleffed of the true ufe of the reafon of their minds, that they do fuch acts againft themfelves, as the animal principle keeps all creatures below us from ; (for what creature was ever known to be accefiory to its own deftruction) and which *they* would never have done, had they continued in the true ufe of their underftandings. This therefore is one way, that God can challenge the arbitrarinefs of his creatures ; either by fuffering the *foundation of nature to fail*, fo that men may *not* have *the true ufe* of their reafon and underftanding ;

underſtanding ; or what they have left, they have
for their own diſadvantage : as you often ſee perſons
of wit and cunning have had no better uſe of their
reaſon and underſtanding, than to reaſon againſt all
counſels that are given them for their advantage.
This is a dreadful way, and we have reaſon to thank
God, that he doth uphold the foundation of our natures, and continues us in the uſe of true and ſolid
reaſon.

2. This may be brought to paſs, by *diſaffecting
the mind of man toward worldly contentment*, and ſatisfaction ; ſo that the *ſubſidia vitæ*, the conveniencies and accommodations of life are not reliſhed,
but prove ſapleſs, without ſavour or reliſh. The pa-
late of the ſoul is out of taſte ; ſo as to reliſh nothing, *Eccleſ.* i. 24. It is beſt freely to enjoy : but
through this judgment of God, there is no more
taſte than in the white of an egg, *Job* vi. 6.   God
can throw men out of the poſſeſſion of thoſe things
as to ſelf-enjoyment in them, whereof they continue the legal owners, in *foro hominum.* For a man
may poſſeſs ſeveral things which he may call his
own ; and yet he himſelf *enjoy* no contentment in
them, no ſatisfaction from them. This *Solomon* hath
obſerved in his ſurvey, in the book of *Eccleſiaſtes* :
a man that hath right and titles, and no enjoyment,
Eccl. vi. 2. And he reſolves, that it is beſt for a man
to take his part of all things he calls his own in the
world. And a man is twice his own in thoſe things
he calls his own, if he have the power to uſe and
enjoy them.   And he tells us that *there is one alone,
and there is not a ſecond, yea, he hath neither child nor
                                    brother,*

brother, &c. *Eccl.* iv. 8. and yet he pincheth himfelf, and ftraitneth himself, and never asketh himfelf the queftion for whofe fake he doth it, and he concludes that it is the blessing of God upon a man when he can afford himself the free ufe of all, that he calls his own : And it is the judgment of God upon bafe minds, that though they have, they have no enjoyment ; they have no power to ufe that which they have ; neither can gratify themfelves, nor do any good with it. They are flaves to their own eftates ; they *have* and they *have not.* This I reckon God's plague upon a man's mind, that he hath no true enjoyment of that which is his own.

3. This may be done by Gods inhibiting, or *fufpending* the *virtue of feveral creatures,* which otherwife would be very proper to give a man diverfion, or eafe, or fitting fupply. For, *nothing is any thing any longer than God will have it. That God that ftopped the mouth of the lions* that they could not feed upon *Daniel,* Dan. vi. that God, that could forbid the fire from burning the three children, *Dan.* iii, that God can make every creature a comfort and inftrumental for our good when he pleafeth. The hungry *raven* at his bidding will be a messenger to bring wholfome food to a prophet, 1 *Kings* xvii. 6. As God can refresh the earth by drops from heaven fo he can make the *heaven over our head to be brafs, and the earth to be iron,* Deut. xxviii. 23. fo that they fhall not bring forth. Yea, he can make the rain that falls upon a mans ground, powder and duft, *Deut.* xxviii. 24. He can, not only give rain, which all the idols of the nations cannot do, *Jer.* xiv. 22. fo

Job

Job. v. 10. but alfo water the earth with the river of God, making it foft with fhowers, *Pf.* lxix. 9, 10. and give us fruitful feafons, filling our hearts with food, and gladnefs, *Acts* xiv. 17. We are to underftand that all things whatfoever, act in the power and virtue of the principle that God planted in them in the firft moment of the creation.   Now it is in God, that gave them feveral virtues, to inhibit and fufpend them.   This is fo great a truth, that I have teftimony for it beyond all exception.   It was acknowledged by a fpirit, of which we can give no account ; the fpirit that was conjured up to give *Saul* an anfwer ; faith this fpirit (which is fuppofed to be an infernal fpirit) *wherefore doft thou ask of me, feeing the Lord is departed from thee, and become thine enemy ?* if God inhibit, all creatures are at a lofs : if God forfake a man, he is undone to eternity, and this is acknowledged from hell, as all fuppofe ; for *this* fpirit faith it.

4. God may do this by *withdrawing his blessing* from mens endeavours ; fo that they become unprofperous, and the happy iffues of providence are intercepted.   This we have experience of, that many times things politickly contrived, and carried on with power, fail and mifcarry, and come to nothing, and this is becaufe God is not there.   Other times you have things weakly managed, and unlikely inftruments, and yet great fuccefs, and things fall out above expectation : no account to be given of this, but Gods bleffing and affiftance.   This is that which the wife man hath obferved, that the *race is not always to the fwift, nor the battle to the ftrong,* &c.

but

but as himſelf obſerves, *Eccl.* ii. 26. *God gives to a man that is good in his ſight ; wiſdom, and knowledge, and joy : but to the ſinner he giveth travel to gather and to heap up* ; to gather by hard labour, and much pains taking ; but he hath no joy in it ; but he reſerves it *to give to the man that is upright in his ſight.* And this is another way, God's *withdrawing his bleſſings* from mens endeavours : and can any one be proſperous, when God's curſe is upon him ? It is the *bleſſing of God makes rich,* Prov. x. 22. If there be a croſs providence, a man may endeavour, and to little purpoſe.

5. God can do this by *awakening the guilt* of the ſinner upon his conſcience ; making that to ſting and gall him ; and then all the world is nothing. Many ſinners ſin themſelves into ſtupidity and ſenſeleſſneſs. Others relieve themſelves by running into company, and other avocations : but if God do but quicken the guilt of ſin upon mens conſciences they are thrown out of all poſſeſſion. Now to do this, there needs no more, but to call men to advertency ; no more but to hold men to thoughtfulneſs ; there needs no more from God, but to ſhut men up, and confine them, that they be not relieved by avocations and other employments. Where there is malignity, and guilt upon the *conſcience*, unremoved by repentance, there God needs no more than to hold a man to converſe with himſelf : and it is a marvel how this man ſtays in his wits. A great offender being at eaſe, hath no better ſettlement, and ſecurity than this, that he is in a hurry, and hath not yet leiſure to bethink himſelf.

6. This

6. This may be done when men through their *own fear, suspicion and* jealousy, have certain foretastes of Gods refusal and displeasure. We find by experience, that things are as we imagine. Now whether this be the truth of the case, or no, (desertion of God) yet it is all one to me, if I think so. Thus God may give men up to their own melancholy conceits. There is no security to any mans peace or satisfaction in this life ; or substantial self-enjoyment, but two ways. 1st, That he hath always retained his innocence. The 2d is, that he is restored and recovered to his innocence, by his repentance, and Gods pardon, in, and through the blood of *Christ.* And if a man hath not one of these two, he is unsecure, and no man knows the condition he may be in, the next hour.

In these *six particulars,* I have given you an account of these *secret rebukes* of God, which the sinner cannot bear up under; but when he feels them, if he be not upheld by the hand of God, and that he be brought into reconciliation with God, upon the terms of the covenant of grace, he will *melt away,* and come to nothing. This for the *first.* The *Second,* Is the case wherein there is *imminent danger* of such judgments as these ; and I will give you *six cases.*

1. The case of *havocking conscience,* by sinning against the light of our own proper judgment ; and in this case, a man doth himself inward hurt, he gives himself a wound at the heart : and the wounds of the mind are the torture of a man's soul ; and *all the world will not secure that man, that is not in*

reconci-

reconciliation with the reason of his own mind. To be sensible of *this*, that a man hath contradicted his own proper light ; in this case a man doth an act of violence upon himself ; a man cannot do himself greater wrong than by this *voluntary consenting to known iniquity*. And this I account the true notion of sin, *voluntarily to consent to known iniquity*, and this is that which separates between us and our God. If a man once voluntarily consent to known sin, he parts with the truest friend (next to God) that he hath in the world, his conscience of right ; that bosom friend, his only adviser and counsellor, which will keep a man company when he hath no company else ; that will give him content, and satisfaction in all conditions, that will give testimony to him, though he be slandred, calumniated, and though all the mischiefs in the world fall upon him. This friend is never put away, but by that by which God is put away, *viz.* voluntary consenting to known iniquity, and this puts God away, and puts away this home-friend, conscience of right. If a man have no internal guilt, know no fault within himself, he will be able to bear up against all the world, and he will have satisfaction in every condition ; but if he parts with *this*, he parts with his best friend, gives God offence, and causes him to withdraw, 2 *Cor.* i. 12. *Our rejoicing is this, the testimony of our conscience, that in simplicity and godly sincerity, we have had our conversation in the world.* This is the first case of eminent *danger* of these judgments these *rebukes in secret*.

2. The

2. The second cafe that I reprefent as dangerous, is the cafe of *hypocrify*, diffimulation and falfhood ; and this is equal to the other. The falfe-hearted hypocrite is neither true to God nor man, but ferves himfelf, and his own ends of God, of the world, of truth, of religion ; and all thefe he fub-ordinates to his own particular ends and purpofes ; only he pretends otherwife, and to cover a bad de-fign, he doth ufe foft words. But how reftlefs muft this man be in his own thoughts, when he comes to confider ? For can he depend upon thefe, that thefe perfons or things will do him any good at all, when he knoweth he hath abufed the perfons, and mifufed the things ? no certainly, this man cannot *think* that either God or man will be true to him, and fo can have no confidence in either. For who-foever is himfelf falfe, perfidious, and bafe, he doth not know whom he may truft : for he doth not think there may be a better man than himfelf, and being fenfible of his own internal bafenefs, that he doth not mean what he faith to others ; he verily believes all others to be as he is ; and fo finding himfelf unable to defend himfelf, he muft be in fear of all the world. Therefore it is of neceffity, that a hypocrite be in no true ftate of fatisfaction, or felf-enjoyment.

3. The cafe of *fhamelefs apoftacy*, reprefented *Heb.* x. 26, 27, 28. *For, if we fin wilfully after we have received the knowledge of the truth, there remaineth no more facrifice for fins, but a certain fearful looking for of judgment, &c.* Where the fin is a wilful depar-ture ; and the finner doth *defpite to the fpirit of grace,*

and he doth this knowingly, and confidering what he doth ; the danger is, there is no hope of recovery, becaufe he hath taken his choice, and contracted fenfelefnefs of mind ; that he is in a condition without hope. For thus will men think with themfelves ; when thefe men come to confider, they cannot but think that God fhould do with them, as he finds caufe to do, fince they have done by God what they had a mind to do. Certainly, *they who do worft by religion, fhall fare the worft by irreligion.* Ignorance and incapacity, on any terms whatfoever, hold no proportion in malignity, with this wicked averfation from God, and the ways of righteoufnefs. The apoftle puts the cafe, 2 *Pet.* ii. 12. Do but confider : what do men in fuch a cafe as this ? If one of great acquaintance and converfe prove an enemy and become perfidious ; men had rather truft a ftranger than him ; for it is the maxim of the world, (I confefs it is not chriftian) never truft a reconciled friend.

4. When men *take up with the world, and leave God out,* give themfelves up to take delight and fatisfaction in their worldly accommodations, and leave God out ; *this,* though it be far fhort in malignity, of the other three, yet *this* hath in it the full fpirit of irreligion, and 'tis a high provocation of God ; for it comes to this, God is little in their thoughts, *God is far from their reins.* For is it not very fit that we have a lively fenfe of God, of the benefits we receive from him ? Now for a man to fit down in the world, and enjoy his affluence and abundance, and make no acknowledgment of God, this is downright

right irreligion : and this is, *to make him, that is all in all to us, and better than all ; nothing at all to us, and lower than all* ; and these men cannot but think if ever they come to a strait, that this may be God's answer, what come you now to me for, in your necessity ? as it is said in *Judges* x. 14. *Go and cry unto the God which ye have chosen.* Relieve yourselves by these things you take delight in ; you thought not at all of me ; you thought yourselves sufficiently provided for, and wherefore come you now to me ? go to the idols you have chosen, let them deliver you in the time of your tribulation. So here I have represented to you four desperate states. But,

5. There is the case of priviledge and *exemption from outward punishment.* A man that is an evil doer, and a constant practiser of sin, hath cause to fear , if through his *power*, or the advantage of the times he is not in fear of any ones stroke ; undoubtedly *that man* is more in danger in respect of God, and these internal strokes of God dispossessing him of what he hath. This you must know, that it sometimes comes to pass, that the all-gracious God will not, (notwithstanding the high provocations of some irreligious persons) he will not disturb the outward peace, for such reasons as these ; *sometimes* for his infinite patience, and no man knows the length of God's patience ; *sometimes* he will forbear, for the sake of those that worship him. God hath special regard to the multitude of innocent, harmless creatures, such as are *persons of mean estates*, but harmless ; and *children*, yea, for the *beasts themselves* as in the case of *Nineveh*, Jonah iv. 11. Now in such

cases

cafes as thefe, that God will extend his patience
beyond what in reafon we can imagine ; and that
he will fpecially gratify the number of his worfhip-
ers, and that he will fufpend judgments in refpect of
harmlefs people, and children ; then in this cafe,
great finners have caufe to fear God's dealing with
them *in private*. For God hath ways to deal with
men in private, by letting them fink down into
darknefs of mind, *&c*. And therefore if any man
knows he is deeply obnoxious to God, and yet
profpers in the world, he hath great caufe to fear
that he fhall hear from God, by *fecret rebukes*,
whereby he fhall *melt away and come to nothing*. The

6th, And laft cafe is, the cafe of *high fpiritual advantages*, where there is powerful, and effectual
means ; but through a contracted hardnefs, they
prove altogether inoperative, and without effect,
and *this* was the condemnation of *Capernaum*, *Coraizin* and *Bethfaida*, Luke x. 13, 15. But of this I
fhall give you a further account, the next opportunity.

And thus have I reprefented to you, as the *ways*
whereby thefe *fecret rebukes* of God are brought a-
bout ; fo alfo the eminent cafes of *danger*.

D I S.

DISCOURSE VII.

The fecret BLASTING of MEN.

PSALM xxxix. 11.

When thou with rebukes doft correct man for iniquity,
thou makeft his beauty to confume away like a moth ;
furely, every man is vanity. Selah.

WHEN I took this fcripture in hand, I thought
I had but little to offer to your confideration, and thought, at once, to have difpatch-
ed all : but well weighing and confidering the confequence and import of the matter of thefe words,
(than which, nothing more in all the world, tends
to the laying a folid foundation of confcience, and
engaging of men in refpect of the fecret fenfe of
their minds, to ftand aright in the fight of God)
I therefore cannot take my hands off ; and though
I have offered many things, yet fome few more remain.

I have given you an account why I have expli-
cated thefe words of thofe things that pafs *immedi-*
ately between God, and the fpirit of man, whereof by-
ftanders know but little. They may difcern the
effects, fee men wither, and come to nothing ; but
the caufe (which is in fecret between God and
them) they feel not, they know not. The laft day,
I gave you an account how the *Hebrew* words in

G 3

the

the text led me to this notion of thofe impreffions that God makes upon the minds of men by way of reafon and argument, when he comes to challenge, convince and reprove them ; the reafon of their own mind fails them, they cannot juftify themfelves, or bear up againft God. And therefore I read the words, *when thou with fecret rebukes, doft charge a perfon for his fecret iniquities, thou makeft his beauty,* viz. *his reafon and underftanding ; his wit and parts, thofe things that he values himfelf by, to confume away like a moth,* &c.

I have fhewed in *fix* inftances, whereby this comes to pafs.

I have alfo fhewed you in part the great provocation of God to deal thus with men ; to confound them in their inward parts, to beat them out of the fenfe of their own reafon ; and leave them felf-condemned, fo that they retain no priviledge of felfenjoyment. And I have inftanced in *fix cafes*, which do properly lead men into this condition.

1. The cafe of *havocking confcience,* by finning againft the fenfe of their own judgment.

2. The cafe of *hypocrify,* diffimulation, and falfehood : when men do not honeftly mean, or really intend.

3. The cafe of fhamelefs *apoftacy.*

4. (Which is yet inferior to the other three, but yet bad enough) The cafe of *irreligion,* when men give God no place, are taken up with their own outward accommodations, and have no fenfe of God; when he is not, by thofe good things, endeared or recommended to them ; this is downright irreligion.

5. The

5. The cafe of *exemption from outward punish-ment :* as whenfoever it pleafeth God (as fome-times it doth) to make ufe of his infinite patience : for who amongft us knows the length of Gods pa-tience ? and upon that confideration, he will forbear the world, notwithftanding profaneneſs and declar-ed atheifm.

Or whenfoever God is pleafed out of refpeſt to his *worſhippers,* or out of his compaſſion towards in-nocent infants, and harmlefs creatures, to keep off judgments ; then is it to be thought that thofe per-fons that are wilful finners, *&c.* ſhall hear from God *in private* ; to abate their confidence, and to ſhew how exorbitant they are, in their ways. This God can do, by letting them fink down into mental dif-traction, *&c.* For God can difpoſſeſs a man of all his comforts, by not giving him power of felf-enjoy-ment, and taking content. For *this* of the two, is a far greater mercy of God, for a man to have lefs, and a contented mind ; than to have much more, and not have fatisfaction. For power of felf-enjoy-ment is a far greater thing than right and title.

It comes to pafs fometimes, that great offenders do avoid the hands of men, either through the un-due favour of partial judges, or fometimes by great friends, or fome worldly intereft, or craft, or cun-ning ; or fometimes a thing is acted in fecret, and cannot be legally proved (as what more ordinary than fecret murders ?) when it cannot at all be pro-ved at a diftance of time, the guilty cannot be at peace, and their own mouths muft betray them. In thefe cafes, it is moft likely, thefe perfons will hear from God. 6. In

6. In the laſt place the caſe of *high ſpiritual ad-*
vantages. That was the aggravation of the ſin of
Capernaum, Coraizin and *Bethſaida,* that they were
lifted up to heaven ; and they are threatned, to be
thrown down into hell, Luke x. 13, 15. *For if the*
mighty works that were done in them, had been done in
Sodom and Gomorrah, they had repented, Matt. xi. 21,
23. and this is the aggravation. And this is an ob-
ſervation, you never read of a ſin that cannot be
pardoned, till you read of the extraordinary gift of
the Holy Ghoſt. The caſe that is repreſented, *I-*
ſaiah vi. 9, 10. all deſperate caſes refer to.   And he
ſaid, *Go tell this people, hear ye indeed, but underſtand*
not ; *and ſee ye indeed, but perceive not.* *Make the*
heart of this people fat, and make their ears heavy, and
ſhut their eyes : *leſt they ſee with their eyes, and hear*
with their ears, and underſtand with their heart, and
convert, and be healed, Mat. xiii. 14. Mark iv. 12,
Luke viii. 10. John xii, 40. All deſperate conditions refer to this ; every one of the four evangeliſts
relate that our Saviour refers caſes to it ; it is referred to, in the acts of the apoſtles, *Acts* xxviii. 26.
and by St. *Paul* to the *Romans* xi. 8. Here it is in
the firſt copy, and all after inſtances are after this
example. When men dally in religion, diſſemble
with God, give God high offences, provoke and ex-
aſperate him to diſpleaſure, by their trifling and dal-
lying, and hypocriſy, and diſſimulation, and irreligion, and living in ſin ; then it comes to the caſe
which is repreſented in the prophet *Iſaiah.* This notion is declared, *Amos* iii. 2. *You only have I known*
of all the families of the earth; *therefore I will puniſh*
you

you for all your iniquities. And this beft complies with the reafon of the thing, and holds the fitteft proportion; that they who have had the greateft opportunities and have been moft wanting to themfelves, and continue in their iniquities, and give themfelves leave to fin, which are the worft of finners; that judgments fhould befal *them.* And it is reafonable, that God fhould recompence fpiritual fins by *fpiritual judgments*, and thefe are a reprobate ftate, a feared confcience, a blinded underftanding; and this is the worft condition : for this man is remoteft from repentance, and repentance is the recovery. Or elfe that they be under the dreadful and fearful apprehenfions of an illuminated and mifgiving mind; and fo, upon a continual rack and torture. Now thefe *mental judgments* they have a peculiarity to the vifible church : and are much more within the compafs of the vifible church than in the wildernefs of the world. Thus I have reprefented to you the *cafes* : now I come to make fome application, I will make thefe inferences.

1. Hence we have an account of men's withering in the world, taking little or no delight in their affairs; though in no bad circumftances, do not enjoy themfelves. We wonder fometimes that men cannot be content; they want nothing, neither friends, nor eftates, nor any other convenience of life; men in fhorter conditions by far, enjoy themfelves upon much better terms; here is the account, there are fecret judgments of God; judgments that work in darknefs. There is no wonder that men cannot hold up their heads when they are neither

at

at peace with God, nor at peace with their own
confciences : and all thefe things that are without
a man will make no more recompence for the want
of the peace of confcience, than it will make a recompence for the pain of the gout, to lie upon a bed
of down. Men have *no peace* neither *with God*, becaufe not reconciled to the nature, mind, nor will
of God ; nor have they *peace in their own confciences*,
becaufe under guilt. Therefore no wonder that
friends and revenues &c. will not relieve them ; they
have an internal wound. In this repect I may truly fay that mens *fin go before them into judgment*, 1
Tim. v. 24.

I will give you fome inftances.

It was from fomething in fecret between *Cain* and
his confcience, that his countenance fell, *Gen.* iv. 5.
for he had facrificed as well as his brother *Abel* :
but it was fomething within him. Another inftance,

In *Nabal*, his heart died within him upon his
wife's words only, *Sam.* xxv. 37. which is ftrange,
for a covetous miferable wretch will moft commonly endure words hard enough : for words break no
bones, but the text tells us *God ftruck him*, verfe 38.

Another inftance ; God defeats the counfel of
Achitophel, 2 Sam. xvii. 14, 23. and he cannot bear
it, but goes and makes away with himfelf.

Again ; *Judas* he had his bargain ; he had received the price of innocent blood, *Matt.* xxvii. 3,
4, 5. why could not he enjoy it ? he might have
enjoyed it for any demand of thofe that paid it him,
for they would not meddle with it again. Had *Judas* been in the fame temper of mind he was in before

fore he did that ill act, he might have enjoyed himself as happily as so much money would have made him ; but it was too hot for his fingers. We are not sure of taking any comfort, if we leave God out.

Another instance ; *Ananias* and *Sapphira*, Acts v. 9. They might have come off for noble benefactors, and received the thanks of the church, had they not diffembled with him who fearcheth the hearts, and had he not found them guilty of *lying to the Holy Ghost. It is a dreadful thing to fall into the hands of the living God*, Heb. x. 31. of him that can not only kill the body, but the foul, *Matt.* x. 28. And how doth God *kill the foul*, which is immortal, but by difcountenancing it, and letting it fall down into darknefs ?

Here are instances of *bad* men : but I will instance in better kind of men, that make fad complaint, when there is any thing in this kind.

The firft is of *Job*, Job iii. 20. *Wherefore is there life to the man that is bitter in foul ?* and *Job* xiii. 26. *Thou writeft bitter things againft me.* Here is a reprefentation from a *good* man, of the fadnefs of this condition.

Next, the cafe of *David*, Pfal. li. 9. *Make me to hear of joy and gladnefs, that the bones which thou haft broken, may rejoice.* 11. *Caft me not away from thy prefence, and take not thy Holy Spirit from me.* 12. *Reftore unto me the joy of thy falvation ; uphold me with thy free Spirit.* When *David* felt this cafe, fee how he expreffeth it.

Another

Another good man, *Psal.* lxxvii. 2. *In the day of my trouble I sought the Lord ; my sore ran in the night, and ceased not ; my soul refused to be comforted.* 3. *I remembred God, and was troubled ; I complained ; and my spirit was overwhelmed. Selah.* 7. *Will the Lord cast off for ever, and will he be favourable no more ?* 8. *Is his mercy clean gone for ever, doth his promise fail for evermore ?* 9. *Hath God forgotten to be gracious ? hath he in anger shut up his tender mercy ? Selah.* See the sadness of men in this forlorn and left state and condition, when God comes to apply himself secretly to mens spirit, and doth inwardly reprove. The like you have in *Psal.* xc. 11. *Who knoweth the power of thine anger ? even according to thy fear, so is thy wrath.* You know, *fear* antedates evil, and multiplies evil ; men commonly fear more than there is. The like case you have in *Isaiah,* lvii. 16. *I will not contend for ever ; neither will I be always wroth, for the spirit should fail before me, and the souls which I have made.* This scripture holds forth this notion fully to you, that I have been so long upon v. 17. *For the iniquity of his coutousness was I wroth, and smote him ; I hid me, and was wroth ; and he went on frowardly in the way of his heart,* v. 18. *I have seen his ways and will heal him ; I will lead him also, and restore comforts unto him, and to his mourners.* 19. *I create the fruit of the lips, peace, peace to him that is near, saith the Lord, and I will heal him.* 20. *But the wicked are like the troubled sea, when it cannot rest, whose waters cast up mire and dirt.* 21. *There is no peace, saith my God, to the wicked.* So *Deut.* xxxii. 39. *See now that I, e-*

*ven I am he, and there is no God with me ; I kill, and
I make alive, I wound and I heal : neither is there a-
ny that can deliver out of my hand.   God killeth, and
God makes alive*, 1 Sam. ii. 6. by these internal rebukes, by these impressions that God makes upon
the mind in case of offence ; in case of consenting
to iniquity. These are called God's killing a man's
soul : for no man can bear up against God ; neither
can he live under the reproofs of God.   This is a
true account, that man cannot be happy in the world
though he may call never so much of the world his
own ; tho' he hath estate, friends, power, authority, *&c.* unless God be with him in some measure,
he is not sure to have content ; so true is this, that
when God with rebukes, &c.

　　But to prevent *mistakes,* I here suggest two things
to you, which being taken into consideration I cannot be misunderstood in any thing that I have said.

　　1. This notion doth concern the *two opposite
states ;* reconciliation with God, and the contrary :
if men trifle in religion, or if they continue profane
and irreligious.　None can be himself longer than
God is with him ; or at least will suffer him.

　　2. Which I must take in (for I must discourage
no body) you must give great allowance for the
mind's misapprehension through *mistaken notions,* and
to persons that are under the power of *melancholy.*
He that is *melancholic,* believes nothing from any
body ; he saith nothing right to any body, and he is
too severe in his measure of himself : and then
there are some good people, who are under false
apprehensions, and under the power of *mistaken no-*
tions

tions ; and till they be rid of these, their peace is not well secured.

This is the *first inference.* The *second* thing that I *infer* upon the former discourse, is this ; if men would be true to themselves, and not depart from their own mercy ; if men would, in a true sense, favour themselves, not do themselves that mischief that the devil and the world cannot do ; let them then keep within compass, let them not betray themselves ; let them *not give voluntary consent to known evil* ; let them not become obnoxious to God, but let men have God greatly in regard, and above all things, keep in good terms with him, and endeavour by all means, to approve themselves to him. Undoubtedly a man is altogether insecure, unless there be terms of right understanding between God and him. If a man have not a conscience free from guilt, he is in danger, obnoxious to God, and is not secure against the malignity of the world. This for certain, the security and solidity of our peace, is settled upon the reality of the terms that are betweeen God and us. But, if men are obnoxious to God, by having knowingly consented to iniquity ; for that is the *characteristical* form of the degenerate state, that they do *voluntarily consent to known iniquity* : if men become obnoxious to God, by giving their voluntary consents to that which their judgments tell them is evil ; if men contract guilt to their consciences, and repent not, and ask pardon, in and through the blood of Christ ; then they are in fear and danger every moment : for at God's sentence, our souls live, or die : by his judgment,

ment, they are abfolved or condemned. Wherefore
it is fundamental to our intereft, that God be obferved. It is a very lamentable cafe, that many
men have religion to very forry ends and purpofes;
not for this great end of fettling folid fobriety,
not for the laying a foundation of right and equity,
not for the determination of good and evil, not for
rectifying of confcience, not for directing them in
all cafes and particulars of life; but it is taken up
for a profeffion in credit; and it hath no regenera-
ting power on men, inwardly to fanctify them, and
make them Godlike : in which cafe, *as they have
not the effect of it, fo they have not the comfort of it* ;
for they are never fafe, never fecure. Whereas,
where religion is in fincerity, perfons are provided
for, as to all cafes, and for all times : and thefe perfons never think of God but with great complacency and delight; and have great expectations from
him, and they converfe with great fatisfaction. Our
weal and wo depends upon our intereft with God.
This is the *fecond* thing I infer from the words.

Thirdly, Upon this confideration how liable we
are to God's demand and challenge, through failings
and mifcarriages in our lives, what caufe have we
to think ourfelves beholden to God, that we have
incouragement to go to him, and that we find in ourfelves any *difpofition God-ward*; any confidence in
him. For we have reafon to think that God may
have taken offence, and juftly refufe us, and remember againft us our former offences, when we
make application to him : for as guilty perfons are
n danger, fo are they alfo full of jealoufies, and
fufpicions

suspicions and fears, &c. *The wicked flee when none purſue but the righteous is as bold as a lion Prov.* xxviii. 1. So that it is the wonderful grace of God to fortify and encourage our minds to come to him ; and to caſt ourſelves upon his mercy ; whereas we know we have given him offence. We find it ſo in our fellow creatures ; where we have given offence, we have no confidence. We are therefore as much beholden to God for this, as for any thing elſe in the world ? let us therefore think of ourſelves modeſtly, how ſhort, and unworthy we are ; and think of God ingenuouſly, and be thankful to him for his goodneſs. What cauſe have we given to God to diſpoſ-feſs us of ourſelves, and to diſaffect our minds towards worldly contentment, or to ſuſpend the virtue of the creatures to us, or to withdraw his bleſ-ſing from our endeavours, or to awaken the guilt of ſin upon our conſciences, or to let fall ſome drops of his own wrath upon us ; and yet notwithſtand-ing all our faultineſs, through his great compaſſion, none of theſe evils have befallen us : but we con-tinue in life, and health, and ſtrength, and power of ſelf-enjoyment, &c. and (which is more than all the reſt, and ſettles all the reſt) confidence in God, and boldneſs to make application to him.

Laſtly, What value then ſhould we put upon the *grace of the goſpel*, which hath declared to us a new and living way to approach to God. That for us, who have fruſtrated the firſt contrivances of wiſdom, and loſt the confidence of creatures, there is a *new and living way* through the grace of the goſ-pel, to approach to God ; in which we may

come

come to God with affurance and confidence. It is
a mighty place of fcripture, *Heb.* x. 22. Let us
draw near with a true heart, in affurance of faith, &c.
The grace of the gofpel doth contain in it, as well
the difpofition qualifying the fubject, as warranty
for the authorifing of the perfon. So that there is remedy againft all manner of exception ; either the
incapacity of the perfon, becaufe he is guilty ; or
the indifpofition of the party, becaufe of malignity :
fo fovereign is the ufe of repentance and faith in the
Lord Jefus.

Thus have I finifhed this great point : and that
which hath made me fo long upon this argument,
is, becaufe I have not found a more folid foundation to fettle and eftablifh confcience toward God
upon, than this is : fince finners become obnoxious
to God ; and no power, no priviledge, no wit nor
cunning, no friendfhip, no worldly intereft, nor
advantage can give defence againft the ftrokes of
God, to whofe eyes all that is done, lies open.
Therefore it is apparent, no man's eftate hath fettlement, unlefs a man be in reconciliation with the
rule of righteoufnefs. If men be inwardly guilty,
though no man be privy, yet they are unfafe and
infecure. If men be obnoxious to God, if he once
come to reprove, the foundation of their confidence
will fink, and all that they think to fhelter themfelves by, will fail and difappear, and come to nothing. Therefore it is very neceffary for men, to fear
God, and have him in due regard and be in reconciliation with him.

IV. The next observation is, that which is *infer-red* : *surely every man is vanity* ; of which I will speak but a little, and so conclude.

Upon the consideration of the whole, the *psalmist* doth *infer, Surely every man is vanity.*

1. Vanity, as being so subject to be *mistaken* ; so liable to miscarry.

2. Vanity, as being so *unable* to bear himself up against God, against whom he doth offend ; when God comes to require an account, and to reprove and challenge.

But a little further, to give you an account, though these two were enough. Vanity may be charged upon men in a *threefold way.*

1. In a *negative* sense.

2. In a *comparative* sense ; and

3. In a *privative* sense.

1. In a negative sense, man is vain : every crea-ture is so, because he is *short of divine perfection.* For a creature is primary to nothing, he hath no ab-solute being ; for he comes into being at God's call, continues in being by his maintenance and allow-ance, and must leave this being at his appointment. He is subject to God's pleasure, so is vain in a ne-gative sense ; in no moment of his life is he inde-pendent, neither for existence, nor in execution : for *in God, we live, and move, and have our being,* Acts xvii. 28.

2. Vain, in a *comparative* sense, because he is short of the perfection of other beings ; short of the divine perfection, nothing in comparison, *Isaiah* xl, *15, 16, 17. Behold, the nations are as a drop of a*
bucket,

bucket, and are accounted as the small dust of the balance, behold he taketh up the isles as a very little thing ; and Lebanon is not sufficient to burn, nor the beasts thereof sufficient for a burnt-offering. All nations before him are as nothing, and they are counted to him less than nothing and vanity. And then short in perfection of some of his fellow-creatures, short of angelical perfection. *Thou madest him a little lower than the angels,* Psal. viii. 5. *Yet it is said, God chargeth the angels with folly,* Job iv. 18. Not imputing any moral defect to the angels, but an incompetition to the divine perfections; and man *made lower than the angels.* Now shortness in these two considerations is no body's disparagement ; for this is to be a creature, and herein any man is as good as God would have him. But I wish I could excuse mankind from vanity in the

3d sense : that is our fault and our shame, for man is vain in a *privative* sense. This is that that doth sink and deface, and deform the glorious workmanship of God in the moment of his creation : and this lies in six things.

1. A man is *divested of his innocence.* He is out of the image of God, his high perfection, which he was invested with in the moment of his creation : he has lost his proper perfection, hath lost more than the whole creation can repair.

2. By his iniquity, he hath *contracted impotency.* By giving God offence, and departing from God, we have lost our innocence; and brought upon ourselves dread and terror, and horror of conscience : for this always accompanies guilt. And then

3. By

3. By *unnatural ufe,* our *faculties* are *marred* and *fpoiled* ; the ingenuity and *modefty* of a man's mind, and the noblenefs of his underftanding, is marred and fpoiled moft grievoufly. In this a finner miferably wrongs himfelf by fin. For if a man do but one act that is unnatural and horrid, he abufes the ingenuity, candour and noblenefs of his mind for ever.

If a man once let go the fairnefs of his nature, no man knows where he will ftop. He is fit to do every defperate act of fin. So that man is vain, becaufe he hath loft his innocence, and deformed himfelf by his fin ; he hath *marred his principles,* and made himfelf unfit for many good acts that he might have done.

4. A man is vain, by his lying apprehenfions. *Man walketh in a vain fhew,* Pfal. xxxix. 6. A man is his own fool, flatters himfelf into a fool's paradife, cheats, delufions, lies rule in mens lives. Man gives his confent to impoftures. Man will believe, becaufe he would have it. Man feeds upon lies, fancies, imaginations. Mens hopes and fears, confidences and refuges are laid, as lying apprehenfions and conceits mifguide, *If.* xxviii. 15.

5. By his foolifh undertakings. Man goeth rafhly forth into act, neither well refolving concerning the enemies of his action, nor duly confidering his fufficiency to grapple with, and overcome difficulties, *Luke* xiv. 31.

The vanity of man in iffuing forth to act, confifts in this. (1.) That man is *finifter* in his *intention :* aims not right, miftakes the world for God. (2.) That man is *irregular,* and inordinate in *motion* ;

tion, errs in choice, and application of *means* to his end. (3.) That man is *frustrated*, and disappointed in the issue : after all costs, curseth his labour. After promising expectations, expensive ways in the close of all, has a shadow for the substance. Hope deferred makes his heart sick, and the desire is not accomplished, which is a tree of life.

6. By his inward *perturbations*, man is vain. The affections of the soul, have as well changed their *name* as their *use*. A man is always at difference, in contestation with himself. *'Tis not in man, a monarchy of reason, but a democracy of humours.* Man disturbs his own content and quiet. To enjoy a man's self, is the greatest good in the world : the serenity and sweet composure of his mind, is happiness within ; yet men easily discompose themselves, and throw themselves into mal-content. Were all the world else in a calm, yet man will not be at quiet ; he raiseth storms and tempests, makes foul weather within. We have not ourselves in our own hands : we are not masters of our passions, ends, and undertakings.

Man *fears* where no fear is, and so creates himself an enemy, by his own fancy : he dotingly *loves* what will return nothing for affection : he runs out in hope, where there is no ground for expectation.

The *uses* to be made of this, are these.

1. There is no cause of *pride*. Presumption, pride and conceit, are the most ungrounded things in the world. Self-denial is the most rational act. Why should we believe a lie ? Why do we make tools of ourselves, by fond self-flattery ? man is *vain*

in

in his exiftence : by *opinion* a liar, *Pfal.* lxii. 9.
Things are not to conform to our apprehenfions ;
but our thoughts are to anfwer things. 'Tis our mifery to be deprived, but 'tis our madnefs to be deceived, befooled ; otherwife we affect to know
things juftly as they are ; why are we not willing to
know ourfelves ?

2. What caufe have we to magnify the rich grace
of God, who gave fo great a price for us, fo little
worth. The great phyfician hath dearly bought difeafed patients. God hath bought chaff inftead of
wheat ; *vanity* inftead of fubftance. It could not
be therefore his gain by us, that did direct his choice,
but his compaffion of our mifery, that procured us
mercy.

What the grace of God finds us, and how grace
leaves us, are two things of greateft confideration. From the depth of mifery, to the height of
excellency. Who deals with the blind, halt and
difeafed, but God ? *Luke* xiv. 21. We may fay as
Job, Doft thou open thine eyes upon fuch an one ? Job
xiv. 3.

3. Let no man believe himfelf, or *lean to his own
underftanding,* Prov. iii. 5. *He that trufteth in his
own heart, is a fool,* Prov. xxviii. 26. Let the grace
of God be acknowledged, both for wifdom, and for
ftrength. Nothing is better grounded than that advice of wifdom ; *In all thy ways acknowledge him,*
Prov. iii. 6. If *Egypt* be a *broken reed,* Ifa. xxxvi. 6.
which was never ftrong, becaufe a *reed* ; which will
pierce him that leans on it, becaufe *broken* : is not
he rafh and unadvifed, that trufts, and hath confidence

dence in fuch things ? *better have no confidence, than·
felf-confidence* : *which is a refuge of lies* ; *an hiding
place·that waters·will overflow*, Ifa. xxviii.17. And
man is never fo broken, as when he is fruftrated in
his expectation..

·4. Hence we have an account of the general
madnefs that rules in the commonwealth of men.
·What can the tranfaction be, when the convention
is made up of vain and empty perfons ? the world
is a very chaos, and confufion ; fo that, if things
be *tolerable* in the world, that is much more than we
can groundedly expect from men.

· Whatever is of any confideration in the world is
to be accounted to God, who made a *chaos* and confufion the ground-work of a glorious creation.

DISCOURSE VIII.

Preached before· the Honourable H o u s e of
C o m m o n s, *February* 4. 1673.

J E R. vi. 8..
*Be thou inftructed, O Jerufalem, left my foul depart
from thee ; left I make thee defolate, a land not inhabited..*

TO awaken your apprehenfions upon this occafion, I fhall make ufe of the words of
king *Hezekiah*, when he rent his clothes,
and covered himfelf with fackcloth, and went into·
the houfe of the Lord, upon an occafion of *Senna-*
cherib's

cherib's invading *Judah*, and fending reviling *Rab-fhakeh* to infult, and triumph over them : his words were, *This is a day of trouble, and of rebuke, and of provocation*, Ifa. xxxvii. 3. For our further advantage upon this account, I will adjoin the words of the prophet, *Joel* ii. 2. *A day of darknefs and of gloominefs, a day of clouds and of thick darknefs* : v. 3. *A fire devours before them, and behind them a flame burneth.* By fears and apprehenfions people are appaled, and *all faces gather blacknefs*, v. 6. This feems much to fuit with our condition ; and if fo, it becomes us (as *Ezra* fometimes did, *Ezra* ix. 13.) to make a due acknowledgment to God, and to ftate things right : *for all this is come upon us for our evil deeds, and for our great trefpaffes ; for God hath punifhed us lefs than our iniquities deferve, viz.* in the late devouring fire, and a little before, in the raging peftilence, and by feveral other judgments. But now God hath given us a very great deliverance, and we have out-lived all thefe judgments, and we have caufe to fay that God is righteous, not in the fenfe that fometimes the word is taken, *viz.* to punifh condignly; but righteous in the fenfe of the prophet, *Dan.* ix. 7, 8. *O Lord, righteoufnefs belongeth unto thee* ; which he explains v. 9. *To thee, O Lord, belongs mercies and forgivenefs, though we have rebelled againft thee.* God hath been gracious, and God is righteous ; he hath been gracious and merciful ; for we are before God, all of us in our tranfgreffions, and we cannot ftand before God becaufe of them : wherefore let us be ingenuous, and let us reafon God's caufe with ourfelves, as *Ezra* once did with
the

the people of *Ifrael, fhould we again break thy commandments, and join in affinity with a people of fuch a-
bominations ; wouldeft not thou be angry with us till
thou hadft confumed us, fo that there fhould be no rem-
nant nor efcaping,* Ezra ix. 14.

We profefs, by our affembly this day, to do what
king *Hezekiah* did ; to make hearty application to
God, to humble ourfelves before him, to deprecate
his offence and difpleafure, and to reprefent before
him, the fad and deplorable condition of the nation,
and to do alfo what the prophet *Joel* called the people to : *Thus faith the Lord, turn ye even to me, with
all your heart, with fafting, with weeping, and with
mourning, and rent your hearts, and not your garments,
and turn unto the Lord your God.*   And alfo what
we find the prophet *Jeremiah* iv. 4. in the like cafe
directing to ; *Circumcife yourfelves to the Lord, and
take away the fore-skins of your heart, left my fury
come forth like fire, and burn that none can quench it,
becaufe of the evil of your doings.* Let us clofe with that
of *Daniel* iv. 27. *Break off your fins by righteoufnefs,
and your iniquities by acts of mercy, if there may be a
lengthning of your tranquillity.* For a day of humili-
ation, is a day of repentance, in order to reconciliation with God ; and the truth of repentance lies
in real reformation, in leaving off fin ; in converfion and turning to the Lord. *It is not to bow down
the head as a bulrufh, and to fpread fackcloth and afhes
under us,* Ifa lviii. 5. But as the *Ninevites* did, who
though a people that were not under any inftitution
of God, before the prophet *Jonah*'s denunciation a-
gainft them (that we know of ;) yet they teach us
the

the true nature of a faft ; for they fay, *Cry mightily unto God, and let every one turn from the evil of his ways, and from the violence that is in his hands,* Jonah iii. 8. So the prophets upon all occafions do infift, and lay ftrefs upon the indifpenfible neceffity of morals ; by which I underftand things that are good in themfelves, good in their own nature, and quality ; that are not only recommended to us by inftitution, *Ifa.* i. 16. *Wafh ye, make ye clean, put away the evil of your doings from before mine eyes, ceafe to do evil, learn to do well.* This is the prophets direction. And he fpeaks undervaluingly of facrifices of all forts, tho' the foundation of them was divine inftitution. And as the prophet begins, fo he ends, *Ifa.* lxvi. 3, 4. *They have chofen their own ways, and their foul delighteth in their abominations.* Wherefore, what do facrifices in this cafe fignify ? No more than *flaying a man, or cutting off a dog's neck, or offering of fwines blood : he that burneth incenfe, is as if he bleffed an idol.* Thefe things were once commanded by God, and were acceptable to him, if men were not wanting in moral duties : for there is no difpenfation for immorality, there is no diffembling with God ; he will not take facrifice at our hands, if we be not refined in our fpirits, and reformed in our lives. It is but to cozen ourfelves, to think that any thing will be an apology with God if we ourfelves do only pretend to repent, and do not reform. *To do juftice, to walk humbly before God, and to fhew mercy,* thefe are things beyond *thoufands of rams, and ten thoufands of rivers of oil* ; more pleafing to God than if a man fhould *give his firft born for his tranfgreffion, the fruit of his body for the fin of his foul,* Mic. vi. 6. *&c.*   It

It fhall be my bufinefs this day, from this fcrip-ture, to prefs not only what is external, and in fhew, but what is vital, internal, folid and fubftantial in the motion of repentance, which now the nation doth profefs in this folemn application unto God. Our great and loud fins, they are the things that ex-pofe us to God's difpleafure, indignation and wrath. And becaufe generals do not affect, I fhall inftance in fome particulars : our falfenefs and treachery to the true religion, in which this nation hath profper-ed above a hundred years : our affected atheifm, and avowed profanenefs, beyond what former times have had experience of : our wantonnefs and licen-tioufnefs, difgraceful to human nature : our high im-moralities and debaucheries in feveral ways. Thefe have brought the judgments of God upon us, and turned God from us in difpleafure. And none that is fober-minded can think otherwife, if he acknow-ledges God's government of the world, and doth confider that wickednefs and unrighteoufnefs are an abomination to him. For as *Mofes* told the chil-dren of *Ifrael*, Num. xxxii. 23. *Our fins have found us out* : and as the widow of *Sarepta* faid, *Art thou come to call my fins to remembrance ?* 1 *Kings* xvii. 18. which words carry this intimation, that if we hear from God in a way of difpleafure, we fhould fufpect ourfelves, and find out the *Achan* that is among us. The prophet *Micah* vi. 9. faith, *The Lords voice cri-eth unto the city* ; and then it follows, *hear the rod, and who hath appointed it.*

In the words of the text, you have thefe things confiderable.

I. The

I, The *caution* or admonition ; *Be inſtructed* .

II. The *ground* and reaſons thereof ; *leſt my ſoul depart from thee ; leſt I make thee deſolate, a land not inhabited.*

I. Concerning the former, the *caution* or admonition, there are three enquiries to be made.

Firſt, Whereby we are to be inſtructed ?

Secondly, Wherein we are to be inſtructed ?

Thirdly, What it is to be inſtructed ? or the import of the words.

Firſt, For the firſt, *whereby* we are to be inſtructed ? I anſwer,

By the ſtate of affairs, and by the reaſon of things, or the right of caſes.

Things themſelves ſpeak to us ; *Hear the rod, and him that hath appointed it* ; and this the prophet calls the Lord's voice crying to the city, *Mic.* vi. 9. and tells us, that *the man of underſtanding will be inſtructed by it.* Caſes and things, and the ſtate of affairs, gives us hints and intimations of what may befall us ; they give notice and preſages of future events, and by theſe, offer notions to our minds, not to be neglected : by theſe, *Solomon*'s prudent man is inſtructed, and he doth foreſee the evil, and ſhunneth it, *Prov.* xxii. 3. He foreſeeth the evil conſequences in their antecedents. Now, this is to be ſuppoſed, that God teacheth us, by the ſtate of affairs, or by the reaſon of things, becauſe all things are ſome way or other, under God's management. Some things are appointed, ordered, and diſpoſed

by

by God ; in thefe he takes pleafure, he declares his will, purpofe and intention ; and here our fubfervience is required and commanded. · Things not allowed nor warranted by God, yet are permitted by him, elfe they could not be ; for God could hinder them, if he pleafed ; but God permits them for reafons of great wifdom and prudence, and doth not pleafe, by his irrefiftible power, to hinder them. By thefe we may alfo be inftructed ; and we do not enough acknowledge God in the world, if we do not think that he doth interpofe where he is concerned : and wherein is he not concerned ? Since we are required, that *whatfoever we do in word or deed, to do all to the glory of God,* 1 Cor. x. 31. Since God makes overtures to us, and gives us intimations of what becomes us to do, and how we ought to behave ourfelves in the various occurrences of human life. This is a great point of divinity, and it ftands upon thefe foundations.

1. That God is a being of *all perfection,* of infinitely vaft comprehenfion and underftanding and power : and therefore he is able to attain thofe effects, and to teach men by all things that fall under his government.

2. That things *managed* by divine wifdom are intenfely virtual, fignificative, expreffive of notions, becaufe they do partake of the excellency and fufficiency of their caufe.

3. That God doth *nothing in vain,* nor to fewer, or leffer purpofes than the things are capable to promote, or be fubfervient unto. For it concerns the wifdom of any agent to make the beft improvement

of

of his means : for a means is inconfiderable but as it
is conducible to its end, which in itfelf may be
foul, or coftly ; only confiderable, as in refpect to
it's end.

4. Becaufe the affairs of mankind are the *choice
piece* of the adminiftration of *providence* : and God
doth in a fpecial manner, charge himfelf with teaching the mind of man knowledge. Wherefore we
may gather fomething directive of us, from all God's
operations, or permiffions in the world. *In that day*
(faith the prophet, *Ifa.* xxii. 12.) *did the Lord of
Hofts call to weeping and mourning, and to baldnefs, &c.*
viz. by the ftate of things. And it is this our Saviour complains of, *Luke* xii. 56. *Ye hypocrites, ye
can difcern the face of the fky, and of the earth : but
how is it that ye cannot difcern this time ?* Upon this
account it is faid, that the *goodnefs of God leads men
to repentance* ; and therefore he complains, *Rev.* ii.
21. That *he gave them fpace to repent, but they repented not.* The patience of God, in not inflicting
punifhment, was an intimation to repent. And becaufe men were wanting herein, the Pfalmift faith,
Pfal. xxviii. 5. *They underftood not the works of God,
nor the operation of his hands* ; but went on to tempt
the Lord, and to provoke him to anger. In this fenfe
it is faid, *Job* v. 6. That *afflictions rife not out of the
duft* : no man's afflictions are wholly cafual or con-
tingent, but are directed by an intelligent agent ;
of which he may make a certain interpretation to
his own advantage ; and may make the interpretation to a determined ufe : for all things, fome
way or other, refer to God ; and as God is concerned

cerned in them, they are inftructions of righteoufnefs, whether God does them, or only fuffers them to be done ; whether he rewards or punifhes ; as I might inftance in feveral things. When *Jofeph*'s brethren fold him into *Egypt*, in refpect of fecond caufes, there is one account of it ; and in refpect of the firft, another ; *they did it for harm, but God defigned it for good*, Gen. xlv. 5. There was a very different intention in our Lord and Saviour's death as it referred to the malicious *Jews* : in thefe 'twas an expreffion of the greateft malice and wickednefs ; but God turned it to good, intending it as an *expiatory facrifice* to all thofe that repent. *Sodom* and *Gomorrah* were not barely punifhed for their own fakes, but for an example to all generations that afterwards fhould live ungodly, *Jude* vii. and *Heb.* iv. 11. and 1 *Cor.* x. 6. *Thefe things are our examples, to the intent that we fhould not luft after evil things, as they alfo lufted.* I will fatisfy myfelf with one place more, and that is the anfwer which our Saviour returned to *John Baptift*'s queftion *whether he was the perfon that was to come, or they were to look for another ?* Our Saviour doth not anfwer them that *John* fent, as it may be they expected, by words, but by things, *Go and tell John what things you have feen and heard,* (Luke vii. 22.) *how the blind fee, the lame walk, the lepers are cleanfed, the deaf hear, and the dead are raifed.* Our Saviour would have him to underftand by things, as well as by words ; by things done, rather than by words fpoken ; and by thefe, *John* might underftand who he was. And our Saviour upbraids thofe cities where his mighty works were

done

done, becaufe they believed not : and tells them that *Tyre,* and *Sidon,* yea, even *Sodom* would have repented, if the mighty works had been done among them, which had been done in thofe cities, *Matt.* xi. 20. This therefore is a certain truth, and of great ufe ; and fhews that a man hath fomething to do to know God in the world, that a man hath reafon whereby to make interpretation of occurrences that happen ; for if a man would know God in the world, he muft both obferve and take notice of his providence, and what falls out in the world, and make interpretation of what is under God's management and government. But becaufe there may be great danget of making falfe interpretations of providence, I will lay down this caution.

All fuch *interpretations* of occurrences of providence are to be made according to the principles of common *reafon,* and the plain guidance of the holy fcripture : not particular fancy, but the plain guidance of the holy fcripture : fo fhall we be fecure from rafh cenfure, and uncharitablenefs on the one hand ; and from the folly of fuperftition, and wild enthufiafm on the other hand ; which hath been fo remarkably prejudicial to the world, and brought fuch fcandal on religion.

And for this we have our Saviour's example, *Luke* xiii. 2. When they came and ask'd him how great finners they were, whofe blood *Pilate* mingled with their facrifices ; he told them, that the import of that, and all other occurrences of like nature ferved for their admonition and to inftruct them that *unlefs they did repent they fhould perifh.* But he rejects their
uncharitable

uncharitable application, as if they were greater
finners than others. Let us therefore interpret ourfelves into our known duty, fuch as thefe, to fear
God greatly in his judgments, to reverence him, to
leave off to fin, to repent, and amend our lives : fo
fhall we, as we ought, acknowledge God in all his
works. And fo I have done with that head, *whereby* God doth inftruct us.

Secondly, Wherein are we to be inftructed ? I
anfwer, in two things.

1. In matters of *God's offence.*
2. In inftances of *our own duty.*

1. In matters of *God's offence* ; for we are highly
concerned in God's favour or difpleafure : for in
his favour there is life ; and if we walk in the light
of his countenance, he will put joy and gladnefs into our hearts. By *his favour our mountain is made
ftrong*; *but when he hideth his face, we are troubled* ;
if he withdraw himfelf, we prefently fall into confufion ; therefore prays the Pfalmift, *Pfal.* xxxviii.
1. *Rebuke me not in thine anger, left thine arrows ftick
faft within me.* We have many fad effects of God's
wrath all along in fcripture. *It is a fearful thing to
fall into the hands of the living God; for our God is
a confuming fire.* And therefore, *Mofes* was afraid
of God's difpleafure becaufe of the people's fins, and
*fell down before the Lord forty days and forty nights,
neither eating bread nor drinking water,* Deut. ix. 18.

There is no defence for that man who is in danger in refpect of God ; and the defperatenefs of the
condition lies further in this ; that this mifchief is
not alone : but a wounded confcience accompanies

I it

it : and this is a misery beyond all expression, to
have almighty God, whose power no one can withstand, engaged against a person, and to have our own
conscience accusing, and condemning us also ; this
is a state which causes astonishment, both from without, and from within : a man then will be afraid
to stay at home, or to enjoy his own thoughts, because of the troublesomeness and uneasiness of his
own mind.   And who can interpose in this case ?
what can comfort, when God and conscience doth
condemn, and give testimony against a man ? these
are testimonies, against which there can be no objection ; God's omniscience, and our own conscience.   Upon this comes the case which the prophet represents, *Isa.* xxxiii. 14. *The sinners in Sion
are afraid ; fearfulness hath surprised the hypocrites :
who among us shall dwell with devouring fire ? Who
among us shall dwell with everlasting burnings?* Thus
it is, if there be not a true understanding between
God and us, and if we have not peace within, saith
the wise man, *Prov.* xviii. 14. *A wounded spirit who
can bear ?* : So much for the first thing, wherein we
are instructed ; the matters of *God's offence*.

2. In the matters of *our duty* ; that is, if we
know it, to do it, if we have departed from it, to return unto it. If we have done the contrary, to revoke
it with self-condemnation and humble deprecation.
And if this be our case, let us be gainers at least in
this way, by our former losses ; to become more
sensible of our necessary dependance upon God because of our frailty ; to be more modest and humble,
more cautious and wary, that we do not in like

manner offend again.   And so much for the two
first, *whereby*, and *wherein* we should be instructed.

Thirdly, What it is to be instructed? or the import of the words: and they comprehend these four
gradual acts.

   1. To *search and examine*.
   2. To *weigh and consider*.
   3. To *understand and discern*.
   4. To *do and perform*.

In the book of the proverbs, we have wisdom
personating a loving and tender parent, directing
and persuading his son to receive instruction.   By
wisdom I here understand consideration and discre-
tion, advertency and weighing of things in the bal-
lance of severe and impartial reason ; in opposition
to that giddiness and folly, that betrays men to vice
and wickedness, and all kinds of immorality.   For
folly and inconsideration are the causes of the great
depravation and apostacy of mankind.   There is nothing baser and more unbecoming mankind, since
the beauty and excellency of human nature consists
in the perfection of reason and understanding, than
to neglect the use thereof, and chuse and prefer the
condition of beasts.   Men are vicious, and act like
beasts, because they are wilful, careless, unreasonable, incogitant, inadvertent ; not considering the
rules and measures of nature, and of reason ; for
human nature is indued with rational self-reflecting
faculties ; able to discern the essential differences of
good and evil, and to observe what things conduce
to its happiness or misery.   It is most natural and
easy for these faculties to embrace, and pursue those
objects

objects, which are moſt agreeable to them. All ſober reaſon is for the ways and practice of virtue.
Vice is contrary to nature, and to a man's intereſt;
it is againſt the reaſon of mankind : and till a man
has forced himſelf, and miſerably abuſed his nature
he will not conſent unto it : and then we may except againſt that man's reaſon or judgment, becauſe
of his practice. For the *philoſopher* hath told us,
that the wickedneſs of a man's life and practice, doth
vitiate and marr the very principles of his mind :
and we muſt never bring a monſter as an argument
againſt what is natural.

Be *inſtructed*; that is, capable to receive inſtruc-
tion ; ſo 'tis in the *Hebrew*.* Here God threatens
and menaces. It is God's intention and expectation, that his threatnings, caſtigations and menaces,
ſhould awaken ſinners to conſideration, put them
upon amendment. For *when God's judgments are
abroad in the earth, the inhabitants of the world ſhould
learn righteouſneſs.* 'Tis expected, that his *afflictions
ſhould work the peaceable fruits of righteouſneſs, to
them that are exerciſed thereby,* Heb. xii. 11. And
the prophet *Amos* iv. from the 6. to the laſt, complains, that though they had been ſo and ſo correct-
ed, yet they had not turned to the Lord. And the
prophet ſaith, *Why ſhould they be ſmitten any more, for
they will revolt more and more,* Iſa. i. 5. We ſhould
take it for granted, all that is from God, toward us

* Significat, conſtringere, cohibere, corrigere a-
liquem, diſciplina, legibus, vinculis, pœna.

in

in this ftate ; whether it be declarations of his will, or denunciation of his judgments or fignifications of his difpleafure, or caftigations inflicted, or his patient forbearance : they are all intended by God as teaching piety, and inftructions of righteoufnefs. God is not at all pleafed with our fufferings, for what can finner's neceffitated fufferings fignify ? of what value is it for a man to lie under thofe evils, which he cannot efcape if he would ? how infignificant is this ? nothing is morally virtuous, but what is our choice. It is not at all pleafing to God, or fatisfactory to him, to grieve the children of men.   Yea, rather God looks upon it as a fecond evil, and himfelf as fruftrated and difappointed in his endeavours to bring us to God, if we be not reformed, and inftructed ; if we be not effectually amended.   For *why fhould ye be fmitten any more, ye will revolt more and more,* Ifa. i. 5. And *I will not punifh your daughters when they commit whoredom,* Hof. iv. 14. He accounts it a farther offence, and a new provocation unto him, when men are infenfible or contumacious. In this cafe men are in danger, either of *greater judgments,* or to be delivered up to *reprobacy of mind,* the moft defperate ftate.   It was *Cain's* temper to complain, and not to repent.   It is reprefented as the very cafe of the damned, *Rev.* xvi. 19. that they *blafphemed God becaufe of their plagues, but repented not to give glory to him. Jofhua's* council to *Achan,* was that he fhould *confefs his fin, and give glory to God,* Jof. vii. 4.

If

If we confider the admonition in the text with the context ; we fhall find caufe to take notice of the mercy and patience of God in his unwillingnefs to deftroy, verfe 6. *Thus faith the Lord of Hofts ; hew ye down the trees, and caft a mount againft Jerufalem ; this is the city to be vifited.* God had given the enemies commiffion to deftroy them ; here is deftruction, as it were, in execution : but here, in the text, he feems to make a ftop, and fufpend his difpleafure, and thus to reafon, *muft it needs be fo ?* Is there no remedy ? May we not yet be reconciled ? Is it not poffible to bring them to repent ? Though evil be determined, though upon the execution ; yet if they repent, their ruin may be prevented. Wherefore, as it is, *Amos* iv. 12. *Prepare to meet thy God, O Ifrael.* God intimates thus much ; I am placable, ready to lay afide my difpleafure ; we may yet be reconciled, if thou wilt return to a right underftanding. This I obferve from the relation of the verfe to the former.

But now, to fpeak fhortly to the particulars, *what 'tis,* to be inftructed.

1. *Search and examine* the number, weight and meafure of thine iniquities, verfe 7. *As a fountain cafteth forth waters, fo fhe cafteth out her iniquities ; violence and fpoil is heard in her.*

2. *Weigh and confider* how unjuftifiable, how unreafonable are provocations on our part, while there is patience on God's. *Deut.* xxxii. 6. *Do ye thus requite the Lord, ye foolifh people, and unwife ?* Numb. xiv. 11. *How long will this people provoke me ? How long will it be, e're ye believe me, for all the figns that I have fhewed among you ?*   3. *Under-*

. 3. *Underſtand and diſcern* : have fixed and ſtayed apprehenſions in your mind. Impreſſions of good things ſlip out of our minds, if they be not conſidered : therefore *David* prays for the people, 1 *Chron.* xxix. 18. *Keep this far ever in the imagination of the thoughts of the hearts of thy people.* There are three acts belonging to a wiſe man.

To have an inſpection into things *preſent.*

To have reſpect to things *paſt,* from which comes experience.

To provide againſt *future events,* and prepare for things to come, even for the worſt. Be *inſtructed,* foreſee, and diſcern future miſchiefs following upon pertinacious continuance in ſin : ſee the iſſues of things in their own cauſes, and conſequents in their antecedents.

4. *Do and perform,* as becomes an intelligent agent, when he is made ſenſible and apprehenſive, *Prov.* xxii. 3. *The prudent man forſeeth the evil and hideth himſelf, but the ſimple paſs on and are puniſhed.* Whatſoever was before, was but preparatory to this and incompleat without it, *viz. examining, conſidering,* and *underſtanding* ; we muſt *execute* and *perform* and do accordingly, things muſt be ſecured by future acts ; *things but half done, will quickly be undone,* for things run back again if not ſettled by us into action : we muſt not give over till all be finiſhed. Things are not put *in ultimo actu,* till there be a refinement of our ſpirits, and a reformation of our lives : that is the end of all before. Things unperfected, go back again of their own accord. Nothing is ſettled, till it be in its ſtate. We muſt attain the regenerate.

regenerate ftate, the juftified ftate ; thefe are the
fettlements and foundations of religion. None more
deceive themfelves, than they who think their religion is true and genuine ; tho' it refines not their
fpirits, and reforms not their lives, *James* i. 27. As
by other principles, the fubjects of them are conftituted *in habitu* ; fo it is likewife in this cafe. Humility doth not only *denominate*, but *affect* ; fo in *reli-
quis virtutibus.*

Now finners, who are called evil-doers and workers of iniquity, they fail in all thefe duties : for they
are either ignorant and inapprehenfive, or elfe carelefs and incogitant ; or elfe vainly fraught and poffeft ; or wilful and prefumptuous.

1. *Ignorant and unapprehenfive* ; notwithftanding
all the means they have to attain knowledge and
underftanding, as never having been awakened ; and
a man is no body where he hath not thought and
confidered. For God and nature brought us into this
world with powers and faculties ; but habits are
acquired by confideration and exercife, improving
our powers through God's affiftance. The want
of principles of knowledge proves mifchievous, for
without knowledge the heart is not good : and God by
the prophet complains, *Hof.* iv. 6. That *his people
perifh for want of knowledge.*

2. They are *carelefs and incogitant.* This is generally true of all thofe that live in fin, who are neglective of God, and defective in the right ufe of
themfelves. This the philofopher tells us, *Every
one that finneth, is ignorant* ; that is, he is either fun-
damentally ignorant, as having been a perfon of no
education

education, no use and improvement of his natural powers and faculties ; or else, he hath been inadvertent and regardless.   And thus many live, as it were, *without God in the world* ; forget God, not having their senses exercised to perceive and discern ; having no affection nor devotion towards him ; have no regard to their future glory, nor to their soul's immortality ;· do good and bad, without difference or distinction ; confound the sense of good and evil ; they think not on the future account, nor upon eternity. Thus did not *David* ; for he tells us, *Psal.* cxix. 59. That *he considered his ways, and turned his feet unto God's testimonies.* The wicked, on the contrary, are said to *forget God,* Psal. l. 22. Job viii. 13. *They call not on his name,* Psal. lxxix. 6. They live but to gratify sense, pamper their flesh, and feed the beast, *Rom.* xiii. 14. *They make provision for the flesh to fulfil the lusts thereof.*   They make it the business and employment of their mind and understanding to cater for the body. their reasonable souls only serve for salt to keep the body from stench and putrefaction.

· 3. *Vainly fraught,* and possess'd, so as to flatter themselves, deceive their own souls, put themselves into a fool's paradise, live in a lie, go on blindfold to destruction. Fancy and humour, and not the reason and truth of things rule in their lives. Or else,

4. They are *wilful and desperate,* casting off all obligations to God, and *hold the truth in unrighteousness* ; make havock of conscience ; *turn the grace of God into wantonness,* and contract reprobacy of mind, and say with them, 1 *Cor.* xv. 32. *Let us eat*
and

and drink, for to morrow we muſt die. Come, ſay they, fetch wine, and we will fill ourſelves with ſtrong drink, and to morrow ſhall be as this day, and much more a-bundant, Iſa. lvi. 12.

Thus have you had an account of the *caution,* and admonition : be inſtructed.

II. Now for the *inforcement. Leſt my ſoul depart from thee ; leſt I make thee deſolate, a land not inhabit-ed.*

Leſt my ſoul depart from thee ; theſe words are a metaphor taken from a member put out of joint, that cannot be ſet again ; it is of the ſame import with that we read, *Ezek.* xxiii. 18. *So ſhe diſcovered her whoredoms, and my mind was alienated from her :* and *Heb.* x. 38. *My ſoul ſhall have no pleaſure in him.* The meaning of God in all ſuch expreſſions, is, that we ſhould return unto him ; therefore here ob-ſerve, how hardly doth God forget his relation to his people ? how doth he inforce his arguments ? he gives admonition ; and how doth he inforce and back it, that they may take notice. God's meaning is, they ſhould return to him, becauſe of his for-wardneſs to admoniſh ? in theſe words you have a double argument.

Argumentum amoris, &
Argumentum timoris.

1. An argument of *love and good will,* leſt my ſoul depart from thee. 2. An argument from *fear, leſt I make thee deſolate.* A double argument is as a double teſtimony, by which every word is eſtabliſhed, 2 *Cor.* xiii. 1. Here is an obligation upon ingenuity : and the conſtraints of neceſſity. This double argu-ment ſhews us two things.   1. The

1. The *stupidity and senselessness* of those who are made to the perfection of reason and understanding, and yet act contrary to it.

2. The *impiety* and *unrighteousness* of sinners, who are a real offence to God; cause his displeasure, and bring upon persons and places, ruin and destruction. For can any one imagine that it is a matter of nothing, that man, who is endued with mind and understanding, and so made capable of God, to live in a constant neglect of God, and abuse of those principles, whereby he is capable to serve God?

Since all the ways of *God*, are ways of righteousness, judgment and truth, in whom there is fulness of power and liberty; yet cannot by power pervert that which is right: is it to be endured by the Governor of the world, that a limited creature, of bounden duties, should extend liberty to the confounding of order and right, and all difference between good and evil? that he should take liberty to the introducing of all confusion and disorder in the family of God (for the whole world is his family) and live in the violation of all the laws of righteousness, goodness and truth, which are the laws of heaven. Let us think impartially, and judge righteous judgment.

Now because some think that sin is a trifle, and wonder that God should think himself concerned to restrain and limit his creatures, in what they have a mind to do; that God should refuse to let them enjoy that liberty; that God should deny his creatures satisfaction. I shall therefore shew that those things which we call sinful, have an intrinsick malignity

malignity in them ; and therefore are forbidden by God, becaufe of their naughtinefs.

And for further fecurity to us againft fuch poifon, God (out of his care for us) hath fuperadded the ufe of his *own authority* over us, and *our intereft* (which in all reafon ought to prevail with us) that we fhould not do ourfelves that mifchief ; that we fhould not meddle with what is fo hurtful and dangerous.

This may be faid concerning the liberty, that by our Saviour we are brought into : *that in the ftate of the gofpel, I know nothing forbidden, which one of true reafon would defire to have liberty to do.* There is intrinfick rancour, venom, and malignity in every fin, tho' in feveral degrees : and this I will fhew in four particulars.

1. Sin is a *variation from the law and rule of God's creation* : It is contrary to the order of reafon : and when I fay this, I fay as bad as can be fpoken. Every fin is againft the order of reafon, againft the law and rule of God's creation : and it is unnatural to the ftate of a creature. What other creature in nature doth vary from the ftate of it's creation, but man ? who ought to be moft regular, conftant and uniform. If the reft of the creatures fhould do fo, the world would foon be turned into a chaos and confufion. If the fea fhould do fo, it would foon overflow all its banks. If the fun fhould give no more light, but be the caufe of ftench and putrefaction ; that inftead of the fplendid rays, which he cafts upon the world, and revives thofe things by, which are below, it fhould fend forth noifom vapours, how would the univerfe be unfurnifhed and difordered ?

The

The like may be faid of all other creatures, which if they fhould act as irregularly, and unnaturally as man, every thing would be brought into diforder and confufion, and the world turned into a chaos. What is it in human nature to do contrary to the order of reafon, and law of heaven ? It is a phrafe characteriftical of venom and malignity ; to which there can be no comparifon.

2. In fin, there is open and manifeft *neglect of God*, to whom all reverence and regard is moft due. For whofoever converts himfelf inordinately to the creature, averts himfelf from God ; and then, what becomes of our due acknowledgements to God, and thankfulnefs, than which, nothing in the world is more reafonable ; for, *the ox knoweth his owner, and the afs, his mafter's crib,* Ifa. i. 3.

3. By fin, there is a *difturbance in God's family* : (as the whole world is.) It is an interruption of that intercourfe and communication there ought to be amongft creatures ; *for every finner deftroys much good.* Wherever there is irregular motions, agents will interfere ; and hence arife exafperations, contradiction and offence. Were mankind regular in their motions, and confined themfelves to warrantable actions, there would be nothing of difpleafure, paffion, provocation or offence found among men.

4. By the practice of iniquity we *marr our fpirits,* fpoil our tempers, and acquire unnatural principles, and difpofitions. By fin, we part with the modefty and ingenuity of our natures. Now therefore let the atheiftical and profane perfon be aggrieved if he can, or find fault with God, that he fhould cut

him

him short, and prohibit him all irregular and exorbitant actions : since they are so contrary to human nature and such a disturbance in God's government: and since there is nothing in inferior nature, but what is regular and constant, from the first moment of its creation, to this hour. There is turpitude in every act of sin ; yet sins differ : for there are several degrees of sin ; for sins are aggravated or abated by the disposition, capacities, and principles of the agent that commits them.   As

1. If there be *clear light*, and fulness of *liberty* ; then it is sin with a high hand.

2. If sin be committed in *doubtfulness* and uncertainty, then it weakens and disables conscience. Great regard is to be had to the innocence and tenderness of our own mind. The wise man in *Ecclesiasticus* faith, thou hast no friend in all the world so near to thee as the reason of thy own mind, therefore never treat the reason of thy mind unhandsomely.   Treat kindly thy home reprover ; there is no friend truer to thee, nor can do thee better service; therefore hear it's voice, and give it satisfaction.

3. If men sin through *confusion of thoughts*, then it may be said we were not ourselves.   One may say we were but half ourselves, when we did it.

4. If we sin by *misapprehension* or mistake ; then we did not intend *that*, but *another* thing, when we did it.

5. If we did it by an *assault*, or sudden suprisal, then it was as well another's fault as ours.

6. If upon *provocation*, heat of passion, and we revoke it as soon as we return to ourselves ; by this

we

we make it morally void and null : for you do revoke and morally undo, that which you repent of.

7. If men sin by some *carelessness*, negligence, and
indiligence ; if we recompence it by after care, and
diligence upon this costly experience ; this also helps
to excuse.

I conclude with two words of admonition to two
sorts of persons.

First, To the *atheistical,* and profane, I earnestly
recommend to them the re-examining of things ;
and if they do not pretend to infallibility, I beg of
them to consider their former thoughts and resolutions. Think again, whether the great things of religion may not be realities, *viz.* the being of a God,
the immortality of the soul, the essential difference of
good and evil ; and future rewards and punishments.
At least do not practise against the sense of these
things ; but return, and use thy reason, which if not
vitiated and prepossest, will satisfy the *native sense* of
the mind. To say nothing now of scripture (which
speaks enough of assurance of what it declares ; so
that they which read it will not easily shut their hands
of it, if they intend to be wicked ;) *reason* hath so
much to say for these great things, that the obstinate
are put upon it, to blind and blot out those reasons
and arguments, which they know not what to say
to, nor how to answer; which stick as so many goads
in their sides. No man but he, who is habitually evil,
and hath dethroned his reason, and confederated
with the enemy of his mind, can satisfy himself, that
there is no reason to satisfy him to fear these
great things, viz. the being of a God, the immortality

lity and eternity of the foul, and future punifhments.
If then thefe things be real, have not finners run a
wild courfe? I will only tell them,

1. That many, who have as madly refolved, have
before their deaths found caufe to alter their judgments in thefe matters, and thought it their fafeft
way to deprecate their offence.

2. However they make fhift to ftifle the voice
of confcience at prefent, and go on to fin; fome o-
thers, who have fometime done the like, have never had any true enjoyment of themfelves after fuch
wounds made in their confcience, and breach of
their peace; but either fell into confufion of thought
and perplexity of mind, or diftraction, and have
been fometimes their own executioners, and have
made an end of themfelves; rather then endure the
reproofs of their confciences, have rid themfelves
out of the world.

3. Thofe that are of raifed intellectuals, of refined morals, of fober reafon, would not have upon
them the guilt of fome mens fins (however they may
efcape judgment in this world) for all the titles,
powers and revenues which fuch men enjoy in the
world. It will only give fuch, reafon to know, that
notwithftanding their own incompetent judgment
concerning themfelves, that is true even of them,
which is faid by *Samuel* concerning the wicked fons
of *Eli*; *they have made themfelves vile*, and contemptible. So are thefe profane and atheiftical perfons;
they are bafe in the fight of God, and in the fight
of wife men: for wickednefs doth difrobe any man

of

of his excellency, and makes him vile and contemptible.

Secondly, To perfons engaged in ways of religion.
If thefe be real and fincere in their profeffion, they
are in a ftate of reconciliation with God ; and if in
a ftate of reconciliation with him, then let them be
true to the terms of friendfhip, and not do acts of
enemies in the ftate of friendfhip. *Let them that name
the name of Chrift, depart from iniquity. Where God
fpeaks peace to his people, let them not return again to
folly,* Pfal. lxxxv. 8. To the *fear of God,* in fcripture, is always adjoined the *efchewing of evil* ; and
this is the character God gives of an upright man,
Job i. 8. It is effential to religion, to walk according
to the difference of good and evil. There are o-
ther things which have the ufe and confideration of
the means in religion, which I call the inftrumental
part of religion : but religion itfelf, doth iffue in
holinefs, uprightnefs, integrity, and feparation from
iniquity.

DISCOURSE IX.

The D A N G E R of U N F A I T H F U L N E S S to G O D.

H E B. iii. 12.

Take heed, brethren, left there be in any of you, an evil heart of unbelief, in departing from the living God.

R ELIGION is highly concerned in two things ; the judgment of truth, and the confcience of right : and he doth fubftantially fail upon account of religion, that is wanting in either of thefe.

I fhall now confider the *reafons* of this *caution* in the text, *Take heed, brethren,* &c. We are highly concerned to be cautious and wary, upon a fourfold account.

1. From thofe things that are *within* us.

2. From things that are *about* us.

3. From the great *confequence* and *importance* that truth and goodnefs hath unto our fouls.

4. From not a *poffibility* only, but a *probability of failing*, and mifcarrying, if care be not taken; and the greatnefs of the evil, if we do fall fhort.

1. We had need to be wary, becaufe of thofe things that are *within* us : for if once we confent to iniquity, and acquaint ourfelves with evil, we put ourfelves out of an indifferency to good and e-

vil,

vil, and fo marr the ingenuity and modefty of our
natures. For one evil act doth beget an indifpofition to the contrary virtue ; men become lefs com-
petent to judge, or to do what is right, when once
they have mifcarried. We do not know what wrong
we do ourfelves, when we do an act contrary to
right ; for by this means we come to pafs into the
oppofite nature. The apoftle doth exhort chriftians,
Heb. ii. 1. *That they fhould take heed to the things that
they had learned ; left they let them flip, and become like
leaking veffels.* Good apprehenfions do not always
ftay with us ; and contrary ones are in a fucceffion.
This we find by experience, that we do ebb and
flow, rife and fall, go backward and forward, up
and down, here and there, on and off, do and undo.
Sometimes we fee, and believe, underftand and refolve, and then again, we grow infenfible of thefe
good impreffions that were upon us : and therefore
David being well acquainted with the frail and uncertain condition of man, prays thus unto God, *Keep
it in the imaginations of the thoughts of the heart of thy
people,* 1 Chron. xxix. 18.

Alfo we are inclined and follicited from our *lower and worfer part* ; from the delights of our fenfes,
which many times prove ftrong temptations to us ;
and laftly, we are often befooled by our own fancies
and imaginations. *He is a wife man who is not his
own fool.* Our fenfe of ourfelves is more incompetent, than our judgment of others. We are fo much
given up to felf-flattery, that in favour of ourfelves,
we conceit that of ourfelves that we do not find, and

are

are apt to think that of ourselves that no body that knows us do believe ; and all this from within.

2. And then from *without* us. How many things do impose upon us from our easiness and credulity ; so that we walk as it were in a vain shew, 1 *Cor.* vii. 31. and this occasioned both from *objects* and *agents* 1 *John* ii. 16. The guise of the world, the manners and humours of men, these are supposed to be indubitable and unquestionable : and these prove a mighty temptation to us, when we look about us and see men so sollicitous, and over-busy, designing, undertaking, and engaging about the things of this life ; as if a man's happiness were altogether to be had here, and as if our present actions had no reference to eternity. And then *Satan*, he is a lying spirit in the mouths of all his false prophets : he is an abettor and encourager of evil ; being a liar from the beginning, and one that goeth about seeking whom he may devour. And then men are deceitful and uncertain, and use their wits and parts to circumvent and over-reach one another. Fair representations of things are made, when their real existence is otherwise ; so that we are many times deluded and deceived, and this is our weakness, we love to have it so ; we would have men speak according to our sense, and not according to the reality of things. Thus it often happens, that they are grievous unto others, that do not speak according to their sense. We read of *Ahab*, that he hated *Micaiah*, because he did not speak according to his sense, and as he would have him, 1 *Kings* xxii. 8. And so St. *Paul* saith, that he was their enemy because he told them the truth, *Gal.* iv. 16.

3. Then

3. Then also, the *consequences* of truth. and real virtue to ourselves. For, it is the proper employment of our intellectual faculties, to be conversant about God ; to make enquiry after him, and to find him out in all his ways and works ; to conceive aright of him, and then to resemble and imitate him; Religion is an obligation upon us to God. The first motion of religion is to understand what is true of God ; and the second is, to express it in our lives and to copy it out in our works : the former is our wisdom, and the latter is our goodness. In these two consists the health and pulchritude of our minds : for health to the body is not more than virtue is unto the mind. A depraved, vitious mind is as really the sickness and deformity thereof, as any foul and loathsome disease is unto the body. And as really as these tend to the death and dissolution of the body ; so the vices of the mind tend to the separation of God and the soul. If therefore it be our care to rid ourselves of bodily diseases; much more it becomes us to look after the cure of our souls.

4. And lastly, the *danger* if we do not take care ; for in this state of probation, exercise and trial there are many things that are matter of temptation to us, and are intended for the exercise of our virtue : and in the course of providence God permits them, partly to awaken us to diligence and consideration ; and partly to make us to betake ourselves to him for protection, guidance, and direction. And then gain or loss is according as we approve ourselves unto, him.

K 3 This

This we may obferve, that there are no effeɕts in the courfe of nature, but the author of nature hath fecured them by vigorous and effeɕtual caufes. And affure yourfelves, God is not more wanting to the higher order of his creatures : but hath taken. care to fecure the intelleɕtual world ; that part which is invefted with reafon and underftanding, with liberty and freedom, and therein doth more partake of him ; and he hath fecured the effeɕts of thefe agents by exerting vigorous and effeɕtual caufes. And what are they. but the exercife of reafon and virtue, together with divine affiftance, guidance and direction ? For when God made a fpirit finite and fallible, he did intend to direɕt, guide and govern it, by a fpirit infinite and infallible. And if any one of us find it not fo, I dare fay fuch a perfon hath negleɕted and forfaken God firft, or elfe God would not have forfaken him. For this we take for granted, that God, in the firft creation of man, did intend to govern his mind by the affiftance of the divine Spirit ; and that there fhould never have been a fpirit finite and fallible, if it fhould not have had relation to, and communication from the divine Spirit.

From what hath been faid, I fhall make two *inferences*.

1. Then you fee, we may not be *carelefs*, felf-negleɕtive or incogitant. Some men live fo carelefly, and upon fuch eafy terms in the world, as if there were no danger, nor any thing before them to gain or lofe ; even as if they had nothing to do, and like *Solomon*'s fluggard, their field is overgrown with

briars

briars and thorns. But we are greatly concerned in this ftate, and there is apparent hazard and danger of mifcarriage : for there is fome difficulty in what is to be done, and this difficulty encreafeth, the longer we negleƈt our duty ; and it multiplies, by how much the more we have abufed ourfelves. For, *a man hath himfelf as he ufeth himfelf*. If a man hath alienated himfelf from God, by confenting to known iniquity, it is the great mercy of God, if ever he be reftored ; and when it is done, it muft be by repentance and renovation. The firft work of religion is to judge and perceive, and this is a work of fkill ; and therefore, for us to be unawakened and carelefs, not to employ our higheft faculties in this work, is irrational and unaccountable, unworthy of an intelligent agent. In worldly affairs that are of any moment, we judge a perfon highly culpable that doth not ufe his reafon and judgment. If a man mifcarry for want of this, we can hardly pity a man in fo fhameful a cafe ; we hardly think him an objeƈt of charity, that will not work for his living, and does not that which in him is, to make provifion for himfelf. For a man that is endued with reafon and underftanding, to fay, *I did not think*, I never took the matter into confideration, is no other than the account of a fool. Really I wonder how any man can fatisfy himfelf, to think that he is religious in any degree, and yet take no care to inform himfelf in neceffary truth : who doth not make it his bufinefs, to fet up a throne of judgment in his own foul. For, if he ftick here, he cannot go any farther. For if he hath any thing

that

that he calls religion, it is but fuperftition and blind
devotion.   But this, though it be what is *firft* in religion, yet it is not *all* a man hath to do : for when
a man hath eftablifhed a throne of judgment in his
own foul, and is able to put a difference between
good and evil, right and wrong ; then, *Secondly*, he
muft reform himfelf according to fuch knowledge,
and always hold himfelf to that, which his judgment tells him is the good and right.   Thefe two
things, I declare to you, are folid and fubftantial in
religion ; neceffary and indifpenfible, and a man
doth but befool himfelf, to account himfelf religious
if he fail in either of thefe : If he fail in the judgment of right and wrong ; and if after his judgment
he doth not anfwerably reform himfelf in his life and
actions : fuch a man's religion is fo cheap, that as
it cofts him nothing, fo it is worth nothing. A man
may pick and gather his religion in the wildernefs
of the world : fuch a man may be born among the
heathen, and converfe with beafts, and never look
after himfelf, and yet be religious upon fuch an account.   If therefore you have fouls to fave, and bear
true refpect to God, be fure you take care for right
information, and then be fure to refine and reform
your fpirits, and your lives, according to your judgments. For, if after this, a man fhould fail in particular practice, he will be felf-condemned ; upon
which doth follow the worm of confcience, and that
fire which goeth not out.   It is a vain thing for a
man to call that an action of religion, which is not
an act of the underftanding : for that is not a religious act, which is not human.   For we all fay,
                                                                that

that which doth not proceed from the judgment of
the mind, and choice of the will is not an human
act, though the act of a man. And if it doth not
arife to the degree of an human act, I am fure it cannot be a *religious* act. It is therefore indispensibly
neceffary to religion, that every man, according to
his capacity, condition, and opportunity, take care
to inform his underftanding, that fo he may have
the judgment of truth ; and after this, to comply
with his judgment in practice.

2. I infer from what hath been faid, that we are
not altogether to *refer ourfelves to others*, but to employ our own faculties, and improve our own advantages and opportunities, and to fee with our own
eyes ; for, otherwife we do not anfwer our ends ;
for, without this, a man grows to be lefs, and goes
backward the longer he lives, and the older he
grows ; unlefs he improves his rational faculties,
which is the proper perfection of intellectual nature.
We ought to look upon this *judgment of truth*, and
difcerning, not only by way of priviledge, and as a
fecurity againft forgery, fuperftition and flavery ;
but alfo as a charge and duty. It is incumbent upon
us to look after information, in order to reformation and amendment : becaufe without knowledge
the heart cannot be good. But then the heart is not
fanctified from knowledge alone : for there muft be
firft knowledge, and then virtue. I dare affure you
no man can be religious by another man's knowledge, nor any thing of another's ; no more than a
man that is fick, can be well by his neighbour's
health. In matters of this nature, 'tis every body
for

for himfelf. For thefe perfections of the mind, virtue and goodnefs, are not communicable, as other things are : they do not pafs as eftates, and money, and the like : but they pafs by mental illumination, by propofing each to other, and by the receiver's confideration, and his own imbibing of that which is offered.

But here now I come to the cafe of *implicit faith,* fo much applauded in the church of *Rome.* I will tell you in few words, the ftate of implicit faith. In fome cafes I think it may and ought to be allowed, but in others not. As,

1. I do exprefs an *implicit faith in God,* in thofe things that God hath not revealed fo plainly and fully : for in thefe things, tho' the fcripture declare them in fome form of words, yet I cannot reach the fenfe that is contained in them. Suppofe there be a place of fcripture about fome notion that doth tranfcend the reach of human reafon, and which is knowable only by divine revelation; and divine revelation is comprehended in a form of words that I cannot fully underftand ; in this cafe I refer myfelf to God, and believe that that is true which God intended in thofe words. This I call an *implicit faith in God.*

2. There are fome cafes, in which God hath revealed himfelf *fo far, and no farther* : here I know no more than God hath revealed ; and it is *learned ignorance* to know no more than God doth fay : and an implicit faith in thefe two fenfes, is the refignation of a man's underftanding to God ; and a great expreffion of our obedience to him. For we fhould

be

be as willing to be ignorant where God hath not declared, as we fhould be ready and forward to know and underftand all that he hath revealed. In this fenfe therefore I applaud and allow an implicit .faith : and I think they have been bufy, and created a great deal of difturbance in the church of God, that have been over induftrious to make out the re-velation of God, beyond what God hath faid, or that will impofe upon others, their own fenfe. But fuch an implicit faith as I have declared, I do allow : for it is becoming, in refpect of God ; and it doth fhew us to be modeft and teachable ; and that we do not make religion for ourfelves, but receive our religion from God.

3. Then again. Another account of implicit faith is this, which is virtuous and highly commendable, being the *neceffity of the cafe*, viz. That every one do reft in his teacher a while. Perfons that are at prefent without inftruction, or the advantage of education, muft believe thofe that have thefe advantages : as thofe that are without learning, muft believe fcholars for the tranflation of the bible : and this implicit faith is not to be blamed, but is the neceffity of the cafe, and cannot be avoided : for the truth is, every man as a *learner* muft believe, and give credit to his teacher, but yet let him not depend upon his teacher more than needs muft, nor no longer than need require : for you ought not to think that you muft be in the ftate of a learner all the days of your life. A child muft believe what is told him at firft, that this letter is fo called, and that two letters put together fpell fo much ; but after a while

he

he comes to see the reason thereof as well as his teacher; and will not be content always to be in the state of a child; but will, as he ought, use the privilege of his nature, and the judgment of discerning, and see with his own eyes. And I must tell you, he is a very unhappy man that hath lived twenty, thirty, or forty years in the world, and hath never done that which is the peculiar and proper action of human nature, that is, to use reason, understanding and judgment; but lived all the days of his life, like a meer animal, and below his kind; having not put forth any of those acts which do most properly belong unto him, as a rational being.

We condemn credulity in the *Romish* church, as we have good reason to do : but I must tell you that absolute reference of a man's self to others, is the very self same thing in the protestant religion; and those men (whatever they profess) are but *Papists* in it; neither can such persons approve themselves to be invested with reason and understanding, for they have not put forth any of those acts of judgment and distinguishing, which belong to reason; which is the height and excellency of human nature : they have not acted as intelligent agents; but have sunk down into the animal life. I confess it is our necessity, for some part of our lives, to believe and give credit; but when we are instructed, we must awaken our own faculties; search, consider, examine, weigh and resolve with ourselves; that it is so upon the evidence of light and reason, that the thing itself speaks. We must not live and die in this state, where there is not a judgment of

discern-

discerning : for in this state, both mens minds and consciences are defiled. How unsatisfactory would it be to a man, were he not in a spiritual lethargy, to be unacquainted with the true principles of life ; and that he should take this to be good, and that to be evil, only because he is told so. In all other matters wherein men are concerned about the things of this life, they would not have patience, to sit down satisfied without making due search and enquiry : but matters of religion are of the greatest importance to us ; and therefore, here is our special employment, and herein we ought to shew our greatest care and diligence. These are things of greatest weight, and moment ; and there is nothing to be alledged to the contrary. And really, we do in substance agree with the papists, that do usurp and impose upon us and we justify their practice : they call men to *blind obedience* ; and we practise it if we do not according to our ability, and parts, set up within us a throne of judgment, by virtue of which we refine our spirits, and reform our lives. This would make a good man ; and if he should happen to mistake, this would yet preserve him, for that which doth proceed from judgment of truth, as the person doth think and suppose, though there be a mistake ; the vice of the mind is abated, and the man will rather be pitied and compassionated, than condemned. He doth act, because it is his judgment, because he hath examined ; and finds cause so to think, after he hath heard, learnt, prayed and considered. If after all this, the man is mistaken at last, he is pardonable, and his case compassionable.

But

But if he hath a private judgment, and hath not ufed due care for better information ; he. is inexcuf-
able : and if he be not reformed according ·to· his
judgment, then he is felf-condemned.

This is a point of great weight, and it.lies at
the foundation of religion.   But alas ! alas ! I lofe
my labour as to the greateft part of the world ; for
though liberty of judgment be every one's right,
yet how few are there that make ufe of this right ?
For the ufe of this right doth depend upon felf-im-
provement by meditation, confideration, examination, prayer, and the like.   Thefe are things antecedent, and pre-requifite ; for a man doth not leap
into a judgment ; he is born only with faculties,
but thefe cannot immediately produce thefe acts.
For it is not in the intellectual world, as in the
world natural : for there doth the fun no fooner
appear, but there is light from the eaft to the weft;
and if the wind blow, it blows, we know not how
far.   But in the intellectual world, a man is born
only with faculties, powers and principles ; but all
habits are acquired; and men attain them by particular acts.   No man is born with habits ; but e-
very man hath himfelf as he ufeth himfelf ; and he
that hath never confidered, weighed and fearched,
he knows but little upon this account.   Hence it is,
that a great many perfons are in an incapacity,
(however they may flatter themfelves) concerning
acts of judgment.   For that man's judgment is not
worth a rufh, in any cafe whatfoever, that hath not
examined, often thought upon, and enquired into
things.· Men fhould confider, and make it their
                                                      bufinefs

bufinefs to be informed in the difference of things, and make due application to God to teach their underftandings knowledge ; or elfe, 'tis not to be expected that they fhould arrive at a true and right judgment. Therefore I do refolve it much fafer of the two, for one that is blind, or is not at leifure to weigh and confider, and fo to receive inftruction, to choofe a wife and good perfon to follow, and to make him his guide, than to attempt to go alone. For he was born only to a poffibility, becaufe of his natural parts : but faculties you muft put no confidence in, unlefs they be qualify'd and feconded by habits ; and no habits are, if not acquired ; and acquifition is by mental, rational, and fpiritual improvement.

None fo mifcarry, as the prefumptuous beyond their own fufficiency ; they who affume to themfelves where they are not prepared and qualified. Such as are fober, and modeft, know much better than others : and yet they are loath to fpeak, fearful of being miftaken. But others there are, that are blind and unawakened ever fince they came into the world, and yet they are confident, arrogant, prefumptuous and felf-fufficient. The modeft man will not venture beyond his own ftrength ; he is very receptive of all direction ; glad of information, but the prefumptuous man, though blind, he is bold and confident ; becaufe he is moft ignorant. So that you fee this argument of private judgment is modeft and humble ; and grows only in God's garden. And this is the privilege of human nature ; yea incumbent upon us all : and we ought fo to employ ourfelves

felves, that we may arrive to a perfection of judgment ; and confequently upon judgment, to a right frame and temper of mind.

Now all this I have difcourfed upon this argument of judgment of truth, and confcience of right, which are things that have great place in religion ; and wherein if we will have any foundation for our profeffion, and denominate ourfelves chriftians, from true and folid grounds ; we muft charge ourfelves with thefe things ; and put ourfelves into a capacity of difcerning the difference of things, and form ourfelves according to that judgment.

DISCOURSE X.

The MALIGNITY of POPERY.

JAMES iii. 18.

The fruit of righteoufnefs is fown in peace of them that make peace.

I Have propofed to make ufe of thefe words as a character, a *criterion*, a note or mark of difference and diftinction : and that not only of perfons in their fingle capacities, but chiefly of *churches*. For we find the great enquiry of chriftendom is, *Which is the true church ?* The *Romifh* they pretend that they are it : and they will tell us, that there is no other ; and that there is no falvation out of their *church*. A very great affuming, and taking upon them-

themfelves. I would not run into other arguments, but let us judge by this temper recommended in the text, *which is likely to be the true church.* If they do make ufe of the name and credit of religion for inhuman and cruel practices, then this character doth not belong to them. Let us try by that : and,

In the firft place they own it, that they may propagate religion with fire and fword : and by woful experience it hath been found, that that which hath been done under that title of extirpating heretical pravity, of which they take to themfelves the cognifance and judgment, hath proved the moft fiery and incendiary principle that ever was in the world. Farther, they do not account themfelves bound to keep faith and truth with hereticks. They fay, that by herefies, men lofe all their right to truth ; whereas we know that keeping our word is the foundation of all converfe : for what is one man to another, more than his word ? If men be not true to their word and promife, by which men are fure of perfons and things, all converfe is to little purpofe, if not for the worfe.

Farther, they *fanctify,* by their notion of religion, treachery, falfhood and perfidioufnefs, murder, maffacre, bloody and cruel practices ; and all this, to extirpate herefy, (as they call it) to plant religion, and bring men into their church. But how this agrees with the character given of religion in the text, and the intent and purpofe of it, let any man judge. Verily, by what thefe men fay and do, one would think that hell itfelf were broken loofe, and come up into the world. So unlike it is to *new*

VOL. I.   L   *Jerufalem*

Jerufalem that fhall come down from above.   Yet
this is that religion which they practife, and which
they own in their principles. And becaufe I am u-
pon a material point, I will give you a few *inftances*
by which it will appear, that what I have faid is
true. *Henry* the third king of *France* was bafely
murdered by *Clement.* *Henry* the fourth by *Ravil-
lac.* And fee how thefe practifes took among them.
Pope *Pius* the fifth that was then alive, applauded
the fact of *Clement,* and reckons it as glorious a work
as God's fending the Meffiah into the world, or raif-
ing him from the dead : that a religious perfon fhould
do fuch an act, for the intereft, fervice, and advantage of the church : becaufe it was done in the defence of the holy league, which was indeed nothing
but rebellion and irreligion.

John Hufs, and *Jerom of Prague* were burnt for
hereticks, notwithftanding the *fafe conduct* that was
promifed them.   But they did all agree, that the
emperor could not give *fafe conduct* to fuch hereticks,
and that no faith ought to be kept with them.   In
this cafe, we may ufe the words of good old *Jacob,*
Gen. xlix. 6. *Simeon and Levi are brethren, inftruments of cruelty are in their habitation. O my foul, come
not thou into their fecret, unto their affembly, mine honour be not thou united. Curfed be their anger, for it
was fierce, and their wrath, for it was cruel,* &c.   In
matters of good and evil, men ought to be governed by the reafon of things, or by plain and exprefs
texts of fcripture.   But thefe men do teach us, as
Gideon was faid to teach the men of *Succoth,* Judg.
viii. 16. *With thorns and briars of the wildernefs, with*
thefe

thefe he taught the men of Succoth. Or as *Joab* did,
2 *Sam.* xii. 31. *He brought forth the people that were
taken, and put them under faws, and under harrows of
iron, and under axes of iron, and made them pafs
through the brick-kiln,* &c.   Thefe are the men that
fulfil what is written by the author to the *Hebrews,*
chap. xi. of men of their fpirit and temper, that ufed thofe men, of whom the world was not worthy,
after this manner : *fome were ftoned, others were
fawn afunder, were tempted, were flain with the fword,
and made to wander about in fheep-fkins and goat-fkins,
being deftitute, afflicted, tormented.*   Thefe men of
whom the world was not worthy, *had trial of cruel
mocking and fcourgings yea of bonds and imprifonments.*
All thefe things are verified of thofe, that have been
perfecuted by the *roman church* : the *Albigenfes* and
the *Waldenfes* ; of whom multitudes were murdered for their confciences toward God.

I might alfo inftance in their manner of convert-
ing the *Indians* and natives : and tell you fuch lamentable ftories, that would even pierce the heart
of any man to hear them. But to come near home,
their maffacre of *Paris,* accompanied with fuch
cruelty and barbarity, as words can hardly exprefs.
Never was it known in the world, that men fhould
all on a fudden, rife up againft their neighbours a-
mong whom they lived in peace ; and without any
provocation, or wrong *done* to them, to rife up and
deftroy fo many thoufands, upon *the fcore* of religion and confcience, as they did here, and in *Ireland.*
The relation of both which is extant.

But

But laftly, their defign all along and continued practice among us, in the days of *Queen Mary* and *Elizabeth.* In the former of whofe reign, who is ignorant of the havock they made upon good and innocent men, haling them not only to prifons, but to the ftake, becaufe they could not worfhip a piece of bread, for God ? And what they are now a doing God only knows ; though in fome meafure their intentions have been difcovered by their actions. Alas ! what have thefe men to do with our faith in God ? Is it any wrong to them, that we have faith in God according as we find caufe to believe ? Is it not enough that we do approve our confciences to God, and to receive from God what he hath fpoken ? Is all this to no purpofe, unlefs we will comply with their novel creeds, none of which were known in the days of the apoftles, nor for feveral hundreds of years after ? I fay, what juft caufe of provocation do the reformed religion give to thefe popifh fpirits : that becaufe proteftants cannot believe as the popifh church doth, but are guided by reafon and fcripture, the moft facred things in the world ; the one being the light of God's creation and the other the revelation and refult of his will. Becaufe we cannot practice contrary to thefe, nor otherwife than our judgments and confciences allow of ; therefore are we ufed, as they in *Daniel* by *Nebuchadnezzar,* thrown into the fiery furnace, and perfecuted with plunders, maffacres, and what the malice of thefe men can invent. Is this any religious motion think you ? which always ought to be in obedience to God, and according to knowledge.

If

If this be a heavy charge, I appeal to thofe that know them beft, whether I charge them with any thing that is not apparently true.

But let us for a while, reafon with thefe men, concerning thefe principles and practices : and I afk them foberly, is *this* like the religion of him that came to feek and fave that which was loft, and that prayed for his murderers, *Father, forgive them, they know not what they do ?* And St. *Stephen,* the firft martyr, he wrote after his copy ; *Lord, lay not this fin to their charge.* Is this the religion of him who *rebuked* his difciples for calling for fire from heaven, to deftroy them that did not follow them ? They did not think of making a fire to do it, but they flew to heaven for vengeance; it muft be fire from thence, and not of their kindling. And then, what was the caufe ? It was for an affront put upon our Saviour himfelf, which, if any thing, would have juftified them : but our Saviour rebukes them, and tells them, that they knew not what fpirits they were of ; and exprefly declares to them, that his coming into the world, was to fave mens lives, and not to deftroy them : and they which carry on our Saviour's work, and are acted by a gofpel fpirit, they do the like. Was this fpirit of popery learnt of the bleffed Jefus, that was meek and lowly in heart, and bid us learn of him to be fuch ? Is it not rather the fpirit and work of him that goeth about like a roaring lion, feeking whom he may devour ? This indeed, is like the work of him that was a murderer from the beginning. Is this the fruit of that religion that allows no evil in any cafe what-

L 3   foever ?

foever ? that requires patient bearing of wrongs, and doing good for evil ? that if our enemy hunger, requires us to feed him, and if he thirft, to g ve him drink, and to win and overcome by genuenefs, and heaping coals of fire upon our enemy's head ; and doing, as God himself, who caufeth his fun to fhine on the evil and the good, and fendeth ; ain on the juft and the unjuft, and that is kind to 'he unthankful and to the evil ? Are thefe the fruits of the Spirit which are fo famoufly defcribed *Gal.* v 22. and *Col.* iii. 12. *Love, joy, peace, long-fuffering, patience,* &c. places that I have had fo often occafion to mention in thefe difcourfes ? And then the apoftle chargeth us to *forgive* one another, even as God for Chrift's fake hath forgiven us : and this was the life of our Saviour. *He went about, doing good, healing the fick,* comforting the difconfolate, and inftructing the ignorant, and reclaiming the difobedient, and bringing them to the wifdom of the juft. This was the work and bufinefs of our bleffed Saviour, all the time he lived in the world, and this is that which he expects from his followers. So that I may truly fay, chriftianity is the beft principle of kindnefs that ever came into the world : but oft it cometh to pafs, that the corruption of the beft proves the worft. And this I have obferved, that where modefty and loving affection, are the natural dowry ; there in the degenerate ftate is the greateft impudence and cruelty. It hath been long obferved, that faction and miftaken zeal, are a kind of *wild-fire.* The more falfe any one is in his religion, the more fierce and furious : the more miftaken, the

the more impofing. The more any man's religion is his *own*, the more he is concerned for it, but cool and indifferent enough for that which is God's.

I will give you a few *inftances* to fhew you the truth of this : that the more falfe any man's religion is, the more furious he will be in maintaining it, *Acts* xxiii. 12. We read of fome men, that out of their great zeal for the mofaical law, banded together and bound themfelves with an oath, that they would neither eat nor drink, till they had killed *Paul.* And 1 *Kings* xviii. we read of *Baal*'s priefts, how that they cut themfelves after their manner, with knives and lances, till the blood gufhed out upon them, and cryed from morning to evening, *O Baal, hear us,* &c.

In like manner, we read of the worfhippers of *Diana, Acts* xix. that they were full of wrath and confufion, crying out, *Great is Diana of the Ephefians.* Alfo, we read of *Balaam,* the falfe prophet, *Numb.* xxiii. how he built altars, and offered facrifice from one place to another, thinking by thefe to bribe God ; and at laft, built feven altars, and prepared feven bullocks and feven rams, hoping, by thefe to effect his defign : fo likewife we read of thofe that burnt incenfe to the *queen of heaven,* Jer. xliv. 17. They confefs this practice of burning incenfe to the queen of heaven, and ferving other gods, whom neither they, nor their fathers had known : and thefe furious *zealots* do fuch things in purfuit of their devotion, that the reafon of mankind condemned. They *made a religion* to themfelves, and then did fuch things in purfuance of

their

their wild and bloody devotion, as the very reason of mankind startled at ; as you may see, *Jer.* xxxii. 35. *They made their sons and their daughters to pass through the fire unto Molech* ; a thing which God commanded them not, neither came it into his mind, *Ezek.* viii. 13, 14. You read of several a-bominations committed by the children of *Israel*, which were represented to the prophet, in the dark. These men even spoiled the good nature they were born with, by cruel practice, and they became the worse for their religion.

I do conclude, that far better is *nature alone*, take it as it is, than that religion which is insincere and false. I say it again, better nature alone, though debased, abused and neglected, the very refuse of God's creation, than *that* religion, which is false and insincere. For, *Aristotle*, who is credible in matters of nature and reason, he hath observed, that man, by his nature and constitution, is a mild and gentle creature, fitted for converse, and delighting in it. Certainly, were I to take an estimate of christianity, either from popery, or any of the gross superstitions of the world, and the affected modes of persons, I would return to philosophy again, and let christianity alone. For philosophy, so far as it goes, is sincere and true, and attains good effects : it mollifies mens spirits, and rids them of all barba-rity. True indeed, it is short of supernatural reve-lation, and these things the princes of the world did not know ; (as we read, 1 *Cor.* ii. 14.) because they are spiritually discerned, that is, (according to the sense of the text) they are known only by revelation

lation from God. For he there doth give an account, that as *no man knows the things of a man, but the spirit of a man which is in him ; so no man knows the things of God, but the Spirit of God :* that is, the results of the divine will are not known, unless they be revealed by the Spirit of God. This is the true meaning of this text ; and it is ill brought, to prove that a man in the use of reason and natural light, cannot understand ought that belongs to his salvation, or the sense of any text of scripture. I am very confident, the apostle never says, nor means any such thing. But as the secrets of a man are known only to the man himself, till he doth reveal them ; so the secrets of God are known only to God, till God reveal them, and till then we are not charged with them ; for negative infidelity damns no man. But those that are acted by the spirit of popery, do corrupt the word of God, as the apostle says, 2 *Cor.* ii. 17. They make the word of God to serve ends and purposes, as the apostle faith, 2 *Pet.* ii. 3. They make merchandise of the word of God, and make gain their godliness : that is, they gain power and wealth, and live in pomp ; these are the ingredients that make up their religion. But since they do usurp upon us, we will put in these few material exceptions against them, and will shew wherein the popish and reformed church differ.

First, They impose upon our belief, things contrary to reason ; self-inconsistent and incongruous.

Secondly, What of truth they acknowledge, they make void and elude, by qualifications, explications, limitations and distinctions.

Thirdly,

Thirdly, They superadd to religion, things unlikely to be true, dishonourable to human nature, and without all warrant from God.

Fourthly, and lastly, they frustrate the effects of real religion, by their pretence of power and privilege.

First, They confound the reason of our minds, by absurdities, incongruities, and imposing upon our belief things impossible and inconsistent.   These are strange things to be said of any religion : yet I will make it evidently to appear, and go no farther than the *monstrous* doctrine of *transubstantiation*, which if we do admit, we must bid farewel to all our natural sentiments. Reason must then be laid aside, and shall be no judge hereafter.   We must then give the lie to the report of our senses.   And if we do this, how shall we think that God made our faculties true ? But if God did not make my faculties true, I am absolutely discharged from all duty to God, and regard to his commands, because I have no faculty that can resolve me that this is of God. Now if I may not believe the reason of my mind, in conjunction with three or four of my senses, how shall I know any thing to be this or that ?   And if I do not know any thing to be true or good, I am not obliged, as to practice.   And if God do require duty of me, he useth power against right, and calls me to give an account, when it was not possible for me to know his mind in any thing.   Therefore, I say, *transubstantiation* doth confound the reason of our mind, by absurdities, and imposing upon our beliefs, things that are impossible, and repugnant to our senses.   *Secondly*,

Secondly, They make void, what they themſeves
acknowledge to be true, by diſtinctions, evaſions, limitations, gloſſes, comments, explications. And to
make this out, I will inſtance in ſix things.

1ſt. Their doctrine of *probability.* If a man can
find any doctor among them that held ſuch an opinion, it makes that doctrine probable.

2dly. The point of *mental reſervation.* You cannot know their minds by what they ſay, becauſe
you do not know what they reſerve in their minds,
ſo that what they ſay may be but half what they
mean.

3dly. The trick of *directing the intention.* By this
they may murder a man, ſo they do not intend to
murder him, but to rid themſelves of an enemy.
They may declare that which is falſe, and deny
that which is true, becauſe they intend the credit of
their church and religion : and this intention ſhall
excuſe them from downright falſhood.

4thly. The practice of *equivocation* is too well
known among them.

5thly. Their way of evaſion, by having a *double
ſenſe.* Whereas, no man ought to uſe wit or parts
to impoſe upon another, or to make a man believe
that which they do not mean. In treating, one
with another, we ought to take care that there be
a right underſtanding between both parties, and
that each do underſtand one another's meaning ;
and in caſe there be a miſtake herein, we ought to
eaſe one another ; for the agreement is only in
that we meant and intended, not in that wherein
they did not conſent and agree.

6thly.

6thly. Their shift of hypocritical *prolocution* ;
that is, to use words of such a sound, when they do
not intend such a thing by them, as a man would
think they did.   Now, all these are contrary to the
simplicity and plain-heartedness that ought to be in
our converse, one with another.   I will not farther
explain these things, because they are abominable ;
and I would not teach any man to be dishonest.
For they are of such a nature, that if you speak
them, you teach them ; and if you declare them,
men may learn them.   But

Thirdly, They superadd things unlike to be true,
and dishonourable to God ; and this I will make
appear in three things.

1st. Their use of *images* in the worship of God·
How far better than this, is that which we find a-
mong the philosophers ?   God, say they, is to be
worshipped by purity of mind ; because a spirit is
best acknowledged by the reason of man's understanding, and the thought of his heart : for this is
the worship most suitable to an immaterial being ;
and it is the use of that in us, which is the highest
and noblest of our faculties.   For the spirit in man
is the *candle of the Lord,* lighted by God, and a
light to direct us unto him, as we read, *Acts* xvii.
27.

2dly. The veneration of *relicks* ; a very vain
thing : for there can be no certainty at this distance
of time, what they are ; and if they were what they
are taken for to be, what is due to them ? for, ina-
nimate things are far inferior to those that have
life ; and we read, that the less is blessed of the
greater,

greater, *Heb.* vii. 7. And *Solomon* saith, *Eccl.* ix.
9. That a living dog is better than a dead lion. And
for the living to worſhip things that are dead, is altogether irrational and unaccountable. And for the wor-
ſhipping of *angels* and fellow creatures, which is the
3d. Thing, why ſhould ſhould any man ſo proſ-
titute himſelf as to worſhip theſe ? I am ſure God
would not have us do ſo : he would not have us a-
dore any creature. For as the apoſtle reaſons, *Col.*
ii. 18. it is but a ſhew of humility to worſhip angels, and they are in the higheſt rank of creatures.
And if they are not to be worſhipped (as it is plain
from *Rev.* xxii. 9. they are not) then ſurely none below them. And God hath declared, that there is
but one God, and one mediator between God and
man, the man Chriſt Jeſus.'

Fourthly, They fruſtrate the effect of real religion by their pretence to power and privilege. That
is, they pretend to make that lawful which is not
lawful. *Bellarmine* ſaith, that the pope may declare
virtue to be vice, and vice virtue. By this practice
they can turn *attrition* into *contrition,* that is, they
can make ſuch a conſternation of mind, as fell upon *Judas,* when he went and hanged himſelf, by
the prieſt's abſolution to be *contrition* ; that is change
it into the notion of true repentance. And alſo bodily penance inſtead of an inward change of the
mind.   They pretend to work ſpiritual effects by
virtue of holy water and the croſs.   They pretend
the efficacy of indulgences, for the pardon of ſin :
the power of abſolving men from oaths and obligations : all which are things unaccountable. There

are

are three great defigns in popery, and I will tell you what they are.

1ft. To keep the civil *magiftrate* in awe.

2dly. To maintain the *clergy* in ftate and honour.

3dly. To keep the *people* in ignorance, and fo to enflave them, and difable them to fee or know. Thefe are three great things in popery. If any of you defire any of thefe three things, popery is for your turn ; but if you would maintain the honour and privilege of human nature, then you muft give your teftimony againft it.

But in true religion there is nothing which the reafon of mankind can challenge or object againft : nothing wherein the reafon of mankind may not have fo good an account, fo as to have fatisfaction.

And to declare the plain truth. I do not at all underftand that there is any religion farther than *that* which is owned among proteftants. What they have more among the papifts is accommodated to ferve ends and purpofes. The moft learned among the church of *Rome* acknowledge the materials of our religion to be true. As for the ignorant, they are of no confideration in point of judgment ; no more than the opinion of a blind man in point of colours, or of a deaf man as to founds.

I conclude this with what a great *abbot* in their church was wont to fay, that he did greatly fufpect that his religion muft needs fail, becaufe there was fo little ground for it in the word of God. I will add to what he faid, that there is as little ground for it in the principles of God's creation, or in that which we call natural religion.

Now

Now I come to give you an account of the *re-formed church*. And I will fay concerning it, that it doth neither perfecute, nor hold any principle of difturbance, but maintain principles of peace. If a-ny man in the reformed church do, I muft declare, that it is the fault of particular parties, and not to be charged upon the reformed church. And to make this appear, I will begin with what the church of *England* declares : and I had beft for that quote fome of the *homilies*, of which there is one concer-ning contention and ftrife, and particularly that which is occafioned by principles of religion.   The words are thefe,   " It is far better and more worthy " for any one to give place to another, and let his " argument fall, than to win the *victory* with breach " of *charity*."   An excellent determination, which you fhall find in the homily againft ftrife and con-tention.   Then for the *ancients*, I will quote you two or three fayings of theirs.

'Tis, faith one, unnatural to religion to be for-ced ; for a man's religion muft be chofen. St. *Au-ftin* gives his account of the *Circumcellions*, the worft fort of *Donatifts*. Saith he, " We bring thefe be-" fore the civil magiftrate, not becaufe they err in " matters of faith, but becaufe they perfecute and " are troublefome to right believers" * they brought

* *Non effe petendum ab imperatoribus, ut ipfam berefim juberent omnino non effe pœnam conftituendo eis qui in illa effe voluiffent : fed boc potius conftituerunt, ut eorum furi-ofas violentias non paterentur qui veritatem catholicam vel prædicarent loquendo, vel legerent conftituendo.* Aug. *ep.* 50. *vid. & ep.* 68, 159.

the

them before the magiftrate, to reftrain their violence
not to compel them to believe.   Thus St. *Auftin.*
And indeed there needs nothing to promote religion
but gentle and friendly ways.   For in point of *natural religion* (which takes in fobriety, righteoufnefs,
and piety) you may eafily fatisfy any man by reafon.   For no man is in any thing more certain, than
that he ought to be fober and temperate ; than that
he ought to deal righteoufly, and fo as he would be
dealt by ; and that he ought to carry himfelf equally and fairly ; and that he ought to fear and reverence the deity : for thefe are the dictates of natural light.   And therefore if we will *fhew ourfelves* to
be *men*, we muft live in the practice of thefe principles, and comply with them.   And then for other
matters, matters of *revealed religion* and truth ;. in
thefe, we are perfuaded by the word of God ; by
the reafon of the things themfelves in matters of the
former fort ; and by the revelation of God's word,
in the latter.   And if the fpirit of God doth not
fatisfy, and perfuade the mind of a man to receive
and entertain thefe, as they are here declared ; then
there is no poffibility of making this man to become
a *chriftian.*   For you cannot force chriftianity, becaufe it is matter of fupernatural revelation : here
you cannot convince men by reafon, which is the
only way to deal with men in other matters.   And
fo the apoftle hath told us : becaufe thefe are the
refults of God's will, therefore it follows that they
are only knowable by God's revelation of them to
us, 1 Cor. ii. 11. *As no man knows the things of a man,
but the fpirit of a man which is in him, fo no man
knows*

knows the things of God but the spirit of God, and he to whom the spirit will reveal them.

Now I will give you an account of the main principles of the *reformed religion* ; what it doth maintain, allow, defend and practise : and lay it out in eight particulars.

1. The reformed religion doth allow and maintain the worship of God, and all the offices in religion, to be performed in the *vulgar tongue* : so that knowledge and devotion may be had and promoted.

2. The reformed religion doth own the *free use of scripture,* both in publick and private ; and call upon men to do as our Saviour adviseth, *viz.* to *search the scriptures,* for by them we hope to find eternal life ; for these are they which make the man of God perfect, and richly furnish him for every good work ; and by these we are able to render a reason of the hope that is in us.

3. The reformed church doth hold that the scripture is the *only rule* of faith : and therefore traditions councils and fathers, and the writings of learned men, are only to be used as helps, better to understand the scripture : but they are *not* to be looked upon as any rule of faith ; but in this case we say as the apostle, *if I, or an angel from heaven preach any other doctrine than that which we have delivered unto you, let him be accursed.* It is well resolved by St. *Austin,* who saith if any one of us offer that which is not in scripture, any man that hears, hath more authority to refuse, than the other hath to declare. But in popery we find *twelve new articles* at once imposed upon us.

4. We of the proteftant religion do affert, that every one hath the right of his *private judgment*. But we do advife, that to the end men may be able to diftinguifh between good and evil, truth and falfhood ; they make themfelves capable of this right by prayer and meditation, and diligent fearch, and conference, and other helps of knowledge. Advifing men to be modeft, humble, fober and temperate and to lay afide all fondnefs and partiality of ferving ends, when they come to read the fcripture : faying as *Auftin* once did, when you take up the bible to read, you muft not feek there for an argument to confirm your opinion, but refolve to entertain that opinion which the text doth direct and warrant. Now the *Romanifts* tell us of what great acquifition they have made, how many they have brought to their church, by their way of force and violence: and particularly they brag of what they have done in the *Indies*. For which I fhall quote you the teftimony of a great *abbot*, that was then a bifhop among them : his words are thefe, " Who after a " brutifh manner drive people to *baptifm*, as men " drive beafts to watering, and butcher far more " than they baptize."

5. We do declare, that the *teachers* of the church ought *not* to be *dictators*, or maftets of mens faith ; but helpers of mens faith ; for they are *not to make religion, but to fhew it*. They do not take away the key of knowledge from the people, as our Saviour chargeth the *Pharifees*, Luke xi. 52. Or as St. *Auftin* faith, they do not command faith in men, upon peril of damnation, to fhew their fuperiority, or to practife

practife as governors : but they do appear in the
good office of direction, and giving men counfel.
'Tis not pride of ruling and fhewing power, but out
of compaffion to lead people into the way of truth,
and to recover them out of error and miftake.

6. We tell people that the *fcripture* is clear, and
full, and *perfpicuous* in all things neceffary, as to all
matters of life and practice.   So that if people be
well minded, and ufe diligence, they may eafily underftand, and be fatisfied.   We never teach them
to refign up themfelves to others, nor to believe as
others do blindfold, to believe as the church believes.
'Tis true, to give you a little account of this, there
are in the *bible*, things of a very different nature.

1. There are matters of *ancient records*, the hiftory of former times ; and thefe things were far
better known then, than they are now, at this diftance of time.

2. There are in the fcripture things that are
wholly expired, and *out of date*; and fo of lefs ufe to
us, as the whole mofaical difpenfation.

3. There are in fcripture matters of *prophecy*, fitted for thofe times ; which they did far better underftand, than we do now : and wherein they were
far more concerned than we are.   For they are
tranfactions partly of things performed, which when
fulfilled were beft underftood.

4. And there are matters of deep *philofophy*, as alfo matters of *philology* ; and thefe do not belong to
the bufinefs of religion.

5. And laftly, there is the *moral part* of religion,
and our Saviour's doctrine ; and in thefe two our

religion

religion confiſts : and theſe are eaſily learnt and un-
derſtood. Nay, the moral part of religion, and the
doctrine of our Saviour, which are eaſy to be under-
ſtood. And for the other parts of ſcripture, they
are not of ſuch concern to the community of mankind. And if we do not fully underſtand them, we
are ſafe enough ; if ſo be we are brought to real
goodneſs and virtue, and to believe in God through
Jeſus Chriſt.

7. The reformed church doth not deceive men
by any ways of *fraud* and *falſhood.* Thoſe of the
Romiſh church, that hold the doctrine of *implicit faith*
and the doctrine of merit, and teach that *maſſes*
ought to be ſaid to relieve ſouls in *purgatory* : theſe
impoſtures and cheats we put upon none. Indeed we
do allow implicit faith in *God,* where we cannot
certainly underſtand what his meaning is, in any
particular text. That is, we do believe that what
the divine ſpirit meant by theſe words is true ; and
when it doth appear unto us, we will receive and
admit it. And this faith we allow.

But an implicit faith in men, or in the *church,*
this is *popery.* We deal honeſtly with men ; for
we plainly declare to men, that without perſonal
holineſs, they cannot ſee the face of God : according as the apoſtle ſaith, *Heb.* xii. 14. and *Eph.* iv.
24. *That we muſt be renewed in the ſpirit of our minds.*
This we declare and inculcate, and admoniſh men
about the effects of regeneration, and the motion of
true godly repentance and turning from ſin to God.
As alſo put men in mind, upon all occaſions, that
this is a probation ſtate, and that men are here to
be

tted and qualified for the state of glory and im
ality. And that men ought to lead christian
, and not refer themselves to a death-bed repen
e, which is very hazardous and uncertain : for
can men get knowledge all in a moment ? Is
ime of sickness a time for men to learn ? when
should come to practise, is that a time to be
ht ? when men are put upon the very last nick
ing. Or to get themselves released from long
naughty habits all on a sudden ; and the facul-
released from such inclinations ; when as the
het tells us, that it is next to washing the black-
r white, for men that have been accustomed to
vil, to do well. So that we deal honestly and
ghtly with men, telling them, as they expect to
appy hereafter, in this state to acquaint them-
s with necessary knowledge, and to get them-
s discharged from all naughty habits, which
not be easy to do upon a sick-bed ; especially
:n have long abused themselves, through ill
custom, and practice.

We do resolve, that all they who do agree in
nain points of religion, may look upon them-
s as members of the same church, notwithstand-
ny different apprehensions in other matters.
this is a principle of peace and charity ; and
:nowledge tends to the reconciliation of men,
o make them live together like christians, in
and good will. And for this I will quote you
tying of the apostle, *Phil.* iii. 15. *Let us there-*
as many as be perfect, be thus minded ; and if in
ing ye be otherwise minded, God shall reveal even
nto you. M 3 L:

I will *conclude* all with that saying of a great school-man, who spake indifferently of the state of the re-formed and *Romish* church. " For men to differ " about matters of particular persuasion and opini-" on it is not inconsistent with that imperfect state " which we are in, while in the way to heaven; " when we come thither, we shall be consummat-" ed, and more fully harmonize : but to differ in o-" pinion, is not repugnant to peace in the way; " though the difference shall be taken away when " we come home."

Now if it be otherwise with any man that owns the reformed religion ; I must tell you that though he may profess he is of the reformed religion, he is *Popish* in the protestant profession. For these are matters wherein they of the protestant religion do agree : and if any man question any of those, he is so far popish in the protestant profession.

DISCOURSE XI.

The Deceitfulness of S I N.

H E B. iii. 13.

Take heed, lest any of you be hardned through the de-ceitfulness of sin.

WE are in this world in a state of probation, and have many enemies to encounter with so that our condition is very dangerous, both from *force* and *fraud*, and from *fraud* the worst of the
two

two. For if a man be ill dealt withal, and forced, he is excufed becaufe he could not help it ; but if any man fuffer from *fraud*, he is both laughed at, and felf-condemned. Now, he is couzened and cheated, that upon any reprefentation made to him of things without, either doth or permits what is in itfelf finful or unlawful. And by *this rule* you may eftimate all that I have to fay.

I fhall,

I. Give you an account of the *deceitfulnefs of fin.* And,

II. Shew you the great *reafon* we have to *take heed*, that we be not deceived.

I. My bufinefs fhall be to fhew you the *deceitful-nefs* of fin, and how much thereby we are in danger. And this I will do in ten particulars.

1. Evil takes *another name*, though it doth always retain its nature ; and becaufe it muft not be known by its own name, it doth adopt itfelf into the family of fome of the virtues, as if it were like to fome of them : and things that are alike do oft impofe up-on unwary perfons. Now becaufe a particular rule is beft known by *inftances*, I will mention feveral. Covetoufnefs paffeth for a thrifty temper, and good hufbandry ; prodigality for being generous ; vanity is reputed neceffary remiffion of mind, and foolifh talking to be affable converfation ; lavifh expence of time, goes for exercife and recreation due to the body ; finding fault with others, is reckoned to be reproof of fin ; fharpnefs and feverity, to be ftrict-

nefs

nefs of confcience ; backbiting is accounted an endeavour for reformation ; jealoufy and fufpicion to
be care for right and truth ; bufy meddling with o-
ther mens affairs, lives, and judgments, is faid to be
activity for the advancement of religion ; and to
controul others liberty, a care for their fouls ; prefumption is thought to be faith in God ; curious de-
terminations beyond fcripture, to be the improvement of faith ; and inconfiderate dulnefs to be the
denial of our reafon ; mal-content to be forrow for
fin ; exceffive ufe of the creatures, to be chriftian
liberty ; compliance beyond meafure to be good fellowfhip ; fond imaginations to be divine infpiration ;
extravagancies of paffion, to be the unavoidable motion of a cholerick temper ; taking too much upon
one's felf, and over-bearing the company in difcourfe
and converfe, to be better improvements of the talent ; fiercenefs in a fect, in a particular way, or
mode, to be a greater care of religion ; fpeaking
without fenfe, to be the fimplicity of the fpirit ;
fheepifhnefs to be modefty ; diffidence to be humility ; affording hard meafure, to be ftanding for
one's right ; petulancy and animofity, to be gene-
roufnefs, courage, good mettle, and like a man of
fpirit ; cunning craftinefs, to be prudence and policy ; neglect and carelefs omiffions, to be infirmities only, the weakneffes of the faints.

Thus there are many things which pafs for a
due temper, and regular motion in religion, which
are not the perfections they are taken for, but rather the contrary. I cannot now ftand to convince
thefe feverally of deceit ; but if they be enquired
                                        into,

into, they will not be found to be the things they pretend to be.

The 2d and 3d I will put together. Sometimes evil suggesteth to us *pleasure and delight,* and sometimes *gain and profit.* And these two, pleasure and profit, are the baits that take with all men that are not of fixed and resolved virtue. Now the scripture supposeth both of these; and therefore we read of the *pleasures of sin,* that they are but for a season. And also it telleth us of the *wages of unrighteousness.* But solid and true pleasure, gain and satisfaction to a mind well instructed, is only to be found in the ways of virtue and goodness. For *Solomon* tells us, that *the ways of wisdom are pleasant :* and *godliness is great gain,* saith the apostle.

4. Evil holds us in hand that it is a matter of our *right,* and that which we may do in the use of our *liberty ;* whereas 'tis not power, to be able to do that which is not fit to be done : this is not liberty, but licentiousness, wantonness, to do evil, or to serve any lust. But we are greatly bent to maintain our right, and shew our power. *Jezebel,* spake thus to *Ahab,* when he was troubled for *Naboth's* vineyard : *dost thou govern Israel, and knowest not how to have Naboth's vineyard ? arise, eat bread, and let thine heart be merry : I will give thee the vineyard of Naboth the Jezreelite.* And she gave it him, but upon strange terms ; by wilful murder, perjury, and subornation thus did she use her power, 1 *Kings* xxi.

5. Evil covers itself with some *probable notion,* or circumstance. Nothing in this vain world is more usual than colours, pretences, representations, excuse

fes, appearances contrary to reality and truth. *Joseph's* brethren's felling him is covered with their *not having their hands upon him* Gen. xxxvii. 2. 7. *David's* murdering *Uriah*, by drawing him out on the forlorn, 2 *Sam.* xi. 15. His numbering the people by the priviledge of a prince, 2 *Sam.* xxiv. When was it known that evil walked abroad without a difguife? a fair pretence for a foul action. The devil's hook is too well baited to be feen. The ferpent propofed to our *firft parents* their being *like unto Gods.* Gen. iii. 5. *The lips of the ftrange woman drop as the honey comb* : *and her mouth is fmoother than oil,* Prov. v. 3. The worfhippers of the golden calf confecrated a day unto the Lord, *Ex.* xxxii. *Balaam* is in fhew for the obfervance of God, *Numb.* xxiii. 26. But he taught *Balak* to caft a ftumbling block before the children of *Ifrael,* Rev. ii. 14. *Saul* takes upon him to offer a burnt-offering contrary to the exprefs command of God. He faith, *the Philiftines are upon me, and I have not made fupplication unto the Lord,* 1. Sam. xiii. 12. And he fpared *the fatteft of the cattle* that he might offer them in *facrifice,* 1 Sam. xv. 15. *Corah, Dathan* and *Abiram* juftified their rebellion againft *Mofes* and *Aaron* with this pretence that they *took too much upon them* : *feeing that all the congregation was holy,* as well as themfelves ; therefore why fhould they *lift up themfelves above the congregation of the Lord,* Num. xvi. 3, 7. Here is a pretence of maintaining the juft *liberty* of the congregation. So they that would take away the life of our bleffed Saviour fay it is *expedient* that one man fhould die, and that the nation perifh not, *John* xi. 50.   6. Evil

6. Evil warrants itself sometimes by the difference of *time* and *place*, sometimes by measure and degree, sometimes by *mode* and *manner*. Forasmuch as that may be done at one *time* that may not be done at another; distinguish but of times, (they will say) and then they think they shall be able to justify themselves. And then by *measure* and *degree* although it be one of the most difficult things in the world to assign mode and measure, yet man will say it may be done in another place, though not in this; and in this manner, though not in that, or after any fashion, and to such a measure and degree. The sluggard was for a little sleep, a little slumber, *&c.* till evil had taken hold of him, and got an advantage upon him. In many cases it is very hard to fix the utmost bounds of good and evil, because these part as day and night which are separated by twilight; so that there is as dim day-light between both. It is a very nice point for a man to know how far he may go, and farther he may not.

7. Evil pleads sometimes the *necessity* of the case, and that it is unavoidable. The *law of the time*, the *necessity of the case*, this answers all objections to the contrary. Though I must tell you, there is no necessity at all to do that which is evil: for the worst that the world can do unto us, is not so bad, as to do evil. And we must rather expose to hazard the loss of our lives, and all we have, than give God an offence. For it is better to die in reconciliation to God, than to live ten thousand years in all the pleasures and jollity of this world. This we find was *Herod*'s justification of himself, when he did

contrary

contrary to the very ſenſe of his own mind. He cut
off *John Baptiſt's* head becauſe of his oath, and becauſe of thoſe that were with him at that time.
But take this for a notion, *neceſſity* may put us upon inconveniencies, but neceſſity muſt never put
us upon iniquity or make us conſent to evil. There
is no neceſſity of ſin: for altho' we live no longer here, we ſhall live in a better ſtate. We muſt not
ſave our lives, and deſtroy the cauſe of life.   To
live is to be in good temper of mind and regular in
our actions and practice.

8. When evil hath once entangled us, there is
another evil (and it may be a greater) thought neceſſary to hide, or *extenuate* it. For evil if it be lookt
into, will be aſhamed of itſelf.   Upon this account
it is that men are aſhamed to own it, and ſometimes
with a lie deny it.   When *Cain* had murdered his
brother, to the very face of God himſelf, he tells a
lie. So *Annanias* and *Sapphira*, when they had ſold
the poſſeſſion, and pretended that they brought all
and laid it down at the apoſtle's feet, when as it was
but a part.   It had been an act of chriſtian *charity*,
to have brought any part, ſo they had been ſincere
and hearty in it : but they are ſaid to lie to the Holy Ghoſt.   Seldom one evil goes alone. *Gehazi* did
the firſt evil action in going after *Naaman* the *Syri-
an* and asking him for gold and change of raiment,
without his maſter's commiſſion : but then this puts
him upon another lie to juſtify it, and then more
followed, as you may ſee in the ſtory.

9:    Evil

9. Evil juftifies itfelf by *prefcription* and *general practice* ; fo it was formerly, and fo it is ftill. And this is taken for a juftification. This was the practice of thofe *Ifraelites* that were not carried away captive, who diffembled with the prophet and with God himfelf ; who, tho' they enquired what they fhould do, yet were refolved to do as their *fathers* did before them ; becaufe then, they faid, it was well with them, when they offered incenfe to the *queen of heaven*, and therefore they would do fo a-again. Things that are in ufe and cuftom, men think they may do ; and what have been done be--fore them. What, will they fay, fhall I be wifer than my forefathers ? This is the anfwer of many *Papifts* among us, who will hear nothing that is faid to them, becaufe they will not damn thofe that went before them, nor pretend to be wifer than their an-ceftors ; others fay, what ! fhall we call into quef-tion common practice ? do not thofe that are wifer and more learned than I, do the fame things ? nay, do not men of place and power do the fame things ? This is juft like *Ahab* to *Micaiah*, 1 *Kings* xxii. Do not all the prophets fpeak fo and fo ? let thy word be like unto theirs. Not a word of what God fhould fay unto him, or what was *true* and *right* ; but let thy word be like unto the reft of the pro-phets. So it is with many men, they follow other mens practice, without confidering what is *right* and *fit* to be done.

10. I fhall obferve in the laft place, that which is moft dangerous of all others, and that is this ; when the firft *motion* towards repentance and converfion

is

is lookt upon as if it were the fovereign remedy of *repentance* itſelf. As if *ſorrow* for ſin, were the whole product of repentance ; whereas indeed, that which is true repentance, muſt be accompanied with the forſaking of ſin and bringing forth the fruits of righteouſneſs. By which St. *John* means the reformation and amendment of our lives.

And that I may the better ſatisfy you in this, I deſire you to conſider, that the *firſt motions* of repentance have been, where nothing that was *good* followed upon it. We read that *Judas* was ſorry for his ſin, in betraying our Saviour ; but what followed upon it ? nothing but deſperation and ſelf-murder. *Cain* was ſenſible of the murder of his brother, and affected with the conſequence that he thought would follow upon it ; for, ſaith he, every one that meets me will kill me : though this fear ſeemed very unreaſonable at that time. We read in the 2 *Pet.* ii. 18. of ſome that were *clean eſcaped* from the pollutions of the world, that were again entangled, whoſe laſt end was worſe than their beginning. And that it is better not to have known the way of righteouſneſs, than afterward to depart from the holy commandment. My *caution* therefore is, that if you look towards God, and your minds ſerve you to make any application to him ; that you purſue that good motion till you bring it into a ſettled ſtate ; for otherwiſe the firſt motion towards repentance may prove an aggravation of your ſin, and heavier condemnation.

Thus I have given you ten inſtances of the *deceitfulneſs of ſin*. And, as I told you at firſt, it will

trouble

trouble us lefs to be over-born and forced, than to be cheated. For the former we may not be able to help ; but we cannot be deceived, if we be but as wife as we fhould, and ought to be. That one man is ftronger and richer than another may not be in our power to help ; but if a man be not as wife and virtuous as another, it may be much his own fault. For this depends upon his own due care, and the improvement of thofe faculties that God hath given him. And I am of opinion, that *we fhould all be wife enough one for another, if we were but equally honeft.* The truth is, if any one be difhoneft, he may deceive a good man : for fuch a man is given to charity, and apt to think of others as he finds himfelf, and fo to have a good opinion. But if I am cheated a *fecond time*, I am a fool. We read of perfons that lay under worldly difadvantages that yet arrived to great wifdom and underftanding. The poor man by his wifdom faved the city, *Ecclef.* ix. 15. And we read of a wife woman that faved her hufband, and a great many people. And poor *Lazarus* was wife for eternity. Therefore, as I faid, we may be over-born by power without any great difparagement ; but we cannot be cheated, but it muft have an ill reflexion upon ourfelves. For no man makes a bargain unlefs he pleafe, and he need not unlefs he will. If he want experience, why hath he not taken advice ? So that, if he be cheated, it is owing to his weaknefs, willfulnefs, or rafhnefs ; for he might have prevented it. No man is afhamed that another is preferred before him in wealth and ability : but the meaneft creature will

be

be impatient to be thought to want wit, or to be
accounted a fool.

Having thus given an account of the *deceitfulnefs
of fin* ; I will,

II. Shew you in fome particulars, how great *reafon* we have, according to the advice of the apoftle
to *take heed* that we are not deceived.

1. Becaufe in this ftate we run all manner of *ha-
zards* and *dangers*, to which God that hath a care
of his creatures, doth yet fuffer us to be expofed ;
and that grace he affords us is not only for ornament, but for conflict. Some ufe the grace of God
more, and fome lefs ; and others wholly neglect it.
God did account, that we fhould ufe and employ
the faculties which he gave us ; and 'tis unaccountable to God, if any man comes into human nature
and doth not fo ufe mind and underftanding (that
is capable of God, and receptive from God, and fit
to make acknowledgments to him) I fay, if he doth
not ufe it for thefe purpofes. For here we are to
fight the good fight of faith, 1 Tim. vii. 12. *To run
a race*, 1 Cor. ix. 24, 26. and *obtain a prize*. In the
work of religion, much is here to be done, many
temptations to be refifted, many conflicts to be
made.

2. Our *feveral* faculties have different inclinations, and fome of them are not at all capable of
reafon, therefore not to be governed by any moral
confiderations, which make it a very hard province
that we are to act in. Many of our faculties are
governed only by reftraint, and are not held or
drawn by the *cords of a man* : as for example, appetite ;

petite ; for which reafon, *Solomon* faith, *Put a knife to thy throat, if thou beeft a man given unto it.* For, reafon will not fatisfy an exorbitant appetite ; and this creates to us great difficulty. This is the rule in all things, that a man act according to *reafon,* which is the *candle of the Lord* fet up in him ; and by this he fhould be directed, and fee his way before him. For even the grace of God doth adjoin itfelf only to our higher principles. For this end it is given to guide and direct them ; but for our lower faculties, they are otherwife to be dealt with : we muft offer violence to them, if they be exorbitant.

3. Things without us, and round about us, prefented with their feveral advantages, do many times *provoke* and *allure* us ; and are hardly to be denied. And a man hath nothing to withhold him, but the virtue of his mind, and refpect to God. And abundance in the world are fo profane, as to decry thefe principles, as things of fancy and imagination. Therefore it is neceffary that we fhould be fettled in a *ftate of virtue,* or we fhall never, like *Jofeph,* be able to refift evil, and to fay, *How can I do this wickednefs, and fin againft God ?* Therefore faith *Solomon,* Prov. ii. 11. *Let underftanding guide thee ; let difcretion keep thee.*

4. That which fhould be for our fecurity, *viz.* company and *converfe* : this oftentimes becomes a fnare to us : though (as *Solomon* faith) two is better than one, becaufe if one fall, the other fhall lift him up. And this was the defign of God in making a *fecond* to be an help unto the firft ; that fo, that

V o l. I.　　　　N　　　　which

which is finite, might be better fecured by another; yet it often falls out that we are in great hazard by our very company and converfe. For company is of a bewitching, moulding and transforming nature: and therefore we fhould take great heed of our company, and affociates. *Go not* (faith *Solomon*) *in the way of finners, avoid it, turn from it, and pafs away.* And *David* faith, *fit not in the feat of the fcornful.* And we have a rule, that *whofoever is not known by himfelf, may be known by his company.* For converfe doth affimilate ; and a man either finds his company fuch as he is, or he will be like them. Ecclus. xiii. 1. *For he that toucheth pitch that defileth, will be defiled ; and he that goeth with vain perfons, fhall be vain.*

5. He that is officious to bring us into his condemnation, he is forward to fit us with fuitable objects that fhall raife our apprehenfions, and draw us into evil. This he did to our firft parents. *It is good for food, and defirable to make one wife,* faid the ferpent to *Eve.* And we read *Mat.* iv. 10. That *Satan* fhewed to our Saviour all the kingdoms of the world, and the glory of them, and faid, *Thefe will I give thee, if thou wilt fall down and worfhip me.* And we read, that he was a lying fpirit in the mouths of four hundred falfe prophets at one time. And that the *devil* is fo bufy to feduce and draw men into evil, may appear to be the common fenfe of *mankind,* by thofe expreffions we find in the *arraingment* of notorious malefactors, who are faid not to have the fear of God before their eyes, but to act by the inftigation of the devil. As he that endeavours

vours to purify himſelf ſhall not want the divine aſſiſtance to encourage and aſſiſt him ; ſo on the contrary he that neglects himſelf and conſents to known
iniquity, ſhall not want thoſe that will drive him on ;
and as we ſay, *he muſt needs go, that the devil drives.*
But then,

6. There are many things impure, and contrary to religion, to which we are tempted, that the
world do not reckon among the greateſt crimes.
There are other evils that are deſtructive to us, beſides *treaſon, murder,* and *theft :* and theſe we are
to beware of, as well as thoſe that make us obnoxious to human laws ; as I will give you ſome *inſtances.* It is a very great evil to make God a *mean,*
and the world an *end* ; to name God, and to intend
the world ; I dread to have to do with any man
that will make uſe of his religion, to gain him credit, and to make a bargain : as alſo to be under the
power of the world, and wholly at its beck or call ;
or to be under the power of ungoverned paſſions ;
to be vainly fraught and poſſeſs'd ; to be out of the
true uſe of reaſon, and ſelf-government. Theſe are
inſtances of evils that are very deſtructive, though
the world takes little notice of them, and do not
reckon them in the number of mortal ſins. Yet if
a man will ſecure his intereſt for eternity, he muſt
take care to avoid theſe things. And herein is our
great danger, becauſe men do not charge themſelves
in theſe things, as in other crimes.

7. Man is ſuch a *compound,* that heaven and earth as
it were meet in him, terms that are extremely diſtant.
Man in reſpect of his mind, is qualified to converſe

with

with angels, and to attend upon God ; and in respect of these noble faculties, he is liable to be tempted to infolency, arrogancy, and great prefumption,
and felf-exaltation. For it cannot be denied, but that
in refpect of his higheft faculties, he is the *image
of God*, which is his honour ; being both intelligent
and voluntary, having underftanding, liberty, and
freedom ; which is his prerogative, above all other
creatures below him. But yet in refpect of thefe, he
is tempted to lift up himfelf, and this was the fall of
Lucifer ; though there be no reafon for it : for
what is a ray that flows from the fun, to the fun itfelf ? which the fun could fpare, without any dimi-
nution. Why fhould any arbitrary and precarious
being lift up itfelf, and leave God out ? what an i-
niquity is this : for fuch beings to act as independ-
ent, felf-fufficient, never to acknowledge God as
original, or referring to him as final, or refting in
him as the centre of his fpirit ! this is a high mif-
behaviour in an intelligent agent, far from duty,
humility, or modefty. Yet this he may be tempted unto, by reafon of his height and excellency, in
refpect of his higher faculties. Now in refpect of
his *lower parts*, he is apt to fink down into fenfuality and brutifhnefs : man in honour, and not underftanding himfelf, is like the beafts that perifh. From
all which you may perceive, in how great danger
man is, and what great need there is that he be
not deceived.

8. I add ; If we do not ufe felf-government, and
moderate our powers, by fubduing the inferior to
the fuperior, we fail in that which is our proper

work

work and province, as we are invefted with intellectual nature ; and if we are led to gratify fenfe a-
gainft reafon, we are cheated and couzened. We
render thofe words of the apoftle, *Rom.* xiii. 14. to
make *provifion for the flefh :* but the *Greek* word fignifies, to make it the bufinefs of mind and underftanding, to *cater for the body ;* which is no lefs than
to make it the employment of the fpirit to feed the
beaft ; when it fhould be the bufinefs of mind and
underftanding, to contemplate God and things divine. For otherwife, the mind of man is as the
field of *Solomon's* fluggard, that inftead of bringing a
good crop, is overgrown with thorns and briars ;
and a man lives in a lie, and hath no judgment.
For the ufe of judgment is to obferve the difference
of things, which he doth not, that knows not how
to value fpiritual and eternal things before thofe
that are prefent and temporal.

9. *Laftly,* If God be not underftood and acknowledged in our worldly enjoyments, and recommended to us by them : if he be not intended in all our
actions, then do we not comply with the relation
we ftand in to God, nor act according to our higheft principles, nor anfwer our capacity ; nor are
true to our own intereft. For it is the work of mind
and underftanding, to feek after God, and to find
him out in his ways and works, as you read, *Act,*
xvii. 27. To be without God in the world, is our
degeneracy in full proportion ; and to alienate ourfelves from him, is the greateft and trueft *facrilege.*
For our higheft faculties are God's peculiar, God's
appropriate, God's referve, made for God, and fit

to

to attend upon him, and to receive from him. Since
therefore there is this danger, *1ſt.* Let us act with
caution and with good advice, by converſation with
the beſt and wiſeſt men.   For 'tis an eaſy, matter
to be deceived without great care and diligence.
2dly. But chiefly, let us make *application to God,* by
meditation and prayer, who will not be wanting to
us. Let us carefully avoid all preſumption, pride,
arrogancy, and ſelf-aſſuming.   Do not on the ſud-
den, but ſee before you do, and underſtand well before you act.   And *in all thy ways acknowledge God,*
and lean not to thy own underſtanding.

DISCOURSE XII.

The Converſion of a S I N N E R.

E Z E K. xviii. 27.
When the wicked man turneth away from his wicked-
neſs that he hath committed, and doth that which
is lawful and right, he ſhall ſave his ſoul alive.

IF we would be true to our great intereſt, and be
wiſe for the great concernments of our ſouls,
and ſecure them for eternity ; we muſt then put
evil from us, and repent of what we have done a-
miſs ; we muſt diſclaim it, and condemn ourſelves
in it ; we muſt be reformed, and return to our duty.
  I ſay,

I. That.

I. That the wicked *aught* to reform.
II. That they *may*.

I. That the wicked *ought* to reform.
And that will appear upon thefe fuggeftions.
Firft, *fin* is contrary to reafon, credit, and fafety.
1. Sin is contrary to *reafon*.

This is the malignant and mifchievous nature of
every finful action. It is in itfelf *unreafonable*, contrary to all wifdom and underftanding : and you
will eafily grant, that what is againft reafon ought
not to be done at all ; or if it be done, that it ought
to be revoked. We cannot fay worfe of a man,
than that he is an *unreafonable* perfon : nor worfe
of an action, than that it is contrary to reafon. If a
man will hear no reafon, who will have to do with
him ? For he that will not hear reafon, will do no
right ; and therefore what is done againft reafon
muft be revoked, and difclaimed. For what is fo
done is done againft right, which is the rule of all
actions. For right is the meafure of all motion,
and the law of heaven. Right is fo facred a thing,
that even poverty, neceffity, calamity, and mifery,
which make cafes very pitiable, and compaffionable,
they are not confiderable, in competition with right,
for fo we read, *Lev.* xix. 15. *Thou fhalt not countenance a poor man in his caufe.* Be the man poor or
rich, the right of his cafe, and nothing elfe muft
be confidered in judgment.

2. A finful action is *difcreditable* to any perfon
whatfoever. It is faid of the fons of *Eli*, that by
their

malady. Men are fenfible of bodily evils, but mental
are the heavieft. Moral evil is the greateft of all
evil ; for it hath the bafeft fymptoms, and moft unhappy confequences and the moft frequent twitches.
For moral evil makes an internal wound, a wound
in the confcience, where there is the quickeft and
tendereft fenfe. For all bodily evils, the creator
of all things hath vouchfafed remedies : but for the
evils of the mind, for wounds in the confcience,
there is no remedy, but the motion of the mind, in
the way of repentance, and application to the blood
of Chrift for expiation, and atonement. *For a
wounded fpirit who can bear*, Prov. xviii. 14.

Now on the other fide, if a man doth repent, he
may be releafed ; for repentance doth alter the
cafe. For this is moft certain, that thofe who are
finite and fallible, if they do fail or mifcarry, upon
repentance may be reftored to favour ; and if the
fault be repented of, it is morally made null and
void. And what we repent of, *God* hath declared
he will pardon. And if we repent, and difclaim,
and God pardon, it is then as if it had not been done.
Then alfo the goodnefs of God is rightly refented,
and his patience underftood, and the means of grace
are in their right ufe ; and thofe that were fpiritually dead are quickened unto life ; for by finful actions
men are faid to be dead, dead in trefpaffes and fins,
and St. *Jude* 12. hath it *twice dead*, once dead by finning againft the rule and law of right ; and dead
again by continuing in impenitency, contumacy
and hardnefs of heart.

Fifthly, There is no expectation either of God's
pardon

.pardon, or of help from him, but in the way of repentance. For who can promife himfelf any thing out of the terms of the covenant of grace ; *viz. repentance* from all dead works, refolution of obedience to God, and *faith in the Lord Jefus Chrift*, Acts xx. 21. Repentance is fo indifpenfably neceffary, that he which hath once done amifs, in refpect of the habit of the mind, he doth it again and again that doth not repent. For he is the fame man ; and men act like themfelves. You have a good form of words, when men are furious, fpiteful, and devilifh, we tell them, that *they fhew their fpirits* ; and it is very right.

. I will now fuggeft to you two places of fcripture for the proof of what I have faid in this fifth particular, *viz.* that there is no expectation of God's pardon, or of help from him, but in the way of repentance, 2 *Tim.* ii. 25. *If God peradventure will give them repentance to life.* Which fhews that there is great hazard of their repentance, who are wilful oppofers of the truth ; and that God will pardon them no other way, intimates this to us, that the cafe is very *hazardous,* whether fuch as are wilful oppofers of the truth, fhall ever be brought to repentance. The other place is, *Acts* viii. 20. where the apoftle fpeaks to *Simon Magus, Repent of this thy wickdnefs, if perhaps the thought of thy heart may be forgiven thee.* Which fhews that his fin was not unpardonable, but that there was no poffibility of pardon without repentance.

. *Sixthly* and *laftly,* We are all under obligation to repent, tho' there would no good come to us by it.

For we are God's creatures, and hold of him ; from
whence it follows, that we ought to serve him, and
to do his will, and to be at his command : for he
created us, and doth maintain us ; and this being
our tenure, we owe duty and observance to him ;
and if we fail in our duty to him, in that case, we
ought to deprecate his displeasure, and to condemn
ourselves.   In that case we owe humble acknowledgments, and we are to repent and revoke what
we have done amiss.   The performance of obedience and duty to God, that is the *first* right ; but
to repent and ask forgiveness, that is the *second.*
Now, that repentance shall have a good effect, and
take place, *that* depends upon *evangelical revelation*:
but the obligation to repentance, that is natural. I
should, in the use of sober reason, think, that if I
had failed and were mistaken, and wanting in my
duty to God, that I ought to humble myself before
him, acknowledge my offence, and ask him pardon,
and doing this, I should imagine (in the use of sober reason) that God was placable.   But this supposition is put out of all doubt and question by the
gospel ; which gives us assurance of pardon and remission of sin, if we do repent and ask God forgiveness, and renounce and disclaim what we have done
amiss. 'Tis true, we are obliged to repent whether God will pardon or not ; because we owe duty and obedience to God, as we are his creatures ;
and if we do not repent, we do, upon account, sin
again.   For this take for granted ; whosoever hath
done amiss, and doth not repent of it, and revoke
it he lives in that sin that he hath committed. For
be

he is in fuch a frame and difpofition, that had he
the like occafion and temptation offered him, he
would do it again.   So that both *nature* and *grace*
do meet here, and fhew the indifpenfable neceffity
of repentance, in cafe of contracted guilt, and a
wounded confcience.

. But becaufe I am to give you *encouragement* ; in
the

II. Place I will haften to *that* : and that which
I fhall fay upon this head is, to give you affurance,
that through the grace, which God doth afford, and
his affiftance of the powers and faculties of his creatures, we *may* repent of all evil done, and make
application to God, and deprecate his difpleafure,
and leave off to fin, and return to our duty, and fo
obtain his pardon.   It is therefore advifable, that
fince we are, all along in this life, in a ftate of
weaknefs, and imperfection ; that we be always in
the motion of repentance, and exercife of faith in
God, by Jefus Chrift. And this exhortation and advice I ground upon the word of God, which tells
us, That *if the wicked man turns from his wickednefs,
and doth that which is lawful and right, he fhall fave
his foul alive.*

.Neither let any man fay, that thefe words fignify no more, than if one fhould fay to an impotent
man, remove this mountain, and thou fhalt have
fuch or fuch a reward : or to bid a man to comprehend the ocean in the hollow of his hand, and it
fhall fo or fo be done unto him.   Thefe are ludi-
crous ways of fpeaking : and fuch as muft not be
put upon God, nor in any cafe attributed unto him.
                                                  God

God doth not mock and deride his poor creatures, when he doth invite them to him. This were to reproach one that were impotent, to bid him come to him, when as he knew he could not ftir a ftep. Therefore, when God faith to the finner, repent and turn from your wickednefs, and you *fhall fave your foul alive*; it doth fuppofe, that either he is able, or that he *will make* him fo. It being madnefs and folly to take into confideration, things that are impoffible: all motion towards fuch things is to no purpofe.

But here fome may be ready to interpofe, and fay: furely God is not in good earneft, becaufe he might if he would; for who can refift the divine will? This is a confiderable *objection*, and doth require an *anfwer*. For fome men put all upon God, and fay when he pleafes to come, with irrefiftable grace, the work will be done; and the man fhall be converted; for *who hath refifted his will?* And till then, the work will not be done, for they can do nothing. But to this I anfwer.

It doth not follow, that becaufe God doth not *inforce*, that therefore he doth not *enable*. That God fhould force agrees neither with the nature of *God*, nor with the nature of *man*; but that God fhould enable, this is natural to the relation we ftand in to God, who is original to our being. And to make this out; this notion is verified throughout the whole creation. For there is not to be found in the whole creation of God, in any part of the world, any thing that is a *procurant* caufe, but is alfo a *confervant* caufe, till the thing be fettled in a ftate of

fufficiency,

fufficiency, and fubfiftency. Even this dull *earth* that we tread upon doth maintain all the plants that do grow out of it. Take a view of the *irrational creatures*, and you fhall find, that every creature that is original to any thing, doth certainly purfue its firft production, by after confervancy, and ready maintenance, and never leave off, till it be fettled in the ftate of fufficiency, and able to fubfift of itfelf.

Now thus I argue : if this be an impreffion of God upon all creatures, and a perfection which he hath placed in them, is not this much more in God? I therefore take this to be a certain propofition ; that he which doth give the firft being, gives farther ftrength for continuance. But *force* agrees not, either with the *nature of God*, or with the *nature of man*.

1. It agrees not with the nature of *God*. An intellectual agent, that hath all knowledge and power, ufeth neither fraud nor violence. This is the neceffity of thofe that are indigent.

He that hath all power, and all wifdom is never put upon the ufe either of fraud or force. This (as I faid) belongs to indigent caufes, and cannot be fuppofed of God, who is infinite in power, and wifdom. Then

2. It doth not agree with the nature of *man*. For fuch is the nature of man, that if he do not mean and confent, it is not reputed a human action ; for nothing is a human act, but what proceeds from the judgment of reafon and the liberty of the will, we are always bound to make ufe of our reafon, for our guidance, and then to exercife liberty in pur-

fuance of the dictates of our mind. 'Tis true, in
this compounded state of flesh and spirit, we are so
addicted to satisfy the inferior appetite, and so a-
verse to the dictates of sober reason and the guidance of the divine Spirit ; that had we any thing
material to alledge to the contrary, it would certainly make us let all alone, come of it what would.
And this would be the greatest discouragement in
the world : if we could allege that we were impotent, and insufficient ; and that though the grace of
God were absolutely n eceffary ; yet we were not
sure of it. 'Tis therefore necessary for us to believe,
that through the grace and assistance of God, we
may be able, and that we shall not fail thereof. For
God is present with us, and puts good thoughts into our mind, and will promote them into execution
if we be not wanting to ourselves.   We are here
in a state of contest and fight against great variety
of enemies abroad ; and there is inclinations of the
sensitive powers within, and the allurements and
provocations of objects : and against all these it is
too little, to oppose nature's strength.   For nature
is divided, flesh and spirit, and flesh in opposition to
spirit.   Now the only foundation of certainty and
ground of encouragement, is from the *grace* and *assistance* of God : and this we are assured of, if we
duly apply ourselves to God. For the infinite, wise
and good God doth not call us to that, which he
doth not enable us to perform.   This were to put
that upon God, which neither scripture nor reason
doth allow.   For this were in effect to say, that
God had not a mind we should do that, which he
calls

calls upon us to ... if he should war-rant in grace, help and ... For our God know... that he is the first ca..., and can do ... our as nothing with... the first, and ... the first must ... gin. For this is ... ... cause should have the place of the first ... : ... be ... self-sufficient ; this is ... to the ... of the creation. Now if any man ... arrogate to ... self a self-sufficiency to do any thing, he would make himself the first cause : whereas, he neither is, nor can be the first cause, nor original. Therefore all good must begin at God ; and nothing that is good, can be done without him ; and therefore he must not only *continue*, but *make*, and when we are enabled, we may do that for which he doth enable us. We may hear the voice of God if God speaks to us ; and we may obey and comply with his motion. I will give you some instance, in scripture for this, *Isa.* xli. 2. God there is said, to call the righteous man to his foot. The righteous man here spoken of was *Abraham*, whom God called to follow him, step by step. And the apostle. *Heb.* xi. gives us an account of this in practice, who obeyed God's call, and *went* at his bidding *not knowing whither.*

Another instance you have of the disciples of our Saviour, of whom we read that when our Saviour called them, there was the virtue, power, and sufficiency in the voice of our Saviour, that they left their relations, and employments, and followed our Saviour, without making any question how they should be maintained, *Matt.* iv. 18. The inferior

creatures they have obeyed God contrary to the very impreſſions upon their natures. The *ſun* hath
left his courſe and ſtood ſtill, at God's bidding,
Joſh. x. 12, 13. Fire hath not burnt, and the ſea
hath riſen up in heaps, and the ſeveral creatures,
though never ſo oppoſite in their natures, one unto
another, came into the ark ; and though before,
they would have deſtroyed one another, yet being
called by God to go into the ark, they became tame
and harmleſs. So that not only intelligent, but inferior agents know how to obey God, if God appear.
Much rather ſhould intelligent agents, who are a-
dapted to hear God's voice, and to be guided by
reaſon, anſwer the call of God, when he ſpeaks to
them.

DISCOURSE XIII.

The Converſion of a SINNER.

EZEK. xviii. 27.

When the wicked man turneth away from his wicked-
neſs that he hath committed, and doth that which is
lawful and right, he ſhall ſave his ſoul alive.

THeſe are words not in vain ; therefore they
do ſuppoſe two things.

I. That the wicked *ought* to reform. And,
II. That they *may*.

I. They

I. They that have committed wickedness *ought* to disclaim it, repent, leave off to sin, and return to their duty. And,

II. That they *may* ; else it might be replied to these words ; *God supposeth that which cannot be done,* and this every where passeth for an undeniable answer. And to suppose this, is a defect in any wise agent : much more in the all-wise God, who never makes a vain shew. It is not only below him, but unworthy of him, to deride men in misery ; when he calls upon them to repent and turn to him. True indeed, if men will not hear his voice, then he will *laugh at their destruction,* and *mock when their fear cometh upon them.* As therefore we may not make a mock of sin, neither doth God mock at sinners. But to make this out, that the wicked *may* turn from their wickedness.

In every nature, there are two things as the provision of God's creation, and its security, *viz.*

1. A principle of *self-preservation.*
2. A motion of *restitution* and recovery.

1st. A principle of *self-preservation* in its true proper and natural state : from which of itself it doth never depart ; but by the violence of other agents, which it cannot resist ; and therefore is sometimes driven from itself. This is the account that some give of storms, tempests earthquakes, and the like. But nature's motion is orderly and leisurely ; as the several seasons of the year, that follow one another : where the former give place unto the latter. This is the first principle in nature : and the

2d Is a power of *recovery,* and self-restoration,

when

when that which did difturb is taken off. Thence
it is, that we expect fair weather after foul ; ferene
after ftormy ; and clear, after clouds. This is an
obfervation from the ftate of the creation, things
without us or about us.

Now, is there any perfection in the *lower nature,*
that is not in the *higher* ? Therefore we are to fuppofe that this is eminently in fuperior nature. Now to
bring this obfervation home to our purpofe. To a
moral agent, fuch as man is ; he being endowed
with reafon and underftanding, and invefted with
liberty and freedom : nothing is more unnatural than
fin and wickednefs. For it is againft the reafon of
our mind, and againft the reafon of the thing. It
is a contradiction to the *reafon of our mind,* which is
our governor ; that which guides the actions of our
will : and to the *reafon of things,* which gives law,
and is the rule of action ; and wickednefs is a great
contradiction to both. Wickednefs in man is as
monftrous and unnatural, as darknefs in the fun,
which is the luminary of the world : wickednefs is
fuch a thing as filth in the water '; as infection in
the air : wickednefs is fuch a thing as a difeafe
in the conftitution of nature, and we fay nature is
every man's beft phyfician. What are agues and
fevers, but nature charged with an enemy that tends
to its diffolution, and therefore labours to fhake it
off ? And therefore phyficians endeavour to help
and affift nature, and put her into motion ; by which
fhe will difcharge herfelf of all malignant and offenfive matter. Now, I fay, fhall nature recover, and
fhall not grace fuperadded to nature, do the like ?
We

We ufe to fay of all habits joined to natural powers that they do facilitate; and we eafily do that, which we do by the help of acquired habits. Now the firft. thing in rational nature is not at all to vary from. the rule of right : and this would be to anfwer the conftitution of God's creation, in man. But in cafe he fails here, in the fecond place, is the motion of repentance ; and herein lies our double fecurity, fafety and perfection. It is therefore highly necef-fary, that we be always in a difpofition towards repentance, and free to the exercife of faith in God, by.Jefus Chrift : that fo the guilt of no fin may lie upon our confciences : for this is the motion of recovery, in human nature.

So that now put the cafe of us men as we find it. Our confciences will tell us, that we have done a-mifs, by departing from the rule of right ; and by confenting to iniquity : for guilt is burdenfome to the mind, and will be a wound in our fpirits. Now if the *firft*, which is beft, fail, *viz.* our *innocence*, and *integrity*, wherewith we were invefted in the moment of our creation : let us betake ourfelves to the *fecond*, the motion of *repentance*; which. is for our recovery, and is the grace of the gofpel : and in fo doing, there will be hope, as we read *Ezra* x. 2. And let us not lofe ourfelves, by adding iniquity to our fin, or by defpair after guilt contracted. For a fecond fin, is not only another of the fame. kind, but the confummation of the former : infomuch that he is reputed to do the. fame evil once again, that he hath once done and doth not repent of it. Let us not live in a lie, flatter ourfelves with that

O 3 which

which will not profit ; for there are in man many
lying refuges, and foolish boastings, and vain glory.
The apostle tells us of some, that *glory in their shame,*
Phil. iii. 19. that do applaud themselves, as if they
were not under the obligation of judgment, and
conscience ; but were free to do any thing, that is
either pleasurable, or profitable, or expedient for
their purpose, or what they have a mind to do. For
of some we say, there is *no fear of God before their
eyes* ; no reverence of the deity in their minds, but
are free to their ungoverned wills, and to their lusts ;
whereas this is worthy of human nature, to overcome a man's own will, and to bridle his lusts. For
will is no rule, nor can justify any thing ; and lusts
are very importunate, *Jam.* iv. 1. *Whence come wars
and fightings ? come they not hence, even from your lusts
that war in the soul ?* Whereas he that ruleth his
own spirit, doth a greater act *than he which taketh a
city* : nothing is the true improvement of the rational faculties but the exercise of the several virtues,
of sobriety, temperance, chastity, modesty, gentleness, humility, obedience in all things to God, and
charity and good will to men. These are acts of
excellency, these are indeed acts of power ; by these
the minds of men are regulated, and refined, discharged of fury, rage and exorbitant passions. By these
a man is made to act *like himself* : whereas, without these, a man acts like a person in a frensy, dif-
tracted and mad, like savage people, or like beasts
of prey, that worry and destroy one another :
whereas by moderate use of the conveniencies of nature ; by modesty, humility gentleness ; by patience

ence and obedience to God, by charity, love and
good will towards men, a man is qualified for the
enjoyment of God, and reconciled to the law of
heaven, the rule of righteousness, and fitted for attendance upon God in the other state, and to enjoy him for ever.

Now, if it may be said of common education,
viz. of learning, and the study of the *liberal sciences,*
that it doth qualify and calm the minds of men, and
bring them to gentleness and sobriety ; upon
which supposition the *Roman* emperors that were
such great warriors, did forbid the study of philosophy, because it spoiled men for soldiers : I say, if
this be true of common education, how much more
of *christian graces,* by which we are taught to imitate Christ, who was meek, and lowly in spirit.
'Tis in the exercise of these virtues, that a man
shews his strength and valour, above the inferior
creation. Whereas on the contrary, by envy, wrath
pride, and haughtiness, men become devilish : but
by doing good, men resemble God. By the several
virtues, the mind is purified, and made fit to converse with God, and to receive from him : and
therefore it is said by the prophet, Isai. i. 16, 18.
Wash ye, make you clean, put away the evil of your do-
ings from before mine eyes, cease to do evil, learn to
do well. Come now let us reason together, saith the Lord.
Wherefore, I say with the apostle, *Eph.* v. 14. *A-*
wake thou that sleepest, and arise from the dead, and
Christ shall give thee life. Awake all you that have
fallen asleep, in the security of sinful pleasures, and
through neglect of God, and your duty : and this

is

¹s my argument ; and the force of my exhortation;
Christ is ready to give you life.

And if I had not good warrant to fay this, there
would be no force in my exhortation ; and I fhould
then labour in vain.   Whereas being fatisfied that
God is in this exhortation, and ready to affift all good.
endeavours with his aid, help, and affiftance ; this
gives great encouragement, and fpeaks to all points,
and anfwers all objeftions to the contrary.   Here is
then an exhortation in the *name of God* ; otherwife
were it only the voice of a man, it would produce
no good effeft.

But this I take for granted, that where there is.
monitions and warning from God in cafe of dangers ; that there the man *is able,* or that God is
ready to *make him fo.*   And if you do not fuppofe
this, all thofe exhortations in fcripture for men to
leave their fins, and to repent, and turn to God,
which are fo frequent, are to no purpofe, unlefs men
be able, or that God is ready by his grace to make
them fo.   I fay, all thofe exhortations do fuppofe
neceffary aid and affiftance. And the apoftle, *Heb.*
iv. 16. hath an excellent form of words to this purpofe, though it be not fo plain in our tranflation ;
for we read it, *let us therefore come boldly to the throne*
of grace, that we may obtain mercy, and find grace to
help in time of need : whereas in the original it is,
grace for a neceffary fupply.

Now this is all that I have aimed at ; to prove
not only that God is ready to receive us, if we repent and turn unto him ; but alfo willing to aid
and affift us.   Therefore depend upon this, as that
                                        which

which you may truft unto ; for without this, neither our religion nor our fafety have any great fecurity : if God, for his part, be not willing and ready to afford neceffary aid and affiftance. But that you may believe this, I can give you all the affurance of reafon and fcripture. Yea, furvey the *whole creation of God*, and you fhall find that God hath provided for all neceffary effects. Hath he not fecured the world, for light and heat, by the fun ? doth the fun fail, after fo many thoufand years, to give light and warmth, any more than it did at firft ? This is the promife of God, to fecure the neceffary effect to the prefervation of the feveral creatures. Hath not God provided the clouds of heaven to drop down fatnefs, and to fend rain to wet the earth, that otherwife would be fpoiled with heat and duft ; I might run through the whole creation, and fhew how every thing is fitted for our ufe, and to fecure the effects that are neceffary and proper for us.

But I go on. No confiderate mind, that is privy to its own flipperinefs, dare be felf-confident. He that is fenfible of his own irrefolution, and fudden furprizal through temptation together with his weaknefs, is, fo far from being felf-confident, or from trufting to his own ftrength that if he fhould leave God out, he would foon give over and fink down into defpair ; and not think himfelf fufficient to manage fo great an affair, as the things of reafon, and the tranfactions of time and preparations for eternity. We are always to underftand, and to remember, that we are but fecond caufes, and have fufficiency only in God, who is firft and principal in every thing that good is ; and if God be with us, we are enabled. Where-

Wherefore be reſolved in this matter, that *God is with us,* and that he is ready to afford his grace and aſſiſtance. And this is a thing of univerſal acknowledgment. For all ſober and conſiderate men, when they do engage in any thing conſiderable, they ſay, *in the name of God* ; and when they part with one another, they ſay, *God be with you.* Let us therefore in every thing begin with God, which is to follow the direction of our bleſſed Saviour, *Luke* xiv. 28. who ſaith, *which of you intending to build a tower, ſitteth not down firſt, and counteth the coſt, whether he have ſufficient to finiſh it. Or who is he that will go forth to war againſt a great and potent enemy, that doth not firſt ſit down and conſider, whether he be able to meet him.*

Now that you may not loſe this great argument and principle of reformation, and true and ſolid ground of encouragement, to leave off to ſin, and to return to God, becauſe of his gracious aid and aſſiſtance, I will give you aſſurance farther by theſe ſix particulars.

Firſt, It was *never* God's intention when he made man at firſt, to put him into a ſtate of abſolute *independency,* or *ſelf-ſufficiency.* And therefore whoſoever aſſumes it to himſelf, doth aſſume that which never did belong to a creature-ſtate. God always did intend, that his creatures ſhould depend upon him, and hold of him : for man was made but in the place and order of a ſecond cauſe, and a ſecond cauſe is no cauſe divided from the firſt. Therefore it was always the report of wiſdom, *acknowledge God in all thy ways ; and lean not to thine own underſtanding*

Prov.

Prov. iii. 5. This was a duty of *Adam* in paradise, e-
ven while he continued in innocency ; before ever
he meddled with the forbidden fruit ; and he mis-
carried, because he did forget his dependence upon
God, and withdrew himself from him. Those
words of the psalmist, *Psal.* xxxvii. 5. *Commit thy
way unto the Lord, trust also in him,* are not directions only for this lapsed state : these are directions
suitable and connatural to the very first institution
of God. As also that of the prophet, *Isa.* l. 10.
Trust in the Lord, and stay thy self upon thy God, and
as he there goes on most excellently. *v.* 11. *Behold
all ye that kindle a fire, that compass yourselves about
with sparks that you have kindled, but this shall you
have at my hand, ye shall lie down in sorrow.* They
are sure enough to fail and be disappointed in their
undertaking, be it never so good, they will end in
sorrow and shame, if they do not begin with God,
and look up to him, as the only self-sufficient cause.
For alas ! *none of us are wise enough for our own direction,* in any of the ordinary affairs of life, *or able
enough for our own defence* : we do not see before us,
nor understand what evils may befal us. If we walk
in the streets, we are not sure of one another ; for
he that despises God or the laws, may be master of
any man's life. So that if we leave out God, or God
be neglected, we shall be frustrated and disappointed ; and then we may justly reflect upon our own
presumption and folly. For we went out in
our own strength, and God was not in all our
thoughts ; and therefore he doth not give issue and
success. This was the state of the creation, the

creatures

creature's reference to God, and the creator's influence upon the creature, and communication of himfelf to him ; and that which was not in the ftate
of innocence, cannot be fuppofed to be in the ftate
of weaknefs, and contracted impotency and debili-
ty. Yea, to tell you of a felf-fufficient creature, is
a contradiction *in fubjecto* ; for all things derive
from their original, and refer thereunto. As *Solomon*
hath obferved, *the place from whence the waters come,
thither they do return*, Eccl. i. 7. This is a reafon
beyond all contradiction. I could triumph in this
argument ; 'tis without all poffibility of anfwer or
evafion.   Therefore there is an abfolute infufficiency in every fecond caufe ; and what is a fecond
caufe, is applied without effect, when the firft caufe
is abfent, or doth not move. This is the firft. But,

Secondly, Could man alledge either *neceffity* of e-
vil, or *impoffibility* of doing good, it would be a plea
when God calls us to an account, and admits us to
reafon with him.   For the fcripture tells us, that
God doth do fo, not only at the *day of judgment*,
but even *now* ; and every one hath heard the voice
of God calling upon him, to give a reafon of his actions.   *Come now* (faith the prophet in the name of
God) *let us reafon together*, Ifa. i. 18. and argue the
cafe, and I will let you judge between me and
yourfelves, *what could I have done more to my vineyard than I have done*, Ifa. v. 4. But what have you
done anfwerable. ? But if fin were neceffary, it
could not be avoided ; and if a man's duty were
impoffible, it could not be done ; this would be an
anfwer to God himfelf.   But, that there is no ne-

ceffity of evil, or any impoffibility of doing good, and becoming virtuous, I will fhew you from that paffage of our Saviour, *Matt.* xi. 21. who faith to that wicked generation, *that if the mighty works that had been done among them, had been done in Tyre and Sidon, they would have repented.* Which fhews, that there was no impoffibility in the matter, but that it might have been done ; otherwife this fpeech of our Saviour had been vain, and to no purpofe. Upon this account it is, that we read, *Jude* 15. That at the day of judgment God will *convince all the ungodly,* and challenge them for *all their hard fpeeches,* and *ungodly deeds, that they have committed* ; and fhew, that they had no reafon, either to fpeak or think hardly of him ; fo that if this could be made out, that it were abfolutely impoffible to avoid evil, and to do good, and difcharge our duty ; *this* would be an anfwer to the indictment, that might be brought againft us at the laft day of judgment. For *neceffaries* cannot be otherwife than they are, nor that which is *impoffible,* otherwife than it is. So that before any judgment of condemnation pafs from a righteous judge ; it muft appear, that neither any one was neceffarily wicked ; nor was it impoffible, to have been virtuous.   Therefore thefe things will appear otherwife, or men will not condemn themfelves, nor juftify God in his dealings. And doth not our Saviour plainly intimate this, when he tells you that *Chorazin* and *Bethfaida,* as they *ought* to have repented, fo they *might* have done it ; and others *would* have done it upon the like means, as hath been already faid. It is true of finners, what *Saul*

faid

said of himself, 1 *Sam.* xiii. 12. *I forced myself,* when he did that which he ought not to have done. So it will be found of all sinners, that they have done that which was *unnatural* and against the reason of their minds; which had they followed, they would not have been wicked.

Thirdly, Where there is *excellency of nature,* there is always readiness to communicate, supply and gratify. We commonly say, 'tis *not majesty without goodness* : all excellency is easy to give allowance to shew grace and favour. A good dispositioned man saith *Aristotle,* is ready to make a candid interpretation, and overlook an injury; and it is more generous *not to take cognizance* of a fault, than to forgive. It is *God-like* to pardon to gratify, to do good. In case of misery, it belongs to goodness, to make a supply. They think meanly of God, that think he doth less to recover his creature, than doth consist with infinite clemency and compassion; that God doth less than what might serve the turn, or that he is wanting in necessaries, to save his creatures harmless, or bring them to good. This I depend upon in a way of reason; that infinite goodness will not do less than is necessary, or than will serve the turn. But then as reason speaks, so also doth God speak of himself, by those impressions he hath made of himself, upon all creatures. For all creatures that are *original* to any other, they have this in them, to take care of their young, and to watch over them, till they are able to make their own defence and supply. This is true throughout the *whole creation* of God; and hear what God hath said of himself,
                                                            Psal.

lcxlv. 9. *God is good to all : and his tender mer-*
re over all his works.   Therefore I will rather
k, *that God did not make the world, than that he*
fail to be very good unto the creatures that he hath
. For I fee it otherwhere quite otherwife.
urthermore, we find good affection every where
nmended, and the contrary every where blam-
ld difparaged.   We admire goodnefs, tender-
and compaffion ; but on the contrary, every
complains of envy, malice, hard-heartednefs,
:y. We therefore may be fure, that goodnefs
)t be wanting in God, the want whereof God
es in his creatures.
urthly, We cannot *fay worfe* of God, than that
ills and monitions to his creatures, are not fe-
, and in good earneft, and out of love and good
. I can make no other explication of that
ction of God's *fecret and revealed will,* but that
lo declare the felf *fame will* in God ; but it is
cret will, before he hath declared it : and his
led will, when he hath made it known.   Juft
: fecrets of a man, knoweth no man, but him-
nd he to whom he will reveal them : fo the
f God is not known, till God himfelf declare
'or to fpeak of a fecret and a revealed will in
contrary one unto another, is without war-
for it is the *fame will in another ftate.* And this
well affured and refolved of, becaufe this would
honefty here below in the very judgment of
:, to pretend and not to intend ; to make a
and overture, and to refolve in a man's mind
ntrary, is a great difhonefty, in the judgment
of

of reason. And we have no other principle to difcern the nature of God by, than the light of reason ; and therefore the prophet faith, *Isa.* xlvi. 8. *Shew your-selves to be men* ; that is, use your reason, and he speaks it in this case, of judging in the ways and things of God. *To whom*, faith he, *will ye liken me and make me equal ?* Will you compare me with your i-dols, that are made of silver and gold, and carried upon mens shoulders, and set in a place from whence they cannot remove ? and though one cry unto them yet cannot they answer, nor save themselves out of trouble. *Remember this, and shew yourselves men, bring it again to mind, O ye transgressors.* Wherefore we cannot think that to be a perfection *above*, which is base and an imperfection *below.* For those things that are true, are eternal truths, always were so, and will be so immutably and unalterably. And u-pon this account, it is very hard to think of God that he will not contribute that which is neceffary to his creature, to do that which he calls him unto, efpecially in fuch things, where the creature is un-done, if the thing be not done ; and where none elfe but God can do it, nor help any otherwhere to be found. In fuch cafe how can we make it out, which is declared of God ; *that he would not the death of a sinner* ; if he do not that which is neceffary to bring him to repentance and unto life ? We are told, *Wifd.* xi. 24. that *he hateth nothing that he made* ; but is the lover of souls. And therefore he cannot be wanting in neceffaries to save them harm-lefs, and to bring them to good. And this acknow-ledgment is made in our publick prayers : and up-

on this account it is, that we are advised, to *cast a-*
way our transgressions, and to make us clean hearts, and
thus expoſtulated withal, *for why will you die ?*
Have I any pleaſure at all that the wicked ſhould die,
or in the death of him that dieth ? wherefore turn and
live, Ezek, xviii. 23. 31, 32. xxxiii. 11. And it is very obſervable, that he which bids us do theſe works
hath alſo promiſed, that he will work them in us,
Ezek. xxxvi. 26. *I will ſprinkle clean water upon you*
and you ſhall be clean ; and a new heart will I give
you, and I will put my ſpirit upon you, Jer. xxxii. 39.
and *Heb.* viii. 10. Now theſe places are very eaſily
reconciled, by acknowledging God's ſuperintenden-
cy, as the original and firſt cauſe ; and mens labour, care, and diligence, as a ſecond cauſe. So
that it may be ſaid, that man doth it, as we [attri-
bute an effect to an inſtrument : and it muſt be acknowledged, that God doth it, becauſe he is chief
and principal. We read, *Jonah* iv. 2. that God
is ſaid to be a God of great pity : and elſewhere we
read, that he delighteth in mercy ; and what
perſons delight in, they do eaſily and readily. Farther, let it be conſidered, that the fault is laid upon
us, and we are charged with careleſſneſs and ſelf-
neglect, if the thing be not done, *Prov.* i. 31. *I*
have called, but ye refuſed, and would have none of my
counſels. So, *Hoſea* xiii. 9. *O Iſrael, thou haſt de-*
ſtroyed thyſelf : and *John* vi. 40. *ye will not come to*
me, that ye might have life. This is the fourth particular.

DISCOURSE XIV.

The Conversion of a SINNER.

EZEK. xviii. 27.

*When the wicked man turneth away from his wicked-
nefs that he hath committed, and doth that which
is lawful and right, he fhall fave his foul alive.*

FIFTHLY, To affert our impotency and difability, and that God is wanting in neceffary
affiftance, is to expofe us to an invincible
temptation ; and that in thefe three particulars.

1ft, To entertain *hard thoughts of God,* and fuch
as are unworthy of him.

2dly, To *throw off the ufe of all means,* and to
take no care at all, in this great affair.

3dly, Finally, to *defpair* ; and we wrong God
more by defperation, than by prefumption. I fay,
to affert our inability, and that God is wanting in
neceffary aid and affiftance, would be to expofe us
to think the *hardeft thoughts* imaginable *of God* ; e-
ven fo far, as to neglect and throw off the ufe of
all *means,* and to final defperation.   For what are
means if the end be not attained by them ? Means
are not valuable for themfelves, nor will any body
be at the charge of them, but in refpect of the end.
And whofe heart will ferve him to act, when he
hath no manner of hope ? and who can have any
hope

hope if he have no confidence, that God will aid and assist ? I add farther ; to think that God is implacable, and irreconcileable, is the way to come unto the very temper of the devils themselves; but that God is ready with his grace and influence, is that which hath an universal acknowledgment ; as appears from these three things.

1*st.* There is not a man among us of any sense and reason, that will engage in any matter of weight but he will say, *in the name of God.*

2*dly.* There is no man of any sobriety if he relate how he hath escaped any danger ; but he will interpose these words, *God be thanked,* or, *as God would have it.*

3*dly.* All men of consideration and sobriety, when they part, will say, *God be with you.* Which observations import, that it is suitable, and connatural to the nature of man, to apply to God, and to acknowledge him, and to think that God will be with us, to assist and direct us.

Sixthly and lastly, God hath *done so much* on his part, that he hath given us all reason to believe, and think that he is well-minded towards us : and that he is resolved in the matter of our recovery, upon terms, that are made easy, and possible. And to make this appear I will offer you these eight particulars.

First. Take into consideration, the length of God's patience : for were God for our destruction, he would take us at the first advantage, and opportunity, as enemies are wont to do. For who lets an enemy go out of his hand ? Men will hardly suf-

fer

fer an enemy to live ; but prevail againft him what
they can ; left, if they fhould let him go out of
their hand, and let him alone, he fhould meditate
their deftruction. And this is that, which is apparent, and the fcripture fuppofes it, *Eccl.* viii. 2. *Becaufe fentence againft an evil work is not fpeedily executed, therefore the hearts of the fons of men are fet in
them to do evil.* But 2 *Pet.* iii. 9. we are told, that,
the long-fuffering of God doth not proceed either
from his weaknefs, or want of power, but from his
willingnefs that we fhould not perifh. He would have
us come to a better underftanding, and take a courfe
that we might live.   This is the firft thing that I
would fuggeft, that God is well-minded towards
us, and willing to do us good.   The
Second thing that I would offer, is the *checks of*
our own *confciences.*   Now the checks of our own
confciences, in all bad ways, we have very great
caufe to attribute them unto God, as his awakenings
of us. And that for this reafon, becaufe finning doth
contract hardnefs and reprobacy of mind ; and dif-
ables the mind for its true and proper work ; and
makes it as falt that hath loft its favour. *We all find
it far eafier, to commit a fecond fin than the firft.*
Therefore we are to look upon the check of our
own confciences as the voice of God.
Thirdly, The abundant provifion, that God hath
made *for our recovery,* fhews that he is in good earneft.   There is *expiation* of fin ; and the affiftance
of his grace and fpirit, for the recovering of us ;
and God would not have done all this, if he had
not been in good earneft. Here, I will take up the
argument

argument of *Manoah's* wife, *Judges* xiii. 22. *We fhall
furely die,* faid he, *becaufe we have feen God.* But
his wife faid unto him, *v.* 23. *If the Lord were
pleafed to kill us, he would not have received a burnt-
offering at our hand, nor fhewn us fuch things as he
hath done.* 'Tis not reafonable to think, that God
having made a large provifion for our relief and recovery ; that he fhould lay a reftraint upon the fovereign virtue of that, which is his own remedy ;.
but fuffer it to grapple with the malignancy of the
diftemper, though it extend never fo far. So that
if a good effect doth not follow, it is not becaufe
God hath been wanting on his part, nor becaufe.
he hath not done that which lay upon him to do.
If fuch a remedy prove ineffectual, it muft be from
fome other caufe, *viz.* from fome obftacle or impediment, or want of due application : or becaufe of
the perfon's impatience under cure, or becaufe
things are allowed and delighted in, [that are of a
contrary nature, and quality ; and not for want of
good will in the all-wife God. For the means that
God ufeth are in themfelves fufficient, and in cafe
they prove without effect, 'tis becaufe they are not
followed.

Men fall fhort in their repentance, becaufe after
men have been forrowful, they return again to their
former iniquities. Whereas, upon repentance there.
fhould follow *works meet for repentance, Mat.* iii. 8.
'Tis an excellent faying that which you find in *Ecclus* xxxiv. 25, 26. *He that wafheth himfelf becaufe
he hath touched a dead body, and goeth and toucheth it
again, what doth his wafhing profit him ? So he that*

hum-

humbleth himfelf for his fins and doth the fame things
again, what doth his humbling profit him ?

So again, for *faith,* which is another remedy of
God's provifion ; for he faith, he that *believeth fhall*
be faved. Now what doth a man's faith fignify, if
a man profefs to believe ; if he do not do thofe
things which naturally follow upon fuch a belief ;
or as they do, who do really and truly believe ;
what profit can a man expect from fuch an empty
and infignificant faith, as S. *James* fpeaks, *Jam.* ii.
14. *Can fuch a faith fave him ?* Who will think that
a man doth believe, who doth things clear contrary
to that which he faith he believes ? Again :

What come the offers of grace unto, which
fhew the favour of God towards finners ; if they
be not clofed with, or if men *receive the grace of God*
in vain ? What doth all this fignify, if that complaint of the prophet may be taken up, *that we have*
laboured in vain, and *fpent our ftrength in vain.* To
what purpofe are thofe prophets fent by God, *that*
rife up early, and fit up late, if men incline not their
ears, and will not liften ? Jer. xxv. 4. Then in refpect of the finner's ftate and condition ; can he be
otherwife than extremely miferable, that is not cured of the rancor and venom that the practice of iniquity hath poifoned his fpirit withal ? For mifery
arifeth from within ; 'tis not by any impofition
from the effects of any power without us : but a
man is miferable from his own inward malignity
and naughty difpofition. So that if a man be not
cured by all the remedies that are applied, he is not
healed of the wound that guilt and fin hath made
in

in his confcience which are the true productive caufe
of his malady and diftemper. And if this effect be
not wrought, it is becaufe the patient is refractory
and ftubborn. And that is the third thing, *viz.*
thofe *provifions* that God hath made which are worthy, honourable, noble, available and effectual, if
we do not obftruct and hinder ; but are patient under God's cure, and application of the remedy.
The

Fourth thing that I fhall inftance in, is the *nature
and quality of the things* that God, upon account of
religion, does require of us, *viz.* Thofe things
whereof religion doth confift : and they are internal good difpofitions and acts that are fuitable, and
do of their own accord follow. I fay, an *internal
good difpofition* and fuch acts as are fuitable and connatural thereunto, and follow of their own accord.
For by our carriage and behaviour, by our words
and fpeech, we fhew our mind and temper ; by
what we do, and practife. In our publick devotion
we make this acknowledgment to God, that *his fervice is perfect freedom,* and we are bid, *Gal.* v. 1. *To
ftand faft in that liberty wherewith Chrift hath made
us free.* And the gofpel is called the *royal law of
liberty, Jam.* ii. 8. For the chriftian ftate is not as
the *Jewifh*; the apoftles did not think fit to lay a-
ny fuch burdens upon believers, as were in the
Jewifh ftate, for that is called, *Acts* xv. 10. *A yoke
which neither they nor their fathers were able to bear.*
Such things were impofed upon them, as had goodnefs only as they were warranted, and enjoined by
him that had power. But all acts in the chriftian
religion

religion, have an *intrinfick goodnefs*, and in their own
nature are fanatory and defirable : and this fpeaks
honourably of the chriftian religion, that whatfoever
it lays upon us, or enjoins, is either good in itfelf;.
or for the fociety, or for recovery in cafe of failing
and mifcarriage. They are either *operative* to fuch
an eftate as is good, or *confervative* of men in fuch
a ftate, or *prohibitive* of the contrary. They are either for our fecurity in a good eftate, or for recovery out of a bad one : they are fuch things as are
good in themfelves, and do fanctify and purify our
minds, and' make us right and found, and fuch as
we ought to be.   I might inftance in all the acts
required by the chriftian religion, and make it good
of every one of them ; which cannot be faid of pofitive inftitution, fuch as was the prohibition to *A-
dam* and *Eve, Gen.* ii. 17. *Not to eat of fuch a tree.*
Neither do we take notice of any fuch prohibition.
in the gofpel : but what we find pleafurable or convenient, 1 *Cor.* x. 25, 27. *we eat, asking no queftion
for confcience fake.* Alfo thofe prohibitions that were
under the *levitical* law, for neglect whereof, the fons
of *Aaron* were fo punifhed as alfo *Uzzah,* for touching the ark ; though with a good mind to keep it
from falling ; and the *Bethfhemites* for looking into.
it.   There are now no fuch things required, fo hazardous and dangerous : for fuch things men had
not the fecurity of their minds, but their fecurity lay
only in their *memories* and not in the rectitude of their
temper. Whereas we have the fecurity of our temper,
becaufe thofe things that are forbidden, are bafe and
unworthy. So that when evil is prefented to us, we
                                                    prefently

presently give an answer *how can I do this wickedness and sin against God?* And out of a sense of the impurity of the thing *we* presently object against it. Whereas *they* had only the security of their memories which is frail and fallible faculty; for we are apt to forget, and do not often think. And this we find, that it is far harder for intellectual nature to do a thing where we see no reason for it, or to forbear any thing, if we do not see any reason why, especially if it be against our way and temper. But in the christian religion those things that are commanded are regular and kindly, because our minds are cast into the same mould with them, and framed into suitableness and conformity with them: so that weact ourselves, without any great consideration; we are ready to make application to God, and to place all affiance and confidence in him; and to do all acts of righteousness and justice; and to govern ourselves according to the rules of sobriety and temperance; because we are reconciled in nature and temper, to all these things: so that it is an easy thing to be religious, upon the terms of christianity. We worship God readily, because we are in temper, Godlike, according to our measure and degree. *Seneca* faith, " If a man would be holy and righteous, let " him *imitate God*; and if a man do partake of " God he is such and will be such." But why should I quote the philosopher, since the apostle faith, we *partake of the divine nature,* by a principle of holiness and righteousness, 2 *Pet.* ii. 4. This is the *fourth* thing, the nature and *quality of those things that God doth require of us.*

Fifthly,

Fifthly, The *equal consideration* that we meet with at the hands of God; in respect of our present weakness, shews that God is ready and willing to do us good. And to make this out, I say, that if any man suffer difficulty in the discharge of his duty, (as I must confess several tempers do, more or less, as to particular virtues ; to some tempers, such acts of virtue are very easy, that to others are more hard and difficult. Now in this disparity, if by consideration, reason and argument a man bring himself to that which is to be done, God accepts it the rather as an act of *high virtue,* and true goodness. And the more of difficulty a man finds in himself, God looks upon it as done with more resolution ; and he will not reject it ; because the man suffered *difficulty* ; but look upon it as the more. *eminently virtuous* ; notwithstanding such indisposition and avocation. Now this is the fairest measure imaginable : God doth make allowance for our temper, complexion, and constitution ; for our prejudices from our education, and suppositions upon mistakes, and for our former converse and acquaintance, which many times doth occasion some difficulty in the discharge of our duty. For *he considers our frame, and as a father pitieth his children, so the Lord pitieth those that fear him,* Psal. ciii. 13. And this is a great encouragement to us, that we shall meet with all fair construction ; and that we are upon good terms with God. And as this is for our encouragement, so doth it declare God's gracious intentions. towards us, and that he is in good earnest desirous to do us good, and that he will not be severe with

us

us. That he will neither neglect nor refuse any
good in us ; for he will not deftroy any thing that
partakes of his own nature ; but will fofter and
cherifh any thing that is God-like. And for our
miftakes, fo our hearts be right, God will mend
them, by his own candid conftruction, and gracious
interpretation. And this meafure *Abimelech* found,
Gen. xx. 6. *I know that thou didft it in the integrity
of thy heart.* Though he was to blame in the mat- ·
ter, yet becaufe he was right in the main, God o-
verlooks his fault. For, if we do not confent, the
action is not reckoned as ours. As on the one
hand, it is no virtue to do well without an intention : fo on the other, 'tis not reckoned as our fin,
if we fall through miftake. I add to this, that
there is great congruity between our own being and
the nature of things enjoyned by religion. The a-
poftle faith, *Rom.* vii. 15. *I confent to the law that it
is good* : here is the congruity of the *agent* and the
object. And *David* faith, *Pfal.* cxix. 142. *Thy law
is truth* that is, it is fuch as it fhould be. *David*
was reconciled in temper, to the law of God. To
the fame degree that we are endued with holinefs,
to the fame degree we are poffeft of *happinefs.* The
mind is the man in refpect of the excellency of the part
for mind is ten thoufand to one above body : and
alfo, in refpect of the *act* that is performed ; what
is done with the confent of the mind is beft done.
What men do againft their minds, is of no value,
though the thing done be good in itfelf ; nor of a-
ny deep malignity, if done with a good mind,
though through miftake. Not only the gracious

God

God, but all good men go by this rule ; they do not value things as they are *materially* confidered, but by the *mind* and *intention* of the party ; not that which is done, but what was *meant* and intended. If it prove an injury, a good man will accept of the good intention ; and that is the *fifth* particular.

Sixthly, Though God begin with lefs, he *will go on* with more. For this I dare fay, if a man be ferious in his religion, and duly fenfible of his own vanity and infufficiency ; and of the many avocations, and temptations from abroad ; the grace of God will not be fhort. Though God doth not give all at firft, yet that which God begins withal, is fufficient for fomething, in the way of converfion and thereby man is enabled to do that for which that affiftance is given. And that being made ufe of, God, of his own grace and good will, will give more. And this we are well affured of by thofe words of our Saviour, *Mark* iv. 25. *To him that hath fhall be given,* (that is, that hath by *ufe* and *improvement,* but *from him that hath not* (that is, that doth not make ufe of what God hath given him) *fhall be taken away, even that which he hath.* But this is moft certain that *God doth never forfake us firft.* That good will of God which did incline him to begin with us, when we were in a way of fin, will move him to go on after he hath begun. For we find in fcripture, that *God* often *makes himfelf, an argument to himfelf, Ezek.* xxxvi. 22. *For my own name fake I will do this.* So *Ifa.* xliii. 25. *I, even I am he that blotteth out thy tranfgreffions for my own name fake.* God here propofeth himfelf, for an argument to himfelf, and
brings

brings this as an argument for a *farther act* becaufe
of his own grace and goodnefs he had *begun.*
For he will not begin, and leave off upon
the fame terms he did begin, when we were in a
ftate of fin, and when we were enemies to him by
wicked works. He did begin then, when he found
us in our blood. It is eafy for us to believe that
God, who of his own accord did begin, when he
found us in a *ftate of fin,* will not give over and
leave us, when he finds us in the motion of *repentance.* And that is the *fixth* particular, tho' God
begin with lefs, he will go on with more. And this
is a great encouragement for any man to fet about
the work of religion, and to make application to
God ; becaufe he does not know how far God will
enable him in time to come. Juft as our Saviour
faid to his difciples, *when you fhall be brought before
princes and governors, confider not before hand, what
ye fhall anfwer ; for it fhall be given you in that hour,
what ye fhall fay,* Mat. x. 18, 19. So that, let no
man be difcouraged, though that which he now
hath, be not fufficient for to carry him through that
which he hath before him ; for as his work fhall
increafe and grow greater, God will furnifh him
with that affiftance that fhall be fuitable, and fufficient for what he calls himfelf unto.

Seventhly, God fpeaketh abfolutely, pofitively,
and without any refervation, that when a finner
*turneth away from his wickednefs, he fhall fave his foul
alive.* When we have but half a mind, we fpeak
with caution, refervation, and upon fuppofition :
but here God fpeaketh abfolutely, clearly and fully,

without

without *if's* or *and's*, that ſo we may ſee his mind,
and know what to truſt to. We uſe to doubt of
mens performance of their words, if they ſpeak
waveringly, and as it were, unwillingly ; but thus
it is not with God, he ſpeaks freely, and without
reſervation. And to aſſure us hereof, we have firſt
of all, the excellency of his nature, and ſecondly,
his truth and faithfulneſs. Alſo, God loſeth nothing by the ſinner's return to him. When his
creature is gained, he accounts it as gain to himſelf; ſo that nothing obſtructs but our own obſtina-
cy, and unworthy refuſal, and for that we muſt
blame ourſelves. *Prov.* i. 24. God ſaith, *Becauſe I
have ſtretched out my hand, and ye refuſed ; therefore
I will laugh at your deſtruction.* It is *God-like,* to
take pleaſure in the good of others. We know
whoſe nature it is, to take pleaſure in the ruin of
others, and who it is that goeth about, ſeeking
whom he may devour ; even the *devil,* whoſe nature is moſt deformed and degenerate.

Eightly, The repentance of a ſinner, and his
turning to God, is a thing ſo acceptable and well-
pleaſing to God, that he will greatly reward thoſe
that have any hand in it, *Dan.* xii. 3. *They that be
wiſe, ſhall ſhine as the brightneſs of the firmament, and
they that turn many to righteouſneſs, as the ſtars for e-
ver and ever.* And our Saviour ſaith, there is joy
in heaven, at the converſion of a ſinner, Luke xv. 7.
And if this may be ſaid to be done by us, which are
but inſtruments, much more by him that is the
principal and chief agent. God himſelf doth ſo
much favour and delight in this work of a ſinner's
                                        converſion

conversion, that when we shall come to know better, how much God was concerned in it, we shall think eternity itself too strait and too narrow for us to magnify and praise so good a God, so well deserving at our hands. What encouragement was it for a prodigal son, to be so kindly received by his father, *Luke* xv. 11. *&c.*

Now, the *conclusion* of all, is this : since, as we have seen, sin is so fatal and mischievous to us, and the condition of every sinner so horrid and lamentable, that is *not* brought to repentance, and into reconciliation with God, and to the law of everlasting righteousness and truth : since, if we are not according to the mind of God, we can never be acceptable to him, nor made happy by him : and since God doth afford us his grace and assistance, let us be encouraged to be up and doing, and set ourselves with all our might to leave off to sin, and to return to our duty. 'Tis very good news to a sick man, to tell him that his disease is not mortal ; and to him that is wounded, that his wound is curable ; and 'tis no less good tidings to sinners, that we can tell them, that their sins are pardonable upon their repentance, and that though they have offended God, they may be forgiven, and become acceptable unto him, upon their conversion, through Christ's recommendation, and intercession. And these things make it credible, which I pray consider.

First, What sin is, either the act or defect of a *fallible creature*, and so reversible. And that by how much the more we are liable to miscarry through temptation, by so much the more is God willing

to

to receive us upon our repentance and return to him. For this doth abate the ſin of us men in this ſtate of weakneſs and contracted impotency ; for our ſin is not like the ſin of the angels, that fell without a tempter, for ought we know.

Secondly, As our act is reverſible, and *made null by our repentance* and ſelf-condemnation, ſo *God hath all right to pardon. Firſt,* as he is lord and *owner* of the creature. *Secondly,* as he is *governor* of the world ſo alſo as he is the firſt and chief *goodneſs.* So that if it doth conſiſt with goodneſs and the honour of his government, a ſinner may be ſure to have it upon the terms of the goſpel. But then you muſt come to God's terms ; for otherwiſe it is good to controul wickedneſs and ſin ; and it is a righteous thing with God, to render tribulation to thoſe that continue obſtinate.

Thirdly, God *de facto, hath* and *will* pardon ſin to the penitent. Such is the excellency of his nature, that he takes delight in it. And I will add one thing more that God concerns himſelf in our affairs and takes care of man ; and this hath an univerſal acknowledgment ; yea, 'tis the very ſenſe of our natures, and the dictates of our reaſon ; as I will ſhew you in theſe inſtances.

1ſt. If at any time, we fall into diſtreſs, what comes ſooner out of our mouth, than, *O God, or God help me.*

2dly, If we do engage, or undertake any thing wherein there is difficulty ; we ſay, *in the name of God.*

3dly,

3dly, In our narration, all sober men say, *as God would have it.*

4thly, In our deprecations of things that are formidable ; we say, *God forbid.*

5thly, In our thanksgivings, we ordinarily say, *God be blessed* ; or, *I thank God.*

6thly, In our protestations, we say, *before God,* or, *as in the presence of God.*

7thly, In our salutations, one of another, we say, *God be with you,* or, *God keep you.*

And though these in the mouths of many men, are formal, and without due consideration, yet the custom of them does proceed from a very good original, and they speak nature's sense, and shew that there is motion in our minds towards God, and some sense of him upon our spirits.

DISCOURSE XV.

The Conversion of a SINNER.

EZEK. xviii. 27.

When the wicked man turneth away from his wickedness that he hath committed, and doth that which is lawful and right, he shall save his soul alive.

I Have purposed, in the *close* of my discourse on this text, to speak to five things.

I. The *time* when the wicked turneth away from his wickedness.

VOL. I.   Q   II. The

II. The *quality* of the person ; *wicked.* When *the wicked man* turneth away from his wickedness.

III. The *motion* ; *turneth away from his wickedness.*

IV. To give an account of. what is *lawful and right* ; when the wicked turneth away from his wickedness, and *doth that which is lawful and right.*

V. To shew the *good effect* of this motion, *he shall save his soul alive.*

I. For the *time* of his conversion and return to God, it is indefinitely spoken, and doth not exclude *late time,* which may be an encouragement to every one, be his case never so desperate.   But then, this is not spoken to encourage mens delays and put-offs ; for there are four great evils consequent upon that.

1*st.* It were to *ill-resent* the goodness of God, thus to requite his grace and favour, that we continue in sin, because God is gracious. *God forbid* (saith the apostle) that we should continue in sin, because *grace doth abound,* Rom. vi. 1, 2. This would be horrid ingratitude, and disingenuity.

2*dly,* It were to *abuse ourselves,* and do ourselves more and more harm.   For evil is against the nature of man ; it is such a thing as marrs his nature and spoils his principle.   Therefore we should never meddle with it, and much less continue in it.

3*dly,* It would make the work which is necessary to our happiness, much more *hard and difficult.* For ill use doth contract bad habits ; and bad habits contracted by long use and custom, are with great difficulty left off.   This the prophet supposeth

eth in thofe words, when he faith ; can the *black-moor change his skin, or the leopard his spots ; then they which are accuftomed to do evil, may learn to do well,* Jer. xiii. 23. Impudence and immodefty, grow upon thofe that continue in the practice of iniquity.

4thly, Continuance in fin doth expofe us to far greater *danger.*

1. Becaufe of the great uncertainty of life, for who can promife himfelf another day, nay, another moment ? and

2. Becaufe of the *devil's* repeated and continued affaults, by which he will ftill get the more advantage upon us ; and fo it will become the more difficult to get him out of poffeffion.

3. In refpect of the infinuations of *bad company* and converfe. For men that are bad themfelves, will keep fuch company as themfelves ; and company and converfe are of an infinuating quality, and *that* is done by treaty and converfe, which is not done on a fudden.

4. All the while you ftand out, you are in a way of *refiftance* of the holy Spirit, and fight againft the motions of God almighty ; which are neceffary to bring you to good, and to qualify you for eternal life. Let therefore no man think, that he may lead a finful life of pleafure here, and immediately repent, and enter into life. For heaven is rather a *ftate* than a *place ;* and doth require a good temper of mind, to qualify us for the enjoyment of it. And we are faid to be faved, in the language of fcripture, when we are delivered from *our fins,* and qualified for the

Q 2

enjoyment

enjoyment of God. And there muft be *falvation of grace*, as antecedent to that of *glory*. For happinefs hath its foundation in holinefs, and there muft be either a confcience void of offence, by abfolute *innocence* ; or eafe of guilt, by our *repentance*, and *God's pardon* : otherwife there is no falvation ; for, a guilty confcience hath hell within itfelf. There are many that would be faved in a negative fenfe, that is, they would not be damned ; but this is not a juft explication of falvation ; for heaven and falvation is begun here, and therefore the apoftle faith, *who hath faved us and called us*, 2 Tim. i. 9. And fo much for the firft particular, the *time* when the wicked turneth away from his wickednefs.

II. The *quality* of the perfon ; *wicked*. And here I muft acquaint you, that fcripture doth not denominate perfons *wicked*, or *finners*, or *workers of iniquity*, from weaknefles, failings, or from error of judgment, or from indifpofition at times, from fudden paffion, or furprifal ; nor from the irregularity of the firft motion, that is fo troublefome and grievous unto us all. But they are called *finners* and *wicked* perfons, who voluntarily confent to known iniquity ; who while they have knowledge and judgment of that which is right, for bafe ends and purpofes act contrary thereunto, and continue in fin and apoftacy from the truth. Sins of the former fort, such as weaknefs and failings, through temptation or fudden furprize, require our modefty and asking God forgivenefs : as alfo our greater care and diligence, and conftant application to God and committing ourfelves into his hand ; and in fo doing,

ing, God doth readily forgive. For he remembers our frame, and confiders and makes allowance for our weaknefs, *Pf.* ciii. 13. and *Mal.* iii 17. *As a father pitieth his children, fo the Lord pitieth thofe that fear him ; and he will fpare them as a man fpareth his own fon that ferveth him.*

III. I now proceed to the third, to fhew when a man may be faid to *turn* from his wickednefs ; to which enquiry I fhall anfwer by three negative, and three affirmative propofitions. The *negatives* are thefe.

1ft. A man is *not* faid to turn away from his iniquities when his fin rather leaves him than he leaves it : either through age and difability of body ; or through weaknefs and infirmity ; fo that he cannot bear to do as he has formerly done. Now, this is the cafe many times of the *riotous* and intemperate, who ufe to *rife up early in the morning, that they might follow ftrong drink ; that continue until night, till wine inflame them,* Ifa. v. 11. But this they cannot do always. Then for the *prodigal,* that profufely fpends all that he hath, and is brought to a morfel of bread, and like him that we read of, *Luke* xv. 14. made to feed with the fwine upon husks ; fuch a man's fin hath rather left him, than he it. The like may be faid of *wanton* lafcivious perfons, that have quite fpoiled and difabled their bodies. And alfo of *falfe dealers,* who have been fo often found out, that no body will truft them, or have to do with them ; you cannot fay that fuch men as thefe, have turned from their wickednefs.

2. Such men as are *not at* their own *liberty* ; but under tutors and governors, whom they dare not difobey ; who are as it were fhut up, and not fuffered to ramble abroad. Thefe men cannot be faid to have turned from their wickednefs.

3. Nor *when fin is made bitter* to men, by fuffering the bad confequences that follow upon it. Sometimes men fuffer in their names, or in their eftates, or in their bodies. Guilt doth always prophefy evil things, and fin is a fhame and reproach to any perfon that commits it, *Pro.* xxiii. 29. *Who hath wo, who hath forrow, who hath contentions, who hath babblings, who hath wounds without caufe, who hath rednefs of eyes? they that tarry long at the wine ; they that go to feek new wine.* It is faid of lazinefs, idlenefs and fluggifhnefs, that it is more painful than induftry and diligence ; and to be employed, is eafier than to be idle. So it may be faid of other vices ; the mifchiefs and inconveniencies that follow upon diffolute living, and naughty practices, are not ballanced by the pleafure that they bring, but are dearly paid for. Whereas ways of goodnefs and virtue are delightful, and end in peace ; as you read, *Pro.* iii. 17. *All her ways are pleafantnefs, and all her paths are peace.* For the feveral virtues, they are fuitable and connatural ; every virtue is according to the nature of man, and agrees with the reafon of his mind which is the fuperior and governing principle. As to inftance, by comparing fome virtues and vices together. Pride, infolence, envy, malice, thefe are troublefome and unnatural : there is no greater torment, or worfe rack, than for a man to live in

malice

malice, and bear envy and ill-will. Those that are arrogant and proud, create to themselves a world of difficulty, besides much ill-will and displeasure: whereas modesty, gentleness, loving-kindness, quietness, is according to the nature of man, and creates no trouble or difficulty to a man. But to return to the matter in hand. There is much difference between these two; between our leaving of sin, and its leaving of us; when we do not act from our own principle; but the bitterness of sin appears by its sufferings, and by this, we are made to desist; in these cases a man cannot be said to return from his wickedness. But then *affirmatively*, in three particulars.

1*st.* When we leave sin out of sense and judgment of its *vileness*, and impurity. For all sin is such in its own nature; and therefore we read, that the sons of *Eli made themselves vile by their wickedness*, 1 *Sam.* iii. 13. and *Jer.* ii. 19. we read *that it is an evil, and a bitter thing to forsake the Lord our God*. For in morals you must know that the ground, motive and reason of the action, doth specificate the action, rather than the matter of it. For two persons may do one and the same action; the same thing materially may be done; and yet the action may be very different, because of the ground, principle and motive, upon which it was done. This for certain you must know, that it is not a virtuous action, if be not done *because* the thing is good; and avoided *because* it is evil. That is the first, when we leave sin, out of sense and judgment of its vileness, badness and iniquity.

2. Whether

2. When we leave fin out of *respect to God*, in obedience unto his laws, and love to him. This was the temper found in *Joseph* ; who when fin was prefented to him, faid, *how can I do this wickedness, and fin against God*, Gen. xxxix. 9. When it is more to us, to give God an offence, than to expose our own lives and liberties. When a man will not deftroy the caufe of God, to fave his own life. Now if it be fuggefted, that this is a notion not practicable becaufe God is at fo great a diftance, *I anfwer*, it is done out of refpect to God, when we do a thing becaufe it is juft, fit and right ; becaufe it is good and ought to be. And this is intelligible; for every man knows what is the ground and reafon of his action ; he knows whether he doth it out of a fenfe of the goodnefs of the thing itfelf, or out of any other reafon. For man, as a moral agent, is only confiderable, as to his *end* and *principle*. For God is beft known to us, by being good, as being the firft and chiefeft goodnefs. To do a thing therefore becaufe it is *good*, is to do it out of love to God, and to avoid a thing becaufe it is *evil*, is the fame as not to do it, becaufe it will give God an offence. And this is an explication of doing a thing out of *love to God*, and out of *refpect to him*. And I have found this among the philofophers, that never had the advantage of a bible, who tell us, " That if any thing be without refpect to God, it is not an " action of virtue, 1 *Cor.* x. 31, 32. There is nothing in the world better known to us, if we fink not down by fenfuality into brutifhnefs, or by malice into devilifhnefs, than that there is a God, and

a difference between *good* and *evil*. These we are all *made* to know, and herein we may not fail. Whosoever doth not know these things, it is matter of his shame, and a sign that he hath greatly neglected himself. For who doth not know that it is better for a man to live in love and good-will than to live in malice, envy, hatred, &c. Who doth not know, it is better for a man to be sober, just and temperate, than to be wanton and lascivious ? For a man to govern himself according to nature and reason, than for to abuse himself ? Who doth not know, that it is better to honour God, and to give him thanks, than to blaspheme him ? That is the second, when we leave sin out of *judgment* and sense of its filthiness and baseness, when we do our duty out of respect to God, and in obedience to his laws, and love to him.

3. A man cannot be said to return from his wickedness, unless he doth conceive displeasure at it and resolve never to have to do with it again. Thus when a man leaves sin, with displacency and abhorrence ; he may be said to turn away from it, otherwise it is but forbearance for a while, upon some reason, and as a matter of prudence, like that of *Felix, Acts* xxiv. 25. *God speaks peace unto his people, but let them not return again to folly*, as the Psalmist hath it, *Psal.* lxxxv. 8. If a man do not continue in a good course, it cannot be said that he is turned from his wickedness, nor that it proceeded from the change of his nature, but was rather a suspension, than a dislike of his former ways. They that *love the Lord*, and do sincerely turn to him, *hate evil,*
Psal.

Pſal. xcvii. 10. We muſt not only depart from e-
vil, and do good, but we *muſt hate evil*, as the a-
poſtle directs, *Rom.* xii. 9. *We muſt abhor evil, and
cleave unto that which is good.* This is the third particular, when men leave their ſins out of *diſplacen-
cy*, and take offence at them ; otherwiſe it may be
forbearance upon ſome prudential account, but doth
not amount to *turning away from their wickedneſs.*
So that you ſee this alteration is by the motion of
the mind and underſtanding ; and is made by the
choice of the will ; the mind is changed, and other
judgment is made, ſo that this man differs from
himſelf. As a man differs that was in a deadly diſ-
eaſe, and is reſtored ; ſo doth a man differ from
himſelf, after he leaves ſin, and doth return to his
duty. And ſo much for the third thing, when a man
may be ſaid to return from his wickedneſs.

IV. In the next place, I am to give you an account of *lawful and right. When the wicked man turns
away from his wickedneſs, and doth that which is lawful and right.* Here are two words for one and the
ſame thing ; and the one is explicatory of the other.
Now, this is that which we all ought to do ; and
there is no pretence of power and privilege to the
contrary. And if every body did confine himſelf
to that which is right, juſt and fit, we ſhould have
a *new world*; and there would be nothing of wrong
or hard meaſure found among us ; we ſhould then
be the better one for another. But here is the miſ-
chief, ſome go beyond their bounds and do not confine themſelves to that which is *lawful* and *right* ;
which are but two words for the ſame thing.

Right

Right gives rule to the ... and the ... will declare what is right; and ... if it be unrighteous and unjust. This must be true of all *human* laws; for I am sure it is true of all the laws of God. The ... saith, *Psal.* ... ... *That thy law is true*; that is ... it ... for *right* is the boundary of power and privilege: ... it is not *power*, if it be not in conjunction with right and truth; for God declares that his throne is established in righteousness, Pro. xxv. 5. It is not power to be able to do that which ought not to be done; for ungoverned appetite is not power but weakness. It is not power to do evil, but impotency, weakness and deformity. *Free-will*, which we so much contend for, and brag so much of, it is no absolute perfection, and we need not be so proud of it. For free-will, as it includes a power to do wrong, as well as right, is not to be found in God himself; and therefore it is no perfection in us. For this is true of God, that all his ways are ways of righteousness, goodness and truth; and there is not in him a power to do otherwise than is just and right. And if we were *God-like*, as we should be, the *fruit of the spirit in us* would be *in all righteousness, goodness and truth*, Eph. v. 9. If *this* were the religion of the world, where would be revenge, malice, spite, and and doing wrong one to another? And as God *doth* that in all cases, which is just, fit, right and good, so doth he require of us, nothing but what is just, right, fit and good: and this he doth require of us, under the promise of a reward, tho' it is our duty so to do, and our righteousness to be found in such

such ways.   And God prohibits us nothing that is
right and good ; and wheresoever he doth impose a
law upon us, he shews us that it is fit for us to be
restrained, and shews us that his laws are easy and
profitable for us.   I am not far from the opinion of
those men that think the prohibition laid upon A-
dam in paradise, was not so much to shew his power, as monitory ; that the fruit was not good for
man, and would do him harm if he meddled with
it.   If it be so, then it doth take off that, which
some men think doth reflect upon the divine goodness. But for this let him receive it that sees cause.

Now if it be so, that God commands nothing
but what is reasonable, just and fit, and prohibits
nothing but what is noxious to us, and for our hurt
and prejudice ; then how comes it to pass, that we,
sorry, impotent creatures, pretend to power and priviledge, otherwise than what is right and just, or
for the best? How comes it to pass that we are so
addicted to set up will for a rule, and for a law ; a
will contrary to God, and to the reason of the thing,
which is a law antecedent to the very creation ?
For upon this supposition, that God will make
such a creature as man, the *reason of things* requires
that he should be made under such a law, and under such obligations.   For if God do make a creature that is voluntary and intelligent ; we must
leave him to the direction of his faculties, otherwise
he should controul his own workmanship. Now
will is no rule at all, nor gives any warrant : the
laws of nature ought not to be varied from ; that is,
what is reason, what is right and fit.   Will stands
for

for nothing, in disjunction from reason and right.
There is nothing gives more offence, than for a man
proudly and malpertly to say, *he will, because he
will.* Our apprehensions of right, are regulated by
the nature of things ; and we have a lie in our
minds, if we act otherwise. For *truth is firft in
things,* and *then* is the *truth* in our *underftandings.*
Truth lies in our regularity and conformity with
our apprehenfion of the reafon of things : and I am
therefore in the truth, becaufe I conceive of things
as they are. But *things* give law to notion and apprehenfion. This is a gallant theme that I am u-
pon, and a more generous argument there is not
under the fun ; and that which would tend to the
fettlement of the world, and every body in their
dues and right.

But a man may philofophife never fo well in generals ; if he do not bring down things to particulars, it will not do. Now therefore go along with
me, and I will particularife this in notion and cafes.

There is a rule of right in all cafes, and 'tis the
charge of all perfons in the ufe of power, to judge
and determine according unto that rule. And *he* is
weak that cannot judge what is the right of the
cafe ; and wicked, that for ends and purpofes will
vary from it. Now that there is a rule of right in
all cafes, I will fhew you in particular inftances.
And

1ft. I will begin with the relation that is between
parents and *children,* and fhew you what is right
for parents to do with their children, and children
to their parents. 1ft. For the parent, who is, in a
fort,

ſort, in the order of God to the children ; as being next after God, the cauſe of their being and original ; yet he muſt not behave himſelf any way, nor after *any faſhion,* towards his children.   For it is ſaid, *fathers provoke not your children to wrath.*   He muſt deal with them tenderly, and in a way of reaſon, and not juſtly give them offence, or provoke them.   This is the *right of the caſe* between *fathers* and *children.*   Then for the *child,* he muſt obey his parents in all things, and muſt do as he is bidden, ſo there be nothing unreaſonable or evil in it.

2. I go to the relation of *husbands* and *wives* ; there is the right of the caſe between them. For the *husband,* that in ſome things hath the ſuperiority, and is the firſt mover, yet, *Col.* iii. 19. we read that the husband *muſt not be bitter againſt his wife* ; nor give her an offenſive word, nor uſe any hard language ; but lead her on fairly, by reaſon ; and ſatisfy her by argument, and in a fair way.   And this is the *right of the caſe,* as to that.   Then he ought to give her *honour,* as *the weaker veſſel,* and give her the advantage of her ſex, as you read, 1 *Pet.* iii. 7. Then for the *right of the caſe,* as to the *wife* towards her *husband* : the wifes converſation towards her husband, ought to be ſuch as to gain upon him, ſuppoſing that he be not in all things as he ought, as that if he be froward and hard to pleaſe, the wifes converſation ought to be endearing, that ſo ſhe may thereby gain upon him, and bring him to temper, 1 *Pet.* iii. 1.

3. Then for *maſters* and *ſervants. Maſters render to your ſervants what is right,* that which is equal, fair,

fair and reasonable. Do not usurp over men, do not use them as if they were irrational creatures, but as those that are of the same species and kind with themselves, not using threatning words, but remembering that they have a master in heaven, and that there is no respect of persons with him. Then for servants, there is the right of the case for them also, and that is to obey their masters in all things, and to be true and faithful to them. And so of the centurion said of his servants; to one he said go, and he went; and to another come, and he cometh. I have in short given you the right of the case, in these three relations of parents and children, husbands and wives, master and servant.

Then in our common converse, we ought to use all humanity, courtesy and affability, giving all respect, despising no body. We ought not in mirth to undervalue any man in company, or to delude to please his sense. For I would never come into that man's company, that I would not bear all love. Then we must be ready to render a reason to every one that demandeth it, 1 *Pet.* iii 15. Then for our carriage towards the *poor*, the right of the case is here also, *Ecclesiasticus* iv. 4. we must not turn away from a poor man, but hear him speak and give him a fair answer, if you cannot answer his request. This is agreeable to the counsel of the son of Syrach, who saith, *Let it not grieve thee, to bow down thine ear unto the poor, and to give him an answer with meekness.*

4. To descend to the creatures below us, there is a right of the case here also. We must not abuse any of those creatures below us. For certain faith,

the

the *righteous man takes care of his beaft* : we muft not abuse fo much as our horfe or our dog. By thefe you fee, that there is in all times and cafes the *rule of right,* which is to do as the cafe requires toward all perfons, in all times, and in all cafes. What is reafon, what is right, what is fit ? even as we our-felves would be done tô, were we in thofe circum-ftances. And it is a man's underftanding, to find out what *that is* ; and his uprightnefs and integri-ty, to do *accordingly.*

Now if this be true, 'tis advifeable that a man be *habituated* and well prepared, that he may not be at a lofs. If a man have pre-confidered, and exa-mined and been well advifed before hand ; when any cafe comes, he is prepared, and fo he will be ready to do as *the right of the cafe* requires. Where-as if he be otherwife, he will be at a lofs, and not know what to do when he comes to act. It is hap-hazard whether he will do right, or wrong : and fo will not act like a man of prudence, and virtue. For this I muft tell you, paffion and felf-will, are no principle of action ; by thefe we are never to act, nor to warrant any thing we do. For he that doth this, acts not like a man, but like a fury ; he doth not act according to the principle of reafon, but like a mad man. The great iniquity in this inferior world, is this, that men affume to them-felves to do becaufe they *will,* which is a very great tranfgreffion, and the higheft exorbitancy of extra-vagant creatures. For a man to do *becaufe he will,* or becaufe he hath a mind, alas, this is nothing to any man elfe. What is this man's mind, to ano-ther

ther man ? for he expects to be dealt with, according to reason and the right of the case. There are some men that are so governed by this rule that a man may know how they will act in any case ; but those *arbitrary* men are men that live in a humour or passion, and no man knows where to have them, or what they will do.

DISCOURSE XVI.

The Conversion of a SINNER.

EZEK. xviii. 27.

When the wicked man turneth away from his wicked-
ness that he hath committed, and doth that which
is lawful and right, he shall save his soul alive.

THE foregoing truth I have declared with great assurance unto you, and I am confident nothing in God's creation can stand up in opposition to this noble and generous notion. And could I but fasten this upon the world, I should mend the world : for reformation must begin *from within*, from the better information of mens minds, before ever their actions will be well directed and governed.

But here some one may rise up and say, may I not *please my own mind ?*

Yes, thou may'st please thyself *in materia libera* ; that is, in matters of thy own right ; where no bo-

dy

dy elfe hath any demand of right. Where the matter is wholly free and indifferent, as whether a man
will ride or go on foot : in which, and a thoufand
other things of like nature, he doth no body any injury. Or,

Where it is only a man's own right, and no o-
ther man hath any demand upon him, there a man
may pleafe his own mind, without any offence to
God, or injury to men. But otherwife, if I have
not the *fole* right, but another hath a demand, then
this of pleafing a man's felf, or doing according to
his own mind, muft be excluded, and fhut out of
doors. I fay, where the reafon of the thing is contrary, or others have a demand of right, there a
man's own mind is no warrant. Therefore this is
that I refolve upon, where-ever a man hath authority, or a lawful ufe, I would always have him have
reafon go along with the ufe of his authority ; and
then he will have a great fatisfaction that doth command ; and *others* will eafily and readily obey. For
a man loves to fee reafon for what he doth ; and
then a man's commands are juftified, when reafon
runs along with his will and pleafure. And he that
obeys, will find it mighty eafy to obey reafon ; but
it is horribly troublefome to do without reafon, and
ftill worfe to do againft it. To obey without reafon, is to be led like beafts, and the nature of man
will be impatient under it : for this is that which
all men call for, *do me reafon, do me right,* and when
this is done men are fatisfied. And this no man
fhould deny ; for God himfelf hath given reafon
for the rule of action and law of right. And 'tis

the

the very self-same thing for a man to obserye God and fulfil his will, and to do that which reafon doth require.   For right is determined by its agreeable-nefs with the *reafon of things* ; and things are driv-en by force and violence, that are not done with reafon : and therefore will return back again, as foon as that force is taken off. As if by power you bend a ftick, it will return to its ftraightnefs, as foon as that force is taken off. If you draw a bow by ftrength never fo much, it will return to its former latitude, when the hand is taken off.   Things will not hold long, if under force and violence ; but if they be according to the right of the cafe, and ac-cording to reafon, they will hold when they are done.   And this is that which God expects, that a wicked man fhould *turn from his wickednefs, and do that which is lawful and right* ; by which *he fhall fave his foul alive.* .Which brings me

V. To the *beneficial part* of the words, the hap-pinefs that follows upon renovation, repentance, and turning to God.   He that doth fo, fhall *fave his foul alive.*   Where you have the principal part put for the whole : not that the body fhall be ne-glected ; for God that takes care of oxen, will take care of it alfo. He fhall fave his *foul* alive ; not as if we were not to look upon the foul as immortal : but this is the account I give of that.   Mifery is worfe than death : to live, is to be well and in good health.   I am fully fatisfied, that it is better not to be at all than to be miferable ; and for this I will take our Saviour's warrant *Mat.* xxvi. 24. where he faith, *that it had been good for that man if he had not*

been born, that should betray the son of God. And
the apostle tells us, of the woman that liveth in
wantonness, that she is *dead even whilst she liveth.* If
any man be under guilt, he is dead while alive.
Whosoever doth amifs, doth abuse himself, and
wrong his own soul : and he that doth continue in
ill doing, doth take a course finally to undo himself.
It is the case of us men, even of us, sometimes in
life to have done amifs, and to have perverted our
way.   But thanks be to God, through the grace of
the gospel, there is a way of recovery : repentance
is a plank after shipwreck, whereby a man may
save himself ; we are therefore not to despair ; but
to turn from our wickedness ; and we have God's
declaration and promise that we shall *save our souls
alive.* 'Tis a great word, but God hath spoken it,
and shall not he make it good ? *He shall save his
soul alive*, Ezek. xviii. 27. It is God that hath spoken it, in whose hands are the issues of life and
death, who hath power to kill and to make alive.
In the five books of *Mofes* you have often these words
that soul shall be cut off from among his people : that
is the punishment shall be inflicted by the hand of
God himself.   And therefore it is said to be *a fearful thing to fall into the hands of the living* God. This
sometimes, yea, very often, is the case of those
which fin so secretly, that they escape the cognizance of men. But the more are such men in danger of falling by the hand of God ; if by the secret-
ness of the fact, the judgment of man cannot lay
hold of it. For this is most certain, that none shall
finally prevail in wickedness : *though hand join in*
band

hand, yet the wicked shall not go unpunished, Prov xi.
21. And where the hand of the magistrate, either
because of power or secrecy, cannot reach, God
himself will judge in those cases ; and he will proceed according as things are. Though before men
not to be proved, and not to be, are the same thing
yet God searcheth the heart, and he cannot be deceived. God hath given us double security for our
lives, and we have just expectation from both : the
first is from innocence, for God made us in his own
image. But because we have failed, here is a second provision that God hath made by the motion
of repentance, and this is God's after-grant. The
first was the state of God's creation : the next was
that of restoration, and recovery by repentance,
which is declared by the gospel. So that now having lost our innocence, let us look after salvation
by the motion of repentance, which through God's
grace is sufficient, and will be effectual to prevent
punishment : which is the true explication of remission of sins. For if sin be committed, no power
can make that not to have been done. Nor, secondly, if a thing hath been done amiss, can it be made
not to be worthy of punishment. But the forgiveness of sin doth prevent the deserved punishment
of sin. Therefore, since we have all of us lost the
snow-like whiteness of innocence, which was the
beauty of our creation : let us now look after that
whiteness which is by blood. For so you have the
expression in the *Revelations* : that they were *wash-
ed white in the blood of the lamb,* Rev. vii. 14. The
faith of the Lord *Jesus Christ* conjoined with our

repen.

repentance and reformation, is now the only way
to obtain pardon and forgivenefs.   Now unlefs a
man repent, he cannot be fenfible of the impurity
of the act, nor of his danger thereby ; and till this
be done, he will not feek after his remedy, no more
than a man will feek after a phyfician, that is not
fenfible of his difeafe, nor of his danger by means
thereof.   No man will go to *Chrift* for pardon, unlefs he be fenfible of the evil of fin and of which he
doth repent, and condemn himfelf, and refolve a-
gainft it ; for no true penitent doth allow himfelf
in fin.

But farther, *fhall fave his foul alive.* From this we
may underftand of how great benefit the good ufe
and improvement of our *time* is.   Time, though it
be of the flendereft entity, yet 'tis of the moft moral confideration, becaufe improveable to the higheft
advantage.   Our time is a day of grace, for we are
in a probation ftate : fo that now it fairly lies before us, to make ourfelves happy for ever. And we
may alfo by the abufe of the grace of God, undo
ourfelves for ever.   Therefore I fay unto you in
the words of Mofes, *Deut.* xxx 19. *I fet before you
this day life and death, bleffing and curfing, choofe life.*
For when a *wicked man turneth away from his wickednefs that he hath committed, and doth that which is
lawful and right, he fhall fave his foul alive.* But if he
continue in wickednefs, he fhall *furely die.*

How many are there that overlook the bufinefs,
purpofe and intention of life ! We are here to run
a race, and fo to run that we may obtain : and
therefore we are to watch over ourfelves, both as
to

to the things of our mind, and body ; and so to keep under our bodies, and bring them into subjection, that we may not ruin and undo ourselves. Now this is another thing, than to gratify our sense, and live in a humour. No, no, we must run the race that is set before us, and as those that strain for the mastery, must be temperate in all things. This is our business, to serve the interest of our souls, in the state that is before us. Therefore I advise every man that is serious, to ask himself these questions.

1*st*. Will this that I have done, or am doing, be accountable, when God shall call me to a reckoning ? When any thing doubtful is proposed, or of a bad quality, then ask this question ; shall I be able to give an account for this, when I shall stand before the tribunal seat of Christ ? The

2*d*. Question is that which *Abigail* put to *David* 1 *Sam.* xxv. 31. *This will be no grief of heart, nor offence unto thee.*

3*d*. Question is, what shall I think of this, when I shall lie upon my death bed ? What judgment of apprehension shall I have of it then ? The

4*th*. Question is, how remediless will the consequence of evil be, when I shall have the least relief by my reason, and be least capable of advice ; and when I shall have the least assistance of God's grace and Spirit ? How shall I be then able to bear up against the intolerable burthen of evil and guilt too ? Let us consider that we die daily in a threefold respect ; in respect of age, in respect of diseases, and in respect of hazard and danger. In respect of age,

W₀

we grow nearer and nearer unto death : and in respect of difeafes, which is death in fome degree :
and laftly in refpect of hazard and danger from a-
broad.   For whofoever neglects God and the law,
may be mafter of any body's life.   How will men
fatisfy themfelves, that take fo little care how they
pafs out of time, into eternity ?   That live and die
in fuch a frame and temper, which is altogether
unfit for the bufinefs and employment of eternity ?
For if we expect to be happy, and to attend upon
God, and holy angels, and faints in glory ; it is neceffary that we free ourfelves from all impurity and
by holinefs of life qualify ourfelves for the enjoyment of God.   For our Saviour hath told us, that
unlefs we be converted, and become as little children, that are innocent and harmlefs, that may fuffer wrong, but will do none, we cannot enter into
heaven.   Thefe three things do utterly unqualify a
man for the ftate of glory and happinefs.

1. Earthlinefs, worldlinefs, and carnality.

2. A fpirit of malice, ill-will, and revenge.

3. Pride, arrogancy, and haughtinefs.

1. *Earthlinefs*, worldlinefs, and carnality.   The
pfalmift tells us, *Pfal.* xvii. 11. That worldly men
have their portion in this life. They being unqualifi-
ed for the ftate of eternity.

2. Then for thofe that live in the fpirit of envy,
malice, and ill-will.   They have the very fpirit and
temper of the *devil*, who goes about feeking whom
he may devour.

3. And for pride : the apoftle *Jude* tells us, that
this was the very temper of the angels that fell, that

kept

kept not their first state, but through pride and arrogance, did assume to themselves.

But to draw to a *conclusion.* Since now we have such a declaration as this in the text, which contains the fulness of gospel knowledge : that *when the wicked man turneth away from his wickedness, and doth that which is lawful and right, he shall save his soul alive.* Let us entertain good thoughts of God, let us have right apprehensions of him in our minds always think so of God, as to encourage our application to him. And never think that he is implacable ; but that he is ready to forgive, and is no hard master, nor difficult to please, nor backward to forgive. Yea, I will say more, that God is such a friend to our souls, and takes such delight in our conversion and turning to him, that he will not be wanting on his part, to afford us what is necessary, for our enablement and encouragement. And should we think otherwise of God, we should fret in our minds against him, and sit down in discontent and despair : just as you have an account in *Rev.* ix. 6. of some that blasphemed God because of their pains. This was the temper of *Cain,* who said, *my sin is greater than can be forgiven.* By this a man doth put himself quite out of the way of forgiveness.

I add, that it is the special and genuine effect of the mercy of God to bring sinners to repentance. But by every evil act that a man doth commit, his recovery is the more difficult ; because sin doth put a man quite out of temper, and sets him at the greater distance from God. For sin hardens a man's heart, and spoils the modesty of intellectual nature, and

much

much more difpofeth a man for evil, than he was before.

Now in the clofe of all, I will reinforce the ad-vice of the text, that the *wicked turn from his wick-ednefs.* And let us not herein be miftaken, for we ought in nothing more to underftand ourfelves a-right ; becaufe it is the cafe of life and death. Therefore in thefe cafes, as I told you, men cannot be faid to forfake their fins, when *fin* rather leaves them, than they their fins ; when his turning from fin arifeth rather from abroad than from himfelf, and is rather the effect of his company, and thofe that have power over him. You cannot fay that men turn from their wickednefs, when 'tis not their own motion, nor what they would do if free and left to themfelves. Nor when a man out of fear of former fufferings, doth not do as formerly he did. For you muft know, that all vice and wick-ednefs is firft contrary to the reafon of our minds ; and fecondly, to the health of our bodies : for by fin and wickednefs men lay the foundation of aches and difeafes, and fhorten their days. In thefe cafes a man *cannot* be faid to turn from his fins : but in the other cafes which I named, a man *may* be faid to turn from his wickednefs.

Firft, When the wicked man loaths his fin out of *fenfe* and judgment *of the bafenefs* and vilenefs of it. For the motion, ground, and principle of an action, doth fpecificate the action. And you can-not upon a moral account, eftimate an action from the materiality of it, but from the intention, moti-on, ground, and principle from which it doth proceeds

ceed. And it is reason in intellectual nature and choice, that makes it an action of virtue.

Secondly, When we avoid sin and evil out of *respect to God*, because we will not give him an offence. For this is religion, to have the *fear of God* before our eyes : and 'tis but the religion of a heathen, to avoid sin upon any other account. Now because God is invisible, if any should ask how he might know what he doth, is with respect to God : you may know by that which is materially the same with it. To do a thing because it is consonant to reason and to avoid a thing because it is contrary to reason, is materially the same as to do, or forbear with respect to God. And I will make this out, because two things are matter of easy knowledge, and the great things of religion.

1*st.* That there is a *God*. And,

2*dly.* That there is a difference between *good and evil.* And if we have not sunk ourselves into brutishness, by sensuality, or into devilishness, by malice, envy, and ill-will ; a man cannot be ignorant of either of these.

That there is a *God* every man must grant, because he did not call himself into being out of nothing. This is plain, because he cannot continue himself in that being which he hath. For to call a thing into being out of nothing, is an act of much greater power, than to continue a being that we have.

And for the difference of *good* and *evil,* nothing is more knowable. Will not every man grant, that there is great difference between living in sobriety
and

and temperance, and living in luxury and wantonnefs ; that the one is far better than the other ?
That it is better for a man to govern his paffion,
and to be affable and courteous, than to be furious,
infolent, arrogant, and tumultuous ?

But *thirdly* and laftly, a man may be faid to turn
from his wickednefs, when he conceives difpleafure
againft it, and fully purpofes never to return to it
again, whatfoever temptations or provocations
he may meet withal. Otherwife it may be but only forbearance of the act ; unlefs a man withdraws
from it through diflike, and take up refolutions never to do the like. Now if the wicked man do
thus *turn* away *from his wickednefs, and doth that
which is lawful and right, he fhall fave his foul alive.*

DISCOURSE XVII.

The true Valuation of MAN.

L U K E xvi. 25.

*But Abraham faid, fon, remember that thou in thy life-
time receivedft thy good things, and likewife Lazarus evil things : but now he is comforted, and thou
art tormented.*

Whether this were a ftory, or a parable, I
will not difpute or determine. It will be all
one as to our inftruction ; for our rule is,
comparifons make facts ; hiftory contains matter of
fact, and parables are reprefentations only ; therefore

fore every thing in parables is not to be obferved, for fome things are put in for decorum's fake, and to make it look like a hiftory. All things in parables that make an appearance, are not intended therefore there is great caution to be ufed, and if there be any point of religion, or any matter of faith grounded upon a parable, it muft alfo have other foundation. For parables and fimilitudes are rather for illuftration, than confirmation.

But, before I come to fpeak to the words themfelves, I will a little look back, and glofs upon the verfes precedent.

Ver. 19. *There was a certain rich man which was cloathed in purple and fine linen, and fared fumptuoufly every day.*

Ver. 20. *And there was a certain beggar named Lazarus, which was laid at his gate full of fores,* &c.

Upon thefe two verfes I obferve the different difpofition of providence, as to mens eftate and affairs : one rich, over-rich ; the other poor, miferably poor. For this, you need not look after any other account, but refer it to God's fovereignty and good pleafure. For neither doth the one make a man certainly happy, nor the other truly miferable.

21. *And defiring to be fed with the crumbs which fell from the rich man's table ; moreover, the dogs came and licked his fores.*

Hereupon I obferve, that it is highly commendable in every one, to comply with the neceffity of his condition, and to fupply himfelf as he lawfully may, and to be contented with his lot and portion,

and

and to make as good a shift as he can, and to go
through this world as well as he may.   Thus did
the poor man ; for his diet, he was content with
the crumbs that fell from the rich man's table, and
for his physick, he was content that the dogs should
lick his sores.   .

22. *And it came to pass that the beggar died, and
was carried by the angels into Abraham's bosom : the
rich man also died and was buried.*   .

From hence I observe, that all sorts of men die :
and after death a great difference.   The rich man
had all the advantages that this world could afford,
of him it is said, that he died and was buried. The
poor man died also, but we have nothing of his funeral : the world had no such kindness for him.
But where this world ends, a better world begins.
For, though it is not said the beggar was buried,
yet it is said that he was carried into *Abraham's* bosom ; and that by Gods messengers, the angels.

Ver. 23. *And in hell he lift up his eyes, being in
torment, and seeth Abraham afar off, and Lazarus in
his bosom.*

These words declare a future state, and the existence of the soul after the body moulders away and
tumbles into the dust.   .   .

Ver. 24. *And he cried and said, father Abraham
have mercy on me, and send Lazarus that he may dip
the tip of his finger in water and cool my tongue ; for
I am tormented in this flame.*

From whence I observe, that there is no great
hope or expectation for bad men, in the future state.
See how little he asks : *send Lazarus that he may
dip*

dip the tip of his finger in water and cool my tongue.
One would think that it was but a fmall requeft ;
yet we do not read that it was granted him. Wherefore, there is very little hope or expectation for bad
men in the future ftate.

Ver. 25. *But Abraham faid, fon, remember that
thou in thy-time receivedft thy good things, and likewife
Lazarus evil things : but now he is comforted, and
thou art tormented.*

From which words I obferve thefe things in general.

Firft, That *Abraham* gives *reafon* for what he
faith ; therefore we fhould not take upon us to
dictate and impofe on others, but it becomes us to
fhew caufe and to fatisfy men by reafon and argument : and this is the direction of the apoftle, who
charges it upon chriftians, to be ready to render a
reafon of the hope that is in them.

Secondly, Where we reprove, we fhould ufe *good
language* ; we fee here *Abraham* faith, *fon* ; though
the man was in a deplorable ftate, yet *Abraham*
gives him no hard language. *Son remember that
thou in thy life-time had'ft thy good things.* He rubs up
his memory, and reproves him by reafon : and thus
we ought to refolve, neither to provoke others, nor
be provoked ourfelves : and this would tend to the
quiet of the world, Let us not provoke any one,
for there is fome good nature in every body : but
if you provoke any man, you put him to act upon
the worft principle. Neither be you provoked, for
then you are not fure of yourfelf ; for in this cafe
a man lofes felf-government ; for every man in a

passion

paſſion is leſs himſelf, if he do not wholly loſe himſelf.

Thirdly, I obſerve, that the poor man who is commended, he is diſtinguiſhed by his name : but for the rich man who is diſparaged, there is *no name* for him.   From whence I obſerve, that prudence and caution are to be uſed, where men reprove and diſparage : reprove with concealment forbear names and perſons ;   convince by reaſon and argument. *Lazarus* who is commended is named : but for the rich man who is diſparaged, there is no name for him.

Again, we are to underſtand, that it is neither a virtue to be poor, nor a ſin to be rich. The explication muſt be, that thou did'ſt uſe thy good things for pride and voluptuouſneſs &c ; and *this* is the condemnation of the rich man ;   not ſimply that he was rich, but that he uſed his riches for pride and luxury ; and not for inſtruments of virtue.

Likewiſe Lazarus evil things.   That is, thoſe evil things in the courſe of this life, did attain the peaceable fruits of righteouſneſs and virtue, a ſubmiſſion to God, and ſelf-ſurrender.

It is a miſtake to think that poverty is a ſtate of perfection, or any ways meritorious, for we are neither recommended, nor diſparaged to God, by either ; and both ſtates have their temptations ; the rich, to inſolency ; and the poor to baſeneſs. If the poor man be ſurly, he gains no advantage by his poverty ; and if the rich man be haughty, he had better have been without his riches. The rich man was not diſadvantaged becauſe he *had* his good things

things in this life, but becaufe he did not well *ufe* them : and the poor man was not rewarded for his poverty, but becaufe it was fubjoined with fubmiffion to God's providence.

But thefe things I only hint by the by.   In the words you have thefe three things reprefented.

1*ft.* In this life, under the managery of ordinary providence, the worft men may abound with the good things of this world, when better men are ftraitned, and want even the neceffary conveniencies of life.

2*ly.* If we would take a right eftimate of man, we muft not only confider him in refpect of the prefent ftate, but alfo of the future.

3*ly.* The ftate of man in the world to come holds a proportion with fomething of him here : the temper of his mind, the frame of his fpirit, the courfe of his actions.

1*ft.* In this life, under the managery of ordinary providence, the worft men may abound with the good things of this life, and better men are fometimes fhortned, and want even the neceffary conveniencies of life.   Of this I fhall fpeak but a word, becaufe it is a matter of eafy obfervation. This *David*, *Job*, and *Jeremiah* ftumbled at.   The pfalmift tells us, *Pfal.* xvii. 14.   That there are men that have *their portion in this life* ;   and that good men are oftentimes in want and neceffity, while thefe are in plenty themfelves, and leave their fubftance to their children.   So *Pfal.* lxxiii. 3, 4, 5, 6, 7. *I was envious at the foolifh, when I faw the profperity of the wicked. For there are no bands in their death, but*

Vol. I,   S   *their*

their ſtrength is firm.   They are not in trouble as other men, neither are they plagued like other men.   Therefore pride compaſſeth them about as a chain ; violence cover-eth them as a garment.   Their eyes ſtand out with fat-neſs.   They have more than heart could wiſh.   The like you have, *Jer.* xii. 1. *Righteous art thou, O Lord when I plead with thee : yet let me talk with thee of thy judgments ; wherefore doth the way of the wicked proſper ? wherefore are all they happy that deal very treacherouſly ?*

This is the ſhort account that I would give of this matter : that the adminiſtration of the things of this life, doth not at all belong to the *kingdom of Chriſt* ; but they come from another hand. To make a man to be a rightful owner, he muſt prove his title, either from deſcent, from ſome that were be-fore him ; or by a fair and lawful acquiſition, by his good employment and improvement of his ſtock and talent in ſome honeſt way, and that he *hath* not got his wealth by violence, fraud, or coſenage : for this is a maxim with us (and they are diſturbers of the world that go upon any other ground) *that right property and title are founded in nature, not in grace.* God gave the world and the things thereof unto the ſons of men. If I would prove this to be mine, I muſt prove my title, not by miracle ; but as the law and uſage of the country where I dwell do ſtate and determine : therefore I will ſay no more in this particular.

2*ly.* This particular is of great importance : If we will take a right eſtimate of man, we muſt con-ſider him alſo in reſpect of another ſtate ; for leſs

of

of him is here, and more in another world. That which is moſt a man's own, may be leaſt in worldly appearance. And

3*ly.* The ſtate of men in the world to come, holds a proportion to mens ſpirits and temper, to the tenour of their lives and actions. And this is clear from the text, *ſon, remember, thou in thy life-time receivedſt thy good things, and Lazarus, evil things ; wherefore he his comforted, and thou art tormented.*

Not that we are to ſuppoſe that it is either a virtue, to be poor ; or a ſin, to be rich : therefore we muſt ſupply theſe words from the *context*, and take the ſenſe of them to be this : ſon, thou in thy lifetime, had'ſt thy good things ; and did'ſt *uſe* them to luxury, exceſs, and riot, pride, haughtineſs, and ſcornfulneſs ; and did'ſt not uſe them, as inſtruments to virtue, and arguments to thankfulneſs : whereas a man ſhould honour God with his ſubſtance, and the rich in this world ſhould be *rich in good works ; and not high minded, nor truſt in uncertain riches, but in the living God.* The want hereof was condemnation of the rich man, not that he was rich, but that he did *uſe* his wealth to pride and luxury ; not as inſtruments of virtue, and arguments to gratitude.

So on the other ſide : *thou in thy life-time receivedſt thy good things, and Lazarus evil things ; therefore he is comforted.* Not that he was therefore comforted, becauſe he was poor in this world, and did receive evil things here ; but becauſe thoſe evil things he received in the courſe of his life, did attain *the peaceable fruits of righteouſneſs,* as the apoſtle

ſpeaks,

speaks, *Heb.* xii. 11. They put him upon the exer-cise of those virtues that his condition required ; that is, submission to God, and self-surrender, and acquiescence in the dispensation of providence. For that is a fancy which the *papists* go upon, that the state of regular obedience, and single life, and poverty, are virtues in themselves, and meritorious, and a state of perfection. For we are neither recommended to God by means of our worldly estate, nor further from his acceptance, meerly for our worldly possessions and riches. Both states, either of wealth or poverty have their difficulties ; and we are concerned to know what temptations we are exposed unto by either of them. If the rich be tempted to pride, and insolence ; the poor may be tempted to baseness, and discontent. And if this be his case, he will receive no advantage by his poverty : and if the rich man become through his riches, haughty, proud, and insolent, he had better have been without them. You must therefore take the explication from the *context*. The rich man was not disadvantaged, because he *had* the good things of this life ; nor the poor man recompenced, meerly for his poverty ; but because it was accompani-ed with humility, submission, and contentation in the divine providence.

These two latter points being of great concern-ment, I shall speak distinctly to them.

I. That if we would take a right estimate of man, we must consider him, in respect to a double state, here, and hereafter.

II. That

II. That the ftate of man in the world to *come*, holds a proportion to his fpirit and temper ; to the tenour of his life, and actions in this world.

I. That if we would take a right eftimate of man, we muft confider him in refpect to a double ftate ; here, and hereafter ; and that for thefe two reafons.

1*ft*. Becaufe there is *lefs* of man here, and more hereafter.

2*dly*. Becaufe man is more *valuable* than this world reprefents him to be.

I. The *firft* of thefe I will make appear in three particulars, that there is *lefs* of man here, and much more hereafter.

1. In refpect of his *time*, and *continuance* in being. Though *we* do but little, confider how uncertain our being is in this world ; yet fee how abundant the *fcripture is*, in admonifhing us of our uncertain abode, and fhort continuance in this world, *Job* vii. 6. *My days are fwifter than a weaver's fhuttle* ; and you know how fuddenly that goes and returns, *Job* viii. 9. *Our days upon earth are a fhadow*, which if once a cloud come, the fhadow vanifhes. *Job* xiv. 1, 2. *Man that is born of a woman, is of few days, and full of trouble. He cometh forth like a flower, and is cut down : he fleeth alfo as a fhadow, and continueth not.* Gen. xlvii. 9. *Few and evil have the days of the years of my life been :* this was old *Jacob's* account of himfelf. And men that have been ferious and confiderate, have thus reported concerning themfelves, and others : 1 *Chron.* xxix. 15. *For we are ftrangers before thee and fojourners, as were all our fa-*

S 3   *thers :*

thers : our days on the earth are as a shadow, and
there is none abiding. Psal. xxxix. 4. 5, 6. *Lord make
me to know mine end ; and the measure of my days
what it is : that I may know how frail I am. Behold,
thou hast made my days as an hand-breadth, and mine
age is as nothing before thee : verily every man, at his
best estate, is altogether vanity. Surely every man walketh in a vain shew, surely they are disquieted in vain.*
Psal. xc. 9. *We spend our years as a tale that is told.*
Psal. cii. 11. *My days are like a shadow that declin-
eth : and I am withered like grass.* Psal. ciii. 15, 16.
*As a flower of the field, so he flourisheth. For the wind
passeth over it, and it is gone.* Psal. cxliv. 4. *Man is
like to vanity, his days are as a shadow that passeth a-
way.* Isaiah xl. 6. *All flesh is grass, and all the good-
liness thereof is as the flower of the field : the grass withereth, the flower fadeth away.* And this is brought
by the apostle, as an argument, that rich men should
rejoice when they are brought low. *James* i. 10.
Because as the flower of the grass, he shall pass away.
And it is referred to in 1 *Pet.* i. 24. *For all flesh is as
grass, and all the glory of man as the flower of grass.
The grass withereth, and the flower thereof falleth a-
way.* And good men have had this sense of the
shortness of their abode in this world. 1 *Pet.* ii. 11.
*Dearly beloved, I beseech you as strangers and pilgrims,
abstain from fleshly lusts which war against the soul.*
And as *knowing they had no continuing city here,* they
look't for one to come. *Heb.* xiii. 14. To all these
places of holy writ give me leave to add one out of
the apocryphal writers. *Wisdom* v. 13. *As soon as
we were born, we began to draw to our latter end.*
                                        And

And fee how he reprefents the condition of men in
this world by things of the greateft fwiftnefs, and
uncertainty ; as a fhadow, and as a poft that haft-
eth by, which no man may ftay ; even fo a man
hurries through time, into eternity, v. 11. 12. *As a*
fhip that paffeth over the waves of the water, which
when it is gone by, the trace thereof cannot be found,
neither the path-way of the keel in the waves. Or as a
bird that hath flown through the air, there is no token of
her way to be found. Or like as when an arrow is fhot
at a mark, it parteth the air, which immediately cometh
together again ; fo that a man cannot know where it
went through. Even fo doth a man pafs through the
world. But I need not ftand to prove this, it being
a point of undoubted certainty and every man's obfervation ; but (the more is the pity) of too little
confideration. Let us therefore pafs over this point
with the good meditation of the pfalmift, *Pfal.* xc.
12. *So teach us to number our days, that we may ap-*
ply our hearts unto wifdom. Time is a thing of the
greateft importance, but of the moft uncertain continuance ; for we may fay, upon the improvement
of a little time, the ftate and welfare of an immortal foul doth depend to eternity.

In this refpect you fee that lefs of a man is in
this world than hereafter : here he is frail, and
weak, brittle, and crafy, obnoxious to difeafes and
all manner of accidents : fo that, were we not the
care of divine providence, when we confider the
many conveyances that are in our bodies, the varie-
ties and changes we are expofed unto : we fhould
think it a thoufand to one, that a man lived to fix-

ty

ty years. That is the firſt thing ; there is leſs of a man in this world, in reſpeſt of his being and *continuance* here.

2. In this ſtate, there is *leſs* of *right judgment* of things, and perſons.   Things here, go under falſe appearances ; and perſons here, are under the pow-er of lying imaginations.   The *platoniſts* have ob-ſerved, that there is a world of diligence, care, and thoughtfulneſs neceſſary for a man to underſtand the truth.   I ſhould not bely human nature, if I ſhould ſay, that the wiſeſt of us live very much in a fools *paradiſe* ; and that in a world of things, we are miſtaken ; and that our ſuppoſitions are not well grounded, nor our apprehenſions well govern-ed, nor our hope and expeſtation well ſecured. There is much of that which is falſe, miſtaken and inſincere, that takes place in the *life* of man. I might here inſtance in wealth and riches, which are thought to be the greateſt reality in the world, and yet one of the wiſeſt men that ever was, and one that had the greateſt experience, hath told us, that it is great folly for a man to ſet his heart upon it. *Prov.* xxiii. 5. *Wilt thou ſet thine eyes upon that which is not ? for riches certainly make themſelves wings, they fly away, as an eagle towards heaven.*   But then, as for the profane and diſſolute part of the world, *they* live altogether in a lie, *and* are falſe in the main.   For the *fool hath ſaid in his heart there is no God.* Pſal. xiv. 1. Not that he hath any ground for ſuch a ſuppoſition or imagination : for ſee what the pſalmiſt ſaith, in the next words as an account from whence this opinion ariſeth, *corrupt are they, and*

have

have done abominable works. So that this wicked principle in their mind, did arife from the wicked practices of their lives.   Whereas, it ought to be, *practice in purfuance of principle* : but here it is, *principle accommodate, and* fuitable *to loofe and vile practice.* And *well* might the pfalmift call .thefe *fools,* becaufe they are bold to controul the eternal and indifpenfible reafon of things, and venture to deny the difference between good and evil, upon a moral account.   And certainly thefe, in a chriftian ftate, are horribly prodigious and monftrous, that fhall take up fuch principles ; when the very philofophers, who had only the light of nature, have fo ftrongly vindicated the difference of things, upon a moral account.   And, if mind and underftanding in man, fignify any thing ; or if a man kuow any thing in the world, by the natural ufe of his mind and underftanding ; he knows the difference of good and evil, upon a moral account. But many mens principles are vitiated and corrupted by the exorbitancy of their practice, and a vitiated fenfe is no true judge. But to fpeak home to the point, that men here *live in a lie,* and are under mifapprehenfion, and led away with falfe appearances, that there is but *little* in the life of man that is fincere, and true : the fool hath faid to himfelf, that *he had goods laid up for many years,* and that his foul might now, *eat drink, and be merry,* Luke xii. 19. But v. 20. God faid unto him, *thou fool, this night thy foul fhall be required of thee* ; *then whofe fhall thofe things be which thou haft provided.* So *Ifa.* lvi. 12. we read of fome that fay, *come let us fetch wine, and we will*
fill

fill ourselves with strong drink : *and to morrow shall be as this day, and much more abundant.* But ftay a little ; that is well, that ends well. He that will make his reckoning of himfelf, and leave out God, he muft reckon again. He that will make up his accounts by his own fancy, may put himfelf into a fool's paradife : but things in the iffue will not anfwer his expectation, and fuppofition. This is the *calamity* of us mortals ; not that which is true, folid, real and fubftantial doth always take place ; but that which is imaginary doth take too great place in the life of man : not that which is honeft, right and good ; but that which is pleafing and profitable : or rather, not things of the mind, but matters of fenfe, do prevail upon many men. And that is the fecond thing : *lefs* of man is in this ftate, than in the other ; becaufe there is fo little of *true judgment* of things, and perfons. But

3. Lefs of *weal* or *woe*, is in this ftate, than in the other ; for men *in* this ftate do not fully reap the fruit of their own ways ; they do not come to the proof of the bargain *they* have made. Here, men only triumph in their imaginations, becaufe they think to carry the caufe, and that things *muft* be fo, becaufe they *would* have them fo. But hereafter, there will be fad reflection, as you have this matter admirably expreffed in the book of *Wifdom,* v. I. &c. *Then fhall the righteous man ftand in great boldnefs before the face of fuch as have afflicted him, and made no account of his labours. When they fee it, they fhall be troubled with terrible fear, and fhall be a-mazed at the ftrangenefs of his falvation, fo far beyond*

all

d that they looked for. And they repenting, and groan-
g for anguish of spirit, shall say within themselves,
his was he whom we had sometimes in derision, and a
reverb of reproach. We fools, accounted his life mad-
ess, and his end to be without honour. How is he
numbred among the children of God, and his lot is a-
ong the saints! Therefore have we erred from the
ay of truth, and the light of righteousness hath not
ined unto us, and the sun of righteousness rose not u-
m us. We wearied ourselves in the way of wicked-
ess and destruction; yea we have gone through deserts
there there lay no way: but as for the way of the
ord, we have not known it. What hath pride pro-
ted us, or what good hath riches with our vaunting,
rought us? All these things are passed away like a
adow, and as a post that hasteth by. This was the
epresentation that is happily made in this book,
which shews the sad and miserable condition that
very sinner will be in at the last.

Whatsoever of good that is here begun, hereafter
vill be promoted, advanced, and perfected: and
he like may be said of evil, for the *backslider in
eart shall be filled with his own ways, Prov.* xiv. 14.
Every sinner *sooner* or later shall receive the fruit of
heir own doings. It is a most signal place, that of
he apostle, *Rom.* ii. 5. &c. wicked men are said *after
heir hard and impenitent heart, to treasure up to
hemselves wrath against the day of wrath, and reve-
ation of the righteous judgment of God; who will ren-
er to every man according to his deeds. To them who
y patient continuance in well doing, seek for glory, and
onour, and immortality, eternal life; but unto them*
who

who are contentious and obey not the truth, indignation and
wrath, tribulation and anguish upon every soul of man
that doth evil ; to the Jew, *first, and also to the Gentile.*
Alas ! we fee but the out-fide of men, and we do
incompetently judge.   But whofoever doth allow
himfelf, in ways of fin and wickednefs ;   at times,
he will have fears and jealoufies, doubts and fufpicions, however he may appear to others, to be jol-
ly and merry ; and to have but little trouble. For
this I dare fay, of all men that continue in fin without repentance, unlefs in one cafe, and that is a
worfe ; unlefs they be deferted of God, and given
up to hardnefs of heart ; faving *in* this cafe, men
that do affect to tranfgrefs the fettled rule and law
of righteoufnefs and honefty ; that make no confcience to approve themfelves to God, the laws of
nature, or of revelation ; the rules of fcripture, or
of reafon ; thefe men undoubtedly have fuch times,
wherein their hearts mifgive them ; have much of
heart-ach, much of fear and jealoufy. And, if they
have none of thefe, it is worfe with them, for then
they are lefs recoverable.   Whereas in the ways of
fobriety, reafon and virtue, religion, and true goodnefs, there is certainly hearts-eafe, and a compofure
·of mind : there is an inward calm and ferenity ;
there is fatisfaction for the prefent, and a well-
grounded expectation for the future.   And this is
to be expected, as that which is connatural ; and
it doth not fail. This mans affairs are here, folid, and fubftantial ; and hereafter they will be
further fettled and confirmed. And fo I have giv-
en you an account of the truth of that reafon, why
                                                    there

there is *lefs of a man here and more hereafter.* For he hath lefs of ftay and continuance in this world; lefs of true judgment, and lefs of weal or woe.

DISCOURSE XVIII.

The true Valuation of M A N.

L U K E xvi. 25.

But Abraham faid, fon, remember that thou in thy lifetime receivedft thy good things, and likewife Lazarus evil things : but now he is comforted, and thou art tormented.

IN the refpects before-mentioned, and others that poffibly might be fuperadded, it appears that there is *lefs* of man in this world. But I may alfo adjoin by way of exception, fome particulars to the *contrary*; for I muft acknowledge, that in fome refpects, our being in this world is very confiderable. I will inftance in three particulars,

1. In refpect of man's *poffibility.*
2. In refpect of man's *opportunity.*
3. In refpect of man's well-grounded faith and *expectation.* In thefe refpects, a man's being in this world, is very confiderable and highly valuable.

1. In refpect of man's poffibility; for *here* we may lay a good foundation, upon which the happy

fuperftructure

fuperftructure of glory *hereafter*, may be ere

For though the worft that can be faid, prove t

that man is a bankrupt, and hath fuffered fhipwi

is confounded in his principles, marred and fp

by his apoftacy, defection, degeneracy, and con

ing to iniquity : admitting that he is perfectly

trary to the true complexion he was in, in the

that God made him, yet all this malady may be

ed, and his condition is recoverable.   Thoug

hath committed fin, it may be pardoned ; the

he hath alienated himfelf from God, yet he ma

turn, and God may receive him ; though he l

given God offence, yet God is reconcileable. I

is a great faying of our Saviour, *Mark* ix. 23.

things are poffible to him that believeth.   This is

both in the active and |paffive fenfe : that is,

man apply himfelf to God, and his mind be cha

ed, it is poffible that he may do all thofe acts t

are neceffary for his fafety and recovery, thro

the affiftance of God's grace.   That for the at

fenfe. It is true alfo in the *paffive* fenfe.   All thi

may be done for him, in him, or upon him :

may be brought out of a condition of enmity, t

ftate of friendfhip with God : all things are po

ble to be done for him, in him, or upon him. A

it is enough to make this out, that God is placal

and reconcileable ; and if this were not true, th

could be no hope. If this were not known to m

there could be no place for repentance, nor co

any man find any difpofition in his heart, G

ward.   But all men are bound to think that G

is placable and reconcileable ; he is not elfe the f

and chiefeft goodnefs. So that, in refpect of man's *poffibility*, his being in this world is very confiderable, But,

2. In refpect of man's *opportunity*, his being is very confiderable ; and this is much more than a bare poffibility. If this were all that I could fay to a man, that a thing is poffible, it would be no great encouragement. But I can tell finners, that they have *opportunity*, and an opportunity is the *nick of time*. Take things in their feafon, and they will be eafily done. Now we enjoy a day of grace, and a day of grace doth import opportunity. We are now under God's call and invitation. Theie is no man in the world, that hath the bible in his hand, or that hath heard any thing out of it, who hath any reafon to doubt but that he is called of God. What we read in the bible, we may build upon, and apply to ourfelves, with as good affurance, as if God did difpatch an angel from heaven to us. We are in this day of grace, God's invited guefts ; and we are all of us under the operation of the divine Spirit, and may depend upon the affiftance of the divine grace. And for this, I offer to you that fignal place, though our tranflation abate a little of the emphafis of it. *Phil.* ii. 12, 13. *Work out your own falvation with fear and trembling ; for it is God which worketh in you, both to will and to do of his good pleafure.* But in the *Greek* it is the participle *working*. The verb is verified by one fingle act : but the participle imports a *continuation of action*. That is, apply yourfelves to God, and fet yourfelves about the bufinefs of your recovery, by acts of righteoufnefs

teoufnefs, goodnefs, and truth ; and look not upon
your own weaknefs, and indifpofition ; for *God is
working* in you, both to will, and to do, of his own
good pleafure.   Apply yourfelves to God, and you
will find him in motion ; and where God is, there
is ftrength, and fufficiency, and any thing may be
done through the divine aid ; and therefore we have
encouragement, to be up and doing, according to
the advice of the apoftle, *Eph.* v. 14.   *Awake thou
that fleeepeft, and arife from the dead, and Chrift fhall
give thee light.*   We are fure of God, by virtue of
his promife : and this we may depend upon, that
wherefoever God begins, he gives in fome aid, and
affiftance ; which aid, though it be lefs than we
may receive afterwards, yet it will enable a man
to do fomething : and that God, who of his own
motion, grace, and good will, begins with lefs ;
yet he will go on with further affiftance, and with
this a man may do more : for it is certain, the failure will not be on God's part : and therefore if
we have fufficiency or the act that God calls us
unto, at prefent, and affurance of further affiftance,
as there fhall be need ; we have encouragement,
not only to engage us to begin, but to continue in
thofe ways that tend to our recovery. *Seek the Lord
therefore while he may be found, call ye upon him while
he is near,* as the prophet advifeth, *Ifa.* lv. 6.   For
there wants nothing but what lies on our part to
perform, and that is our concurrence, our fubfervi-
ency and confent.   For it is irrational for us to
think, that God having made us intelligent and voluntary agents, that he fhould force and conftrain

us ;

us ; and that he fhould not expect the ufe of thofe powers that he hath given us. And this is the 2d. Our being in the world is very *confiderable* in re-fpect of our *opportunity.*

3. Our being in the world is alfo confiderable in refpect of our affured *hope and expectation* which we may have in this probation-ftate.   God's merciful declarations to us fcatter all fears and jealoufies. God's gracious promifes and invitations are a good ground for our expectation : and the fcriptures are full on this account, *Ezek.* xviii. 23.   *Have I any pleafure at all that the wicked fhould die ? faith the Lord God : and not that he fhould return from his way and live ?*   We do obferve, that thefe interrogations do moft peremptorily deny.   *Have I any pleafure ?* that is, I have no pleafure that the wicked fhould die.   And fo you have it expreffed, *v.* 32.   *I have no pleafure in the death of him that dieth* : but my plea-fure and delight is in this, that the wicked fhould return and live.   And again, *Ezek.* xxxiii. 11. *As I live, faith the Lord God, I have no pleafure in the death of the wicked ; but that the wicked turn from his way and live.*   Here we have God's *oath* : *As I live, faith the Lord* ; which is a word fit for him on-ly to ufe, who is the firft caufe and original of be-ing : but it is a word too big for the mouth of any creature.   For our being is altogether arbitrary and dependent ; and therefore though this word is fometimes ufed among men ; if they did confider, they would not do it : For alas ! We are but as a vapour ; and if God withdraw himfelf, we prefent-ly fall into our firft principles, and return unto the

duft. But to return : many fcriptures you have more to this purpofe. God faith, *Ifa.* v. 4. *What could have been done more to my vineyard that I have not done in it ? And how often* (faith our Saviour) *would I have gathered thee, as a hen gathereth her chickens under her wings, but ye would not ?* And again, *come unto me, all ye that are weary and heavy laden, and I will give you reft,* Matt. xi. 28. And fo the fcripture ends, *Rev.* iii. 20. *Behold I ftand at the door and knock,* if any man hear my voice, and open the door, *I will come in to him, and will fup with him, and he with me.* This is the 3d. Our affured *hope and expectation.*

I have now done with the *firft* reafon. If you would make a juft eftimate of man, you muft confider him in refpect *to his double ftate,* his exiftence in time, and his future exiftence in eternity. For as to his prefent being, you find him here but of fhort and uncertain continuance ; you find him here labouring much under falfe opinions and lying imaginations ; and whether he be here happy, or miferable, it is *lefs* than it will be hereafter : yet his being here, is not to be defpifed, and over-looked ; for upon three accounts it is very *confiderable, viz.* in refpect of his poffibility, opportunity, and his well grounded hope and expectation.

2ly. I come now to the *2d reafon,* why, if we would make a juft eftimate of man, we muft confider him in refpect to his double ftate of exiftence, in time and in eternity : for man is a much more *valuable* creature than his affairs in this world reprefent him to be : and this I will make appear in three particulars. Becaufe 	1. Man

1. Man is here in his ſtate of infancy, and non-age ; he is not yet come to the full uſe of his parts ; yea, he is as it were impriſoned, and incumber'd with a groſs, dull and craſy body.

2. In this ſtate, man is neither *as he ſhould be,* nor if he himſelf well conſider, *as he would be.*

3. There are many *appearances* in this ſtate, which repreſent man to be but a *mean and ordinary* thing, whereas he is in truth, a noble and generous creature, made for attendance upon God, and to converſe with angels in glory, as I ſhall ſhew you in ſeveral particulars.

1. Man is here, in his ſtate of infancy and non-age : he is here as a child in his minority, who is not ſo much as truſted with himſelf, or his own af-fairs ; and much leſs with the affairs of other men : who becauſe of his imperfection, is not able to do any legal act, any act that may extend to his own prejudice. Here he is but as a flower in the bloſ-ſom, and in the ſpring of his years : and beſides, he is in a ſtate of limitation and confinement, in reſpect of his body, and in reſpect of his mind. In reſpect of his body, he is impriſoned, and incumber-ed : therefore we read, that this body which we now have, is to be ſo remarkably changed, that it is ſaid it ſhall be a *ſpiritual body*, and that this cor-ruption ſhall put on incorruption, and be made like unto the body of our Saviour, or a *glorified body* ; and this ſhall be effected by his almighty power, which is able to ſubdue all things to himſelf. We now dwell in *houſes of clay*, but we ſhall then have a houſe not made with hands, eternal in the heavens.

Our

Our bodies fhall then be made fit inftruments for our fouls, whereas now, as the philofopher tells us, the body is an impediment to the mind and to all divine contemplation. It was the great confolation that *Socrates* * had, when he was condemned to die ; what (faith he to his friend that came to comfort him) is this, but to do that which I have endeavoured to do all along my life ; that is to lay afide my body, which yet never kept company with my mind ? thus was he able to fay. So that, as a child in the cradle, fo is a man in this world. Our minds are confined in the body : In this tabernacle (faith the apoftle) we *groan being burdened* ; this is the voice of all fpiritually awakened fouls " Let us " take our flight to heaven and fee in the light of " God's countenance, and forfake this low and dirty " world, for here fouls are hindered as to their high- " eft operations of mind, and underftanding, and the largenefs of their wills and affections." As *Plato* faith well, we have here certain inclinations, at times, to move upward towards heaven, and then we fall down again as birds that are tied by the leg. We are as they fay, heavy behind. In this body, the very reafon of our mind is materiated, and the very fentiments of our fouls (to ufe the common phrafe) do tafte of the cask. That is the firft thing : man is a far more confiderable creature than his ftate in this world doth reprefent him to be ; becaufe he is here in his *infancy*, he is not at his full growth, not at perfect liberty ; but is contracted by a grofs and heavy body. 2. Man

* Plato, apologia Socratis.

2. Man in this ſtate is neither ; 1. *as he ſhall be.* Nor,

2. (If he well conſider) *as he would be* : and therefore he is not in perfect welfare here.

1. Man is *not as he ſhould be*, becauſe of non-uſe and miſuſe, and abuſe of himſelf ; of which every one is more or leſs (in ſome degree) guilty.   And therefore as the lawyers tell us, if men do not deſtroy, yet they weaken their title by theſe things. Now we are all of us guilty, in reſpect of *non-uſe* of ourſelves, in that we do not employ ourſelves about God, as we ſhould ; and of *miſuſe*, witneſs the contracted evil habits ; for by cuſtom and practice men may ſo miſuſe themſelves, as to become lame and blind ; and therefore the ſcripture doth apply to us thus *Rev*. iii. 18. *I counſel thee to buy of me eye-ſalve that thou mayeſt ſee* : the remedy doth declare the nature of the malady.   If a man doth but conſider he will be a wonder to himſelf, and he will marvel how it is become ſo with him, as *Rebecca* ſaid, *Gen*. xxv. 22. *If it be ſo, why am I thus !* Every man is ſenſible of contradiction from within, and a diverſity from himſelf ; he is not all of a piece, nor hath the power of his apprehenſions.   That which is *born after the fleſh perſecutes that which is born after the ſpirit*, Gal. iv. 29. I do enlarge the apoſtle's words, and ſpeak them upon a natural account ; that is, things that are founded on the body are not the genuine iſſue of mind and underſtanding ; bodily temper and inclination doth make it hard for us to exerciſe our underſtanding and reaſon.   And he is the moſt valuable man that can ſubdue every

T 3   thing

thing to himſelf, all appetites and deſires to ſuch government. This we have experience of, that we are but weak to diſcern ; and many times unreſolved what to do, and uncertain to perform. If we come to judge, we judge fallibly ; if we come to reſolve, we are off and on ; if we come to execute and perform, we are many times beaten off from ourſelves. There is a whole chapter, *Luke* xv. to repreſent this loſt ſtate of man in three parables, that of a loſt groat, a loſt ſheep, and a loſt ſon. That of the *loſt groat* repreſents the ſtupidity, dulneſs and incapacity of ſinners ; they being void of all underſtanding : for a groat is a thing without any life or motion : by which parable is repreſented the ſtupidity and ſenſleſsneſs of ſinners ; that are ſunk, and loſt. Then there is the *wandring ſheep* : A ſheep is indeed an innocent creature, but very ſilly and expoſed to all ſorts of dangers ; from dogs, wolves, briers, and thorns ; and if once 'tis gone from the food, there is no hope of returning by its own care. This doth alſo repreſent the ſtate of ſinners, who are very fools, when they do part from the way of righteouſneſs ; and very ſeldom return by their own care and conſideration, but even like loſt ſheep wandring from the fold, ſo they wander up and down in the wilderneſs of this world. The third parable is that of the *prodigal ſon*, which repreſents the ſtate of diſſolute and profane ſinners that make havock of their conſcience, that are deſperate and preſumptuous, and very hardly drawn to any true conſideration. Theſe three parables repreſent the ſtate and condition of loſt ſinners. From all which

which you may underſtand, that if we were not called from heaven, and God did not give us ears to
hear, and draw ſinners with power from above,
there were little hopes of reclaiming ſinners from
their deſperate condition. And that is the *firſt*
thing in this particular, man in this ſtate is *not as
be ſhould be,* becauſe he hath contracted guilt, becauſe
he hath marred his ſpirit and ſpoiled his principle :
he hath done that which is unnatural. And you
muſt know, that as the edge of a razor is ſooner
turned, becauſe of its keenneſs ; ſo in this caſe, the
mind of man, being made to carry accuracy of ap-
prehenſion ; if he do a baſe, vile and unnatural act,
he doth more marr and ſpoil his mind that is made
to ingenuity : whereas blunter edges would endure
more violence. Man therefore is a more conſiderable creature than his preſent ſtate doth repreſent
him to be.

2. Neither is he, *as he would be,* if he do well
conſider ; for this we have experience of, that if a-
ny man hath worſted himſelf, and his circumſtances
be grown worſe than they have been, and he ap-
prehends himſelf a loſer ; he will never ſit down
ſatisfied, but his whole thought and contrivance
will be about his recovery, and to become as he was.
This we obſerve in nature, that there is nothing at
reſt and quiet, being in an unnatural ſtate, but every thing endeavours to recover itſelf. Water, if it
be ſullied never ſo much, if it hath time, will work
the dregs to the bottom. And every thing in nature if it may, it will not only preſerve itſelf in its
natural condition : but being diverted from its natural

tural courſe, will recover itſelf, as ſoon as it may.
And do you think that the rational nature will not
deſire to be as well, as by nature, it could be ? Now
we having contracted guilt, and ſpoiled our princi_
ples by conſenting to iniquity : if we do but conſider, it will come into our minds, to recover ourſelves by repentance ; by which there is a revoking,
and as it were, an undoing of what hath been unduly done.   For whoſoever commits a ſin and doth
not repent of it, he lives in it : but he that having
committed a ſin, repents of it, he doth revoke and
undo it as far as it is in his power. Therefore man
in a ſtate of ſin, is *not as he ſhould be*, for ſin is unnatural : neither is he as he *would be*, becauſe he is
in a ſtate of deformity, and impurity ; and it is natural for every thing not only to conſerve, but to
recover its own perfection. That is the *ſecond* particular which ſhews man to be a more valuable creature than his ſtate in this world doth repreſent him
to be : becauſe in this ſtate, he neither is as he
ſhould be, (nor if he conſiders) *as he would be.*

3. There are many *appearances* in this world,
that ſeem to repreſent man a very *mean* and ordinary creature : whereas, upon a true account, he is
very noble and generous, fit for attendance upon
God, and converſe with angels. Now if I can make
this out, you will eaſily grant, that man is a much
more valuable creature, than this world doth repreſent him ; and this I ſhall do in *ſix* particulars.

1. The ſtate of man in this world doth repreſent
him ſubject to the ſame vanity, that all other creatures lie under, as in *Job.* xvii. 14. *I have ſaid to
corruption*

corruption, thou art my father : to the worm, thou art my mother and my sister. And what worfe thing befalls any creature, than to be expofed to corruption and rottennefs ? So *Ecclef.* iii. 19. faith the wife man, *that which befalleth the fons of men, befalleth beafts, even one thing befalleth them : as the one dieth, fo dieth the other, yea they have all one breath ; fo that a man hath no preheminence above a beaft, for all is vanity.* Thus *Solomon* (the great fearcher into things) reprefents man. But this is all as to his outward ftate and appearance ; for in reality, man is made for immortality, and his foul is divine.   For fo *Solomon* faith, *Eccl.* xii. 7. The *fpirit doth return to God that gave it* ; and *Job.* xix. 25. *I know that my Redeemer liveth, and that I fhall fee him at the laft.* And though I do believe that the *firft meaning of* thefe wrods, is to exprefs *Job's* faith and confidence in God, that he fhould have his worldly eftate reftored again to him, as it did afterwards prove, and that with his very eyes, that were then even wafted and deftroyed by his bodily infirmities, he fhould fee his Redeemer : yet according to a *fuller fenfe,* I underftand thefe words of the ftate of the refurrection and glory, which fhould be after this life was ended ; upon which account our Saviour puts that queftion, *what fhall it profit a man to gain the whole world and to lofe his own foul ?* Matt. xvi. 26. A very bad bargain, becaufe that which is given as a price, is of much more worth and value, than that which is purchafed.   If we believe thefe fcriptures, we muft acknowledge, that mens fouls fhall continue after their bodies ; and if fo, he is much more confiderable

able, than his *mean* state and condition in this world
do reprefent him.   This is the firft ? But

2. This ftate reprefents a man as very low and
mean, becaufe he *is fubjected* to low and mean *employments*, fit only to converfe with other creatures.
And accordingly many men condemn themfelves to
the drudgery of this world ; and do make their rational faculties very *Gibeonites*, and employ them to
hew wood and draw water ; and much of this hath
an antecedent foundation in the curfe, *Gen.* iii. 19.
In the fweat of thy face fhalt thou eat bread, 2 Theff. iii.
10. *He that will not work, neither let him eat. And
man is born to labour*, faith *Job.* And he that will
not employ himfelf to the utmoft, to maintain himfelf, comes not within the compafs of other mens
charity.   And therefore *Solomon* fends the fluggard
to fchool to learn of the irrational creatures, *Go to
the ant thou fluggard, confider her ways and be wife*,
Prov. vi. 6. Now this ftate of man reprefents him
as made to common drudgery and fervice. Whereas if we confider, man is made for attendance upon
God, and to be happy in the enjoyment of him :
and that 'tis the bufinefs of man to govern himfelf
according to the dictates of reafon, truth and virtue,
and to maintain converfe and fellowfhip with God.
To this, man was *made* ; this was the very end
and defign of his creation, to have a fenfe of God
as the firft caufe ; and to have reft in him, as the
center : and to have intention of God as the laft
end.   O Lord thou haft made us for thyfelf, and
for thy pleafure we are and were created. And the
wife man faith, *the fpirit in man is the candle of the
Lord.*

Lord. And in this fenfe is that true which *Solomon* faith, *Ecclef.* iii. 11. *God hath fet the world in mens heart* ; not as we fet it, by covetoufnefs, and inordinate defire ; but to fhew that man's foul doth in value and worth tranfcend the whole creation below him. God hath contracted the difperfed excellencies of the creation *in man's heart* ; man in refpect of vivacity and poffibility to act, doth tranfcend the whole creation below him.

3. This prefent ftate reprefents a man in a condition of *beggary, dependence,* and *neceffity,* Job. i. 21. *Naked came I into the world, and naked fhall I go out.* 1 *Tim.* vi. 7. *We brought nothing into this world, and it is certain we can carry nothing out.* We are beholden to every creature, either for food, or for raiment, or for defence, or for fome other accommodation. Man hath nothing, but the ufe of his reafon, whereby he doth outwit the creatures below him, and fpoil them of their feveral excellencies, and by that which is their defence, defend himfelf againft them. Man comes into the world moft fhiftlefs and helplefs, the moft unprovided for of any creature ; he hath no way to help himfelf, but by *crying,* and yet that (without any declaration, of *why,* and *what* it *ails*) is fufficient. Indeed, there is no fecurity to human nature, in refpect of our coming into the world, but only *this,* that man is born in the hands of reafon, and loving affection. Thus man appears to be in a condition of *beggary, dependence and neceffity* ; whereas if we confider man duly, we fhall find him to be the glory of God's creation in this lower world ; the mafter-piece of God's workmanfhip ; that

that there is more of value and worth in him than
in all the creation befides. The fun itfelf, that en-
lightens the world, and fcatters away all ftench,
putrefaction, and corruption ; is yet but darknefs,
and a cloud in compare with the motion of mind
and underftanding, inquiring into and difcovering
the reafon of things. For the mind of man takes
cognizance of God, receives from him, and returns
to him ; and carries a continual fenfe of God within itfelf, whereas the fun can do none of thefe
things, nor no creature in this vifible world, befides
man.   Therefore it was wifely done of *Plutarch,*
that he would not make fo *much* the *ufe of reafon* to
be the formal character of man, to diftinguifh him
from other creatures, as the ufe and *exercife of religion.*   For as to the ufe of reafon, they either have
a participation or an imitation of us : but they make
no returns unto God, nor have any principle of
confcience within them, from a fenfe of the difference of things. Upon this account, our Saviour
faith, *what can be given in exchange for a man's foul?*
Matt. xvi. 26. and the pfalmift faith, *the redemption
of a foul is precious, and ceafeth for ever.* Pfal. xlix. 8.
And that is the third particular, this ftate reprefents
a man in a condition of *beggary, and dependency,* being beholden to all other creatures, for relief of his
neceffities, for matters of convenience or defence ;
whereas in reality, man is the glory of God's creation, and hath that in him, which is of more value
and worth, than the whole world befides.

4. This ftate reprefents a man as *worn out with
follicitude and care for himfelf,* as being tormented
with

with fear and more to feek, than any other creature. He goes about the world as a wanderer and a vaga_ bond, always feeking, and complaining, as the pfalmift fpeaks of the redeemed of the Lord, *Pf.* cvii. 4, 5. even *they wandred in the wildernefs in a folitary way, they found no city to dwell in ; hungry and thirfty, their foul fainted in them.* This is a true reprefentation of man's reftlefsnefs, and uneafy condition in this world. And the preacher goes beyond all this, in reprefenting the fickly and diftempered condition of man in this world, *Eccl.* iv. 8. *There is one alone, and there is not a fecond ; yea, he hath neither child nor brother : yet is there no end of all his labour, neither is his eye fatisfied with riches, neither faith he, for whom do I labour, and bereave my foul of good ?* It doth not fo much as once come into his mind to fay, *why do I wear out myfelf, and deprive myfelf of the comforts of life ?* this is alfo *vanity,* yea it is a *fore travel.* This ftate reprefents a man more follicitous, and more inquifitive than any other creature, for they take little care, but depend upon common providence ; *they* enjoy themfelves more freely in fummer, and are not ftraitned in the winter. But yet in reality, man is God's peculiar care and charge : for *Job.* xxxv. 11. it is faid, *he teacheth us more than the beafts of the earth and makes us wifer than the fowls of heaven* ; which argues that man is under God's difcipline. And the *pfalmift* declares that there was more of curiofity in the creation of man than of other creatures. *Pf.* cxxxix. 14, 15. *I will praife thee, for I am fearfully and wonderfully made, marvelous are thy works, and that my foul knoweth*

right

right well. My substance was not hid from thee when I was made in secret, and curiously wrought in the lowest parts of the earth ; which intimates the care of God in man's creation. And so it is represented in *Genesis ;* for when other things were created, it is only said, *let them be* : they were, accordingly : as *let there be light,* and there *was light,* Gen. i. 3. But when he came to make man, he said, *let us make man in our image, after our likeness.* Gen. i. 26. And for his provision, God intended, that the rich furniture of the sea, earth and air, should be for his use, having put in subjection to him, *all sheep and oxen, yea and the beasts of the field, the fowls of the air, and the fish of the sea,* Psal. viii. 7, 8. The providence of God is no where wanting, but most intensely visible in human affairs. And this our Saviour made an argument, why men should not doubt, but that God would provide for them because he fed the ravens, and took care of the smallest birds, and cloathed the lillies of the field (*Luke* xii. 24.) and therefore he would much less be wanting to those that were made after his own image. And for this reason, God saith he will *require the life of man, at the hand of every beast will I require it, and at the hand of man, at the hand of every man's brother will I require the life of man : whoso sheddeth mans blood, by man shall his blood be shed : for in the image of God made he man.* Gen. ix. 5, 6. And *Satan* acknowledgeth this, in the argument he useth to God *Job.* i. *Doth Job fear God for nought ?* ver. 10. *Thou hast set an hedge about him, and about his house, and about all that he hath.* This is the fourth particular

that

hat the *appearance* of this world doth mifreprefent
he ftate of man. For man feems to be moft expo-
:d, and without defence ; whereas, in reality he
: the peculiar care and charge of divine providence,
nd God; that is no where wanting to any of the
/orks of his hands, doth more efpecially concern
imfelf in his care and government of man, and doth
:verely challenge any one that fhall offer him any
arm.

D I S C O U R S E XIX.

The true Valuation of M A N.

L U K E xvi. 25.

ut Abraham faid, fon, remember that thou in thy life-
time receivedft thy good things, and likewife Laza-
rus evil things : but now he is comforted, and thou
art tormented.

THis ftate reprefents man to be in *danger*
from him that is next him, and of his
own kind ; for fo is the world through *fin*
:come degenerate, that *one man, as it were, is be-*
ne a wolf to another : and it is *de facto* true, that
: who is *born after the flefh, doth perfecute him that*
born after the fpirit. The wars of feveral coun-
es have given too much teftimony to this matter,
ho have been the fo highly applauded men in fto-

ry; but thofe great *conquerours,* the great felf-de-
figners and troublers of mankind ? *David* complains
both of friends, and enemies, *Pfal.* xli. 5. *Mine e-
nemies fpeak evil of me ; when fhall he die, and his
name perifh,* &c. *v.* 9. *yea mine own familiar friend in
whom I trufted, which did eat of my bread, hath lift
up his heel againft me.* Thus it is in this world, whereas God *made the fecond* in order to the *firft,* as you
find, *Gen.* ii. 18. *It is not good that man fhould be a-
lone : I will make him an help meet for him.* This is
fo true, that *Ariftotle* hath obferved, that whofoever
being a finite and limited creature can be alone, he
had need be as *good as God,* or is as *bad as the devil,*
or as *dull as a beaft.* He that can be happy alone,
either he is good, like to God, fatisfying himfelf in
the fulnefs of his own goodnefs ; or elfe is as bad
as the devil, fatiating himfelf, in his own malice ;
or elfe as ftupid as a beaft, pleafing himfelf in his
own dulnefs, taking no cognizance of things, but
fatisfying himfelf in eating, drinking, and fleeping
in his own dullnefs. *Solomon* hath obferved, *Eccl.*
iv. 9. *Two are better than one, and wo be to him that
is alone.* In converfe men receive one from another,
and communicate one to another with great delight
and fatisfaction. If men be of any improvement
in their intellectuals, there is no part of a man's life
more profitable, nor more fatisfactory than rational
and ingenuous converfe. It is highly pleafing to a
man to fee the face of his friend ; it doth often recover a man out of his dumps, and deliver him
from melancholy. So it is, and fo it would be if
the intention of God in his creation of man, did attain its proper effect. 6. and

6. and *Laftly*, the ftate of man in this life reprefents his condition *otherwife than indeed it is* ; that
is, it reprefents a man, the *objeƈ of the devil's envy*,
ufurpation, and tyranny, *Eph.* ii. 2. He is called
the *prince of the power of the air, the fpirit that worketh in the children of difobedience.* A fad account for
men to be under the ufurpation of fo monftrous and
degenerate a creature ! Whereas God made man,
with principles of reafon, and underftanding, the
devil abufeth him by cheats and impoftures, as
we have many ftories in the holy fcriptures. 1 *Kings*
xxii. 22. *I will be a lying fpirit in the mouth of all
his prophets.* And 1 *Chron.* xxi. 1. it is faid, that
*Satan flood up againft Ifrael, and provoked David to
number Ifrael.* Obferve alfo how Satan doth mifreprefent *Job* to God ; he makes him fordid and
bafe in his fervice, *Job.* i. 9,. 11. *Doth Job ferve
God for nought ? Put forth thine hand now, and touch
all that he hath,* (difappoint him, crofs him) *and he
will curfe thee to thy face.* Sometimes he mifreprefents
God ; as to our firft parents, *Gen.* iii. 5. *God doth
know, that in the day ye eat thereof, then your eyes fhall
be opened, and ye fhall be as Gods, knowing good and e-
vil.* This is the notion his words carry in them,
that they were lefs beholden to God, than they
thought : and that if God had not dealt to them
with a ftraight hand, and grudged them that excellency which they were capable of, they might have
been like to God, knowing good and evil. And
this he fuggefts, to draw them from God, and to
abate the fenfe of their obligation to him, and to
work them into an ill opinion of God : that though

V o l. I.   U   they

they were in fome meafure, beholden to him for
their creation, yet, if he had pleafed, he might have
exalted them to a much higher degree, than he had
done.   Thus he works upon men by mifreprefentations, by cheats, and impoftures. And other fcriptures fhew how Satan works upon men by open
refiftance, *Zech.* iii. 1. When *Joſhua the high prieſt
ſtood before the angel of the Lord, and Satan ſtood at his
right hand to refiſt him.*   And the apoftle tells us,
Eph. vi. 12. *We wreſtle not againſt fleſh and blood,
but againſt principalities and powers.* And *Luke* viii.
12. *Then cometh the devil and taketh away the word
out of their hearts.* And *Luke* xxii. 31. *And the Lord
ſaid, Simon, Simon, Satan hath defired to have you,
that he may ſift you as wheat.* 2 Tim. ii. 26. *That God
may recover them out of the ſnare of the devil, who are
taken captive by him at his will.*   This is the laſt reprefentation which makes man to appear a lefs valuable and confiderable creature, than indeed he is.
But to this I fay, that this enemy is extraordinary,
and out of the order of God's creation. God made
no fuch enemy for man; but fo it comes to pafs,
through the degeneracy and apoftacy of his higher
creation.   And fince the angels by their apoftacy,
are become fuch, God put a guard upon the devils, and he will finally deliver us from them, if we
do but wha twe may, through the affiftance of God's
grace to refift him ; though he does what he can
to deceive, if it were poffible, the elect, yet if we
refift him, he ſhall flee from us, *Matt.* xxiv. 24.
James iv. 7. And it is faid, *Rev.* xx. 2, 3. *That
the angel laid hold on the dragon, that old ferpent,*
                                                 which

which is the devil, and Satan, and bound him a thousand years. And cast him into a bottomless pit, and shut him up, that he should deceive the nations no more ; and v. 14. Death and hell were cast into the lake of fire.

I do verily believe, and perfuade myfelf, that God doth generally defend all men in the world, by his fpecial and particular providence, againft the devil ; fo that unlefs men either willfully give God an offence, or betray themfelves to the devil, by their own voluntary confent, he can have no power over them. Neither do I think that every act of fin is of this nature, but it muft be fuch a fpecifick, fuch a mifcarriage, fuch a way of finning in kind, which doth incurr a particular forfeiture of God's protection againft the devil. That you may underftand my meaning, I will give you two inftances, out of the fcripture. The firft fhall be that in 1 *Sam.* xxviii. 6, 7. And when *Saul enquired of the Lord, the Lord anfwered him not, neither by dreams, nor by Urim, nor by prophets. Then faid Saul unto his fervants, feek me a woman that hath a familiar fpirit, that I may go to her, and enquire of her.* A like paffage you have, 2 *Kings* i. 2. *And Ahaziah fell down through a lattefs in his upper chamber that was in Samaria, and was fick : and he fent meffengers, and faid unto them, go, enquire of Baal-zebub the God of Ekron, whether I fhall recover of this difeafe.* If men will not be confined under God's limitation, but will know more than God hath revealed ; or by other means than he thinks fit to difcover by ; or befides what is within the compafs of our rational faculties ; if they will know any how, if God

will

will not, the devil fhall : *this* I think, is fuch a provocation in kind, that they which do fo, cannot
but expect that God fhould take off his fpecial
protection againft the devil : and let it be to them as
they chofe. But faving in fuch cafes, as thefe, it
feems very rational to think, that *Satan* is limited,
and that we are under the protection of God and
his fpecial providence againft the devil ; becaufe he
is able to do us fo little mifchief.

Thus I have run through all thefe rules, *viz.*
that man is not here in an *adult* eftate : neither is
he here as he *fhould be*, nor (if he well confider it)
as he *would* be : and there are many *appearances* in
this ftate that do reprefent him a common and ordinary creature ; whereas in truth, man is a noble
and generous creature, made for converfe with God
himfelf, and fitted for the company of the angels in
glory ; whereby it plainly appears, that man is a
much more valuable creature, than his eftate in
this world reprefents him to be. And that is the
laft argument for proof of the fecond *propofition*, that
if you would make a right judgment of man, you
muft not only confider him as to this ftate, but alfo, to the future.

For the *clofe* of this particular, I fhall add a word
or two of application. And,

1. If fo be, there is lefs of man here, and more
hereafter : if when we would take a right eftimate
of man, we muft confider him in refpect of his
double eftate, hereafter, as well as here ; then thofe
perfons are guilty of the greateft madnefs and folly
that

that confider themfelves only in order to *this life* ;
whereas thefe men have fouls to fave or to lofe ;
and there is another ftate that will commence and
begin after the expiration of this. Man who is now
fubject to uncertainty, mutability, and vanity ; he
fhall be hereafter put into a fettled condition·
Wherefore, with the wife man, I ask this queftion,
Prov. xvii. 16. *Wherefore is there a price in the hana
of a fool to get wifdom, feeing he hath no heart to it ?*
Since he hath neither wifdom nor underftanding to
make advantage of it ? This is the greateft argument of folly, that men can be guilty of, like the
fool in the gofpel, *Luke* xii. 19, 20, 21. to think of
worldly provifion, and accommodations great eftates
revenues, honours and dignity, riches and pleafure ;
but not of being rich towards God. *Thou fool* (faith
our Saviour) *this night thy foul fhall be required of thee ;
then whofe fhall thofe things be, which thou haft provided,* Luke xii. 20. Certainly, he is a very carelefs
and prodigal perfon, who fpends all his portion to
day, and leaves nothing for to-morrow. *Plutarch*
fpeaks of a man, who when he was in a languifh-
ing condition, and nature upon its utmoft decay,
comes to the phyfician to be cured of his *res dubia,* a
petty inconvenience that hung upon his finger.
There are many of this defperate refolution, as to
fay, *let us eat and drink, for to-morrow we die ;* and
look no further. As they are wont to fay, they
will have *a fweet life, though it be fhort :* 'tis well
if they could have their choice. But if there be a
feparate exiftence, and another ftate to commence
after this ; and that this life is but preparatory to

U 3   that ;

that ; then thefe men are guilty of the greateft madnefs and folly. And of thefe men it may be faid, that they have their *immortal fouls, only as falt to keep their bodies from ftench and putrefaction* ; they have their reafonable faculties only to keep their bodies a-live ; and not for the great purpofes of eternity ; not for the fenfe of a deity, and the contemplation of God ; not for the purpofe of adoring the fupreme majefty, and ferving of him here, and refembling of him in holinefs and righteoufnefs, which are the only things that put a value upon man.

2. My next inference from what hath been faid, is, that we fhould not be *tempted* in this life, to do any thing to the *prejudice* of our future ftate ; the ftate of eternity : but to let things be confidered according to the true worth and value, left they find caufe to repent, when it is too late, of the pleafures they took in their unlawful actions. To do any thing to the prejudice of our immortal fouls, is the great-eft folly that men can be guilty of. Let men be never fo much admired and adored, yet they are guilty of the greateft folly and madnefs, if they do not fubordinate all the affairs and tranfactions of time, to ferve the intereft of their immortal fouls. But this often happens to be our fate, or our fault, (I am fure) and our folly : *we are all wife, but too many are wife too late.* Wherefore let me advife you to ufe your power and skill to do things in fubordi-nation and reference to the future account. Do that now, which will not burden confcience ; that will not contradict the fenfe of your minds and under-ftanding ; that which is, and will be pleafing and

acceptable

acceptable to God. This is true wifdom, and in this we fhall have fatisfaction for the prefent, and expectation to eternity. I would fain afk this rational queftion, and leave it with you, doth the fcripture declare concerning God, in whom there is all power, and liberty, *Jer.* xix. 24. That all his ways are ways of goodnefs, righteoufnefs, and truth ? then fhould not a man think, that it doth become him, and is fit on his part, that the *fruit of the fpirit in him, fhould be in all goodnefs, righteoufnefs, and truth*, Eph. v. 9. For, *this* is our religion, a divine participation, and to imitate him whom we worfhip. Let us always remember, that the actions of this prefent life are the matter of the future judgment ; and that we fhall be accountable for all thofe actions which do proceed from the underftanding of the mind, and liberty of the will ; and that men may fin by neglect of their faculties, as well as by abufe of them. Now all thofe actions that are capable of morality, are bound to be governed by moral principles ; and the mind and underftanding ought to be intent, fo as to rule and govern them according to the reafon of things. For we may fin two ways, either by confenting to that which ought not to be admitted ; or by neglecting ourfelves, through want of care and due examination. An evil action fhould never be done ; but if upon any occafion it be admitted, it ought prefently to be judged unfit, and to be condemned, rejected, and revoked by repentance, and the rule of right acknowledged. For whofoever doth willingly commit evil, and doth not prefently revoke and

difclaim

difclaim it, he is reckoned to own, and live in the
fin he hath committed, and to juftify it : otherwife
why doth he not revoke it ? It is abfolutely neceffary that this fhould be done, or elfe we are not
capable of God's grace and pardon ; for we cannot put that upon God, to pardon contumacious
and impenitent finners. If we do not revoke the
evil which we have at any time committed ; the
guilt lies upon our confciences, without any remo-
val ; and the malignity will affect our minds, without any remedy. Thefe are the inferences I have
made from the firft propofition.

II. The fecond propofition, is that the ftate of man
in the life to come holds a *proportion* to his affairs in
this life. We may eafily judge, by what we now are,
and by what we now do, how it fhall be with us in
the life to come. And this is fully laid down in the text
*fon, remember that thou in thy life-time received'ft thy
good things,* but didft abufe them to luxury and excefs, to pamper thy body, to wantonnefs, pride, for-
getfulnefs of God ; and therefore, now thou art
tormented. But *Lazarus* had evil things, but they
became inftruments of righteoufnefs, they brought
him to modefty, and felf-denial ; therefore he is
comforted. From which it plainly appears, that
the ftate of man in the world to come, holds a *proportion* to his affairs in this life. For explication.

1. Let it be underftood, that I have no intention at all to fpeak one word to countenance the
creature's *merit* with God ; for that I conceive to
be incompatible to the condition of the higheft angel in glory, properly to merit any thing at the

hand

ınd of God ; and therefore not at all agreeable to
e infirm, weak and crazy condition of man ; un-
fs you will ufe the word *mereri* in latin,. in the
ırmlefs fenfe in which the ancient fathers did ufe
, in which fenfe it may pafs ; for that is no more
an *confequently to obtain* God's grace and favour.
ut we are fhy of the word, fince it hath been fo
ıuch abufed in the Roman church. And I take it
ı be above the capacity of any creature in the
igheft altitude, properly to *merit* ought at the hand
f God. And if fo, they fail in the very fundamen-
ıl, who tell us of a *treafury of merit* in the church,
ıat is partly fupplied by the merit of faints depart-
1 this life, out of which there may be a fupply for
ıofe that want.

Nothing can be given to God which is not due
ı him, nor that can be profitable to him ; and
ıerefore there is no poffibility of merit, in a ftrict
:nfe. Nothing can be given to God which was
ot *his own* before ; and we have nothing that is
roperly ours, but the confent of our minds ; and
confefs, that is our free-will-offering, and our on-
ı facrifice, and all that we have to give, and that
ʃhich God requires at our hands, and that which
ʒod takes kindly, and doth accept, and will reward
ʃith eternal recompence, *viz.* if we make God our
elight and choice. For it is not worthy the name
f religion that is not voluntary, wherein the heart
f a man is not engaged, which is not the matter
f his delight and choice. For to drudge in religi-
ın, is the bafeft thing in the world ; and I would
ıever charge my confcience with that, which I had
ıot reconciled firft to the reafon and judgment of

my

my mind, and to the frame and temper of my foul.
For it is not worthy the name of religion, that hath
not the freedom of the judgment, and the confent
of the mind and will.   And therefore we read, *my
fon, give me thy heart,* Prov. xxiii. 26. And, *thou
fhalt love the Lord thy God, with all thy heart, and foul,
and ftrength,* Matth. xxii. 37. And this hath God
enabled us to bring to him ; it is but the ufe of his
own talent ; for he hath given us this great priviledge ; and 'tis by the direction of one faculty, and
by the ufe of another, that we determine ourfelves
finally to God, that we do attain the utmoft iffue
and improvement. But to prevent a miftake ; though
it hold a proportion, yet not of merit, or defert.
But then,

2. Again, when I fay, the ftate of man in the
world to come, holds a proportion to his affairs in
this world ; you muft not underftand it means
worldly circumftances of wealth, honour, or pleafure;
ftrength, or worldly priviledges. For thefe are not
confiderable in that ftate, nor will thefe be exiftent
in the future ftate, nor will they be to meafure by;
for all thefe things pafs away, and vanifh in time ;
neither are thofe in conjunction with virtue and
goodnefs ; nor are they acquifitions for which we
are commendable.   I remember, there is an excellent difcourfe of *Ariftotle's,* Arift. Rhet. l. 1. c. 9.
to fhew upon what account men are commendable,
and he refolves, not for any thing that is not of a
man's own acquifition ; nor for their excellent
make, power, and faculties ; not for the fagacity
of their underftandings ; but for the improvement
of

if their feveral powers and faculties. This, you know, is fulfome and naufeous, for any one to be heard to commend himfelf, efpecially for thofe things that are not his own acquifition. A man may fay, I thank God, I have a healthy body, and a good eftate, and the like ; but thefe things do not make us valuable : but we are commendable only from thofe things which we do acquire. And if a man is not praife-worthy for thefe things, they cannot be the ground of his future welfare, which are the foundation of his prefent commendation, Therefore in the *affirmative*.

Two things there are belonging to men in this ftate, which are the meafures of our happinefs in the future ftate. (1.) The *internal difpofition*, and mental temper. And (2.) The *elicit acts*, which follow the temper, and are connatural to it ; thefe are our acquifitions, through the grace and affiftance of God ; which always is to be *underftood* as principal to all good, though it be not always exprefled ; for all good is of God : therefore the meafure of proportion, is the *internal difpofition* and temper, and the *elicit acts* that follow thereupon, and are connatural thereunto : therefore from what kind of *temper* and fpirit a man is of here, and from what he *doth*, a man may guefs how it fhall be with him hereafter. If we are partakers of the grace of God, we fhall be reconciled to the nature, mind, and will of God ; and hereby we pafs into another fpirit, that is, we have the fame fenfe and judgment of things that God hath, and the fame motion and tendency : men do fhew their fpirits by their words, and

and by their actions ; by their carriage and behaviour ; for we use to say, when men misbehave
themselves, that *they shew their spirits*. And the like
may be said of men when they do well.   So that
I lay the measure of proportion, in the *frame and
temper* of mens minds, and in the *elicit acts* of their
souls ; and these cannot be hindred by the devil, or
by the world ; for against Satan and all the world, I
have the immediate acts of my mind, that which
is my internal act, that which I affect, that which
I choose and refuse. I confess the *imperate acts* may
be subject to divers impediments ; a man may be
disturbed sometimes, so that these may be quite
contrary to the *elicit acts* : I mean, that which doth
immediately proceed from a man's judgment and
choice.   To these, I say, the state of men in the
world to come is proportionable.   And if men be
now partakers of the divine nature, and led by an
effectual entertainment of the gospel, into a partic-
cipation of the divine nature, and do act conform-
ably thereunto ; then in the future state they shall
adjoin themselves with the angels of glory and the
saints departed, to employ themselves to eternity,
in acts of acknowledgment of God, in adoration
and admiration of him, in loving him, and taking
pleasure in him : and for this I will give you an account that it must be so.

1. From the *nature of the thing* : for *goodness* and
happiness are the same thing materially : in nature
they are the same ; as *malignity* and *misery* are the
same, in nature too. A man that is wicked, is neither wise nor happy, nor can be so. It is said, *Rev.*
xxii.

xxii. 14. *Bleſſed are they which do his commandments,*
that they may have a right to the tree of life. Mark
the phrafe, *they have a right to the tree of life,* by being in this ſtate, by being in this temper, reconciled to the divine law.

2. From the *judgment of God,* and thoſe declarations which he hath made of himſelf in the ſcriptures ; which every where declare, that he will
render to every one according to right. *Rom.* ii. 6,
7, 8. *To them who by patient continuance in well-do-*
ing, ſeek for glory and immortality, eternal life. But to
them which do not obey the truth, but obey unrighteouf-
neſs, indignation and wrath. So that in this caſe
God doth not uſe an arbitrary power, or do that
which is not ſuitable and agreeable to the reaſon o-
things ; but that which is fit in itſelf, and doth naturally follow, every way ſuitable and correſpond-
ent to the reaſon of things and the right of the caſe.
It is but juſt and fit that thoſe who live in an evil
ſpirit, and exerciſe themſelves in ways of wickedneſs, that *theſe* ſhould be miferable. So far are they
miſtaken, who think that men in a way of evil and
ſin, might be happy, if God pleaſed : for this cannot be ; there is a repugnancy in the caſe ; wickedneſs cannot but end in miſery. And on the o-
ther ſide, it is natural for goodneſs to bring men to
happineſs. An evil-doer, unleſs he repent, comes
not within a capacity of becoming happy ; but by
repentance, his ſtate is recoverable : but, ſaving in
this way, it is neceſſary that he ſhould periſh.　I
ſhall now make an *inference* or two.

·1. Then

1. Then let men look well to their *mental dispo-sitions*, and to their *moral actions* : *this* is of a migh-ty ufe in religion, to underftand the true notion of moral actions.   All thofe are moral actions which ought to be governed by the reafon of the mind and underftanding ; fo that you exclude acts of non-attendancy, as if a man, when he is earneft in difcourfe, fhould take up a ftraw, without any con-fideration : this were the *action of a man*, but not an *human action* : for he doth not attend to this, nor ought to do it.   But that which he doth attend un-to, and is an action of reafon and judgment, this is a moral action ; and every fuch action either is an action of virtue or fin : for if it be voluntarily com-mitted, contrary to the right of the cafe, it is down-right finful.   Or if a man be carelefs and negligent in what he doth, it may be finful, becaufe it did not proceed from the judgment and underftanding directing and governing a man's will and choice. And this we may take for granted, in divinity from all the moralifts, as well heathens, as others ; in this explication we have the confent of all the world.   For though there may be things in their kind, of an *indifferent nature*, yet, when they come to be in particular, they are either good or evil, as they proceed from the judgment and underftanding, and liberty of the will.   Only we do exclude acti-ons that are merely *natural*, and of *non-attendancy*, as concoction, diftribution, and the like : thefe are not fubject to the government of mind and under-ftanding : and therefore there is no morality, or immorality in thefe actions. Men in walking together

her, are not guilty of fin by looking backward, or
forward, being intent upon difcourfe; for that is but
by the by ; but what they fay one to another ;
what they engage in, and undertake ; how they
behave themfelves towards one another; for thefe
things they are accountable ; becaufe herein they
do well or ill. Thus having taken a liberty to make
an explication of *moral actions*, and to free it from
actions purely *natural*, and of non-attendance ; let
us therefore look well to all moral motions, becaufe
thefe are the foundation of our future condition.
For though a moral action be in itfelf tranfient, as
any other action is, yet it hath a *virtual continuance* ;
as you fee a felon, if he be taken many years after
the fact, he may be arraigned and fentenced, as
well as if he had been taken immediately upon the
act. And therefore, though the action pafs away
with time ; yet there is a continuation of it, and
will hereafter be the foundation of reward or punifhment.   The pfalmift faith of good men, they
were difperfed, they have given to the poor ; their righ-
teoufnefs endured for ever, their horn fhall be exalted
with honour, Pfal. cxii. 9. But for a *finful action,*
there is no other way to make it null, and void, but
by repentance ; and he that doth not repent, may
be faid to live in it, to ftand to and juftify it : and
being in the fame fpirit, and temper, will do the
like again, if he have opportunity. Neither can we
expect from God, that he fhould forgive any man's
fin, that joins impenitency, and contumacy to it.
Therefore it is highly advifable for us, not to do
that upon any temptation whatfoever, that will
bring

bring us to mifery if we do not repent and revoke
it. Tho' it is true indeed, the penitent may fay,
I am not the man I was ; I am not of the fame mind
and fpirit I was ; and were that to do again that *I*
have done, I would not do it for ten thoufand
worlds.

DISCOURSE XX.

The true Valuation of M A N.

L U K E xvi. 25.

*But Abraham faid, fon, remember that thou in thy life-
time receivedft thy good things, and likewife Lazarus
evil things : but now he is comforted, and thou art
tormented.*

2. WE may from what hath been faid, learn
how much they deceive themfelves who
hope to be hereafter in *another ftate for
kind,* than they are here. I acknowledge, we fhall be
all in another ftate for *degree* ; but verily, we fhall
be all in the *fame ftate for kind.* He that is *in a good
fpirit,* reconciled to God, and the rule of righteoufnefs, fhall moft fully harmonize with the nature,
mind, and will of God, and with the rule of righteoufnefs, goodnefs, and truth. But he that is in the
fpirit of the devil, and filled with malice, hatred,
rancour, and ill-will, fhall have more of the fame.

For

For you read in the *Rev.* xvi. 9. that they in misery *blafphemed God which hath power over thefe plagues.*
A man in the other ftate, will be *more of the fame,*
or the fame more intenfely. Thofe that are in happinefs, will be more fully, according to the nature,
mind, and will of God, in more perfect reconciliation with him, more perfectly fubject to his will,
and full conformity to him ; will find no difficulty
to comply with him.   For it is the *fame thing* we
call grace and holinefs here, and happinefs hereafter, when God fhall be all in all. And becaufe *this*
is a mighty truth that I have infifted upon, I will
fhew it you from divers fcriptures, which will warrant all that I have faid, *Matt.* xvi. 27. *For the Son
of man fhall come in the glory of his Father with his angels ; and then he fhall reward every man according to
his works,* Pfal. lxii. 12. *Unto thee, O Lord, belongeth mercy : for thou rendereft to every man according
to his work.* Rom. ii. 6. *Who will render to every
man according to his deeds.* To the like purpofe, you
have 1 *Pet.* i. 27. *Rev.* xx. 12. 13. *Rev.* xxii. 12.
God will bring every work into judgment, Ecclef. xii.
14. Rom. ii. 16. 2 Cor. v. 10. *Every man fhall be
judged according to that which he hath done in the body.*

From the words of the text, I fhall obferve brief-
ly two things *more.*

Firft, That *worldly profperity* is no certain forerunner of future happinefs ; for this is a thing he-
terogenial, and is from diftinct and quite other caufes. The providence of God which governs the
world, and the laws of the kingdom of Chrift, are
quite differing things. And we expect happinefs

VOL. I.   X   according

according to the laws of Chrift, and his government ; and do not proportion things of that ftate
according to the rules of common and ordinary
providence. Alfo external things do very differently affect the minds of men : no man knows what
may be the effect of worldly profperity ; for as it
is ufed, it may tend to happinefs or mifery. Therefore, let us value things equally. True indeed,
worldly profperity hath an advantage, becaufe he
that is rich, hath great opportunities of doing good,
and tools to work with, if God give him an heart ;
but if he have not an heart to improve this advantage, he is not led into a divine fpirit by it.   And
he that is in a ftate of adverfity, and expofed to neceffity, he is fubject to be envious, bafe, and fordid.
But if adverfity and a ftraitned condition in the world
make a man humble and modeft, his poverty will
tend much to his advantage.   So that you fee both
of the one and the other, the operation is very uncertain ; and therefore,

1. Let no man make himfelf a flave to that,
which is no part of his happinefs.   Let a man ufe
moderate care for the things of this life, and be a
good hufband ; but not make himfelf a flave, and a
drudge to acquire them.

2. Let him take his chief care about *that* which
is in certain conjunction with *happinefs*, and that is
the noble generous temper of his foul, and the elicit acts of his mind.

Secondly, We fee from hence, that men change
terms, circumftances and conditions, one with another in the world to come.   Here we have a *rich*
man,

man, one that had plenty of all things in this world, comes to be miferably tormented ; and a *poor La-zarus* that was very neceflitous, he comes to be comforted.   For an account of this,

1. Things many times are *wrong here* ; but they will not be wrong *always.* . Things though force be upon them, are in fome inclination to return to a right ftate again. Now this is right, that it fhould be well with thofe that are good ; and that they which are evil fhould fuffer evil.   And things will never be at reft, till it comes to be fo ; for like will have like ; light will have light, and darknefs meet with darknefs. Thofe that do evil, will fuffer evil ; and thofe that do good, fhall be happy.

2. The prefent work is to exercife virtue ; this is a *probation-ftate* ; a ftate of trial ; and if fo, there muft be freedom and liberty of action. And there-fore things are to be permitted to go on in confufi-on ; and men are to find fome follicitations from the things of this world, contrary to the true incli-nation of virtuous fouls. It is fit that virtue fhould be expofed to fome difficulty, for this is a probation ftate.

3. The final refolution, and laft ftating of things is referved to another time, when no corrupt judge fhall fit ; but he fhall come that fhall judge the world in righteoufnefs.

The *ufe* I will make of this, is,

1. Therefore, do *not envy* any one's condition; it is not fafe though glory attend upon it for a while, *Pfal.* xxxvii. 1, 2. *Fret not thyfelf becaufe of evil do-ers, neither be thou envious againft the workers of ini-*

quity :

quity : for they shall soon be cut down like the grass, and wither as the green herb.

2. Satisfy thyself in thine *own condition,* if it be good and virtuous ; for then it is safe.   Thou art built upon a solid and lasting foundation ; and that which will be final in thy state, will compensate for any trouble thou mayst meet withal in this life.

3. Have a right notion and judgment of the *bu-siness of time,* which is to prepare for the future state in.   Time hath its order and reference to eternity, and is of no value in itself, but of the greatest value in respect of the future. *The improvement of a little time, may be of gain to all eternity ; and the loss of a little time may be the greatest loss in the world.* There-fore let us consider, what the improvement of time is.   Look upon the world as a *stage* whereon man is at liberty to act ; and what he doth now, will be of account hereafter.   They that are *in a divine spirit,* and have no guilt upon their consciences (through any evil voluntarily committed) they are free from internal trouble and torment, and from that inward vexation that men of evil minds and guilty consciences suffer, even in this world.   I do verily believe, that many a man that is tempted to envy men of great estates, if they were but sensible of the internal acts of their guilt, they would not change conditions with them.   Let us have true sentiments in ourselves, for this is a solid ground of contentment to our minds, without which there is no happiness.   For if we have not quietness in our minds, we cannot be happy.   There is no happiness

nefs or peace but between the temper of our minds
and the reafon of things, and our compliance there-
with, and with the everlafting law of righteoufnefs, goodnefs, and truth.

I will *conclude* this difcourfe, with thefe four inferences. Since it appears that there is *lefs* of man
in this world ; and that his future ftate in the world
to come, holds *proportion* to what is moft himfelf,
the temper of his fpirit, and the courfe of his life,
in this world.

1. Then it is *folly* and madnefs for men (as frequently they do) to eftimate or confider themfelves
wholly, or *chiefly* by their affairs in this world, and
by the good things thereof, fuch as are power, riches, pleafures.

This is juft the cafe propofed, *Prov.* xvii. 16.
A price in the hand of a fool, and no heart to it. And
the fatal mifcarriage, reprefented, *Luke* xii. 20. A
fool over-provided for this world, and unprovided
for the other, and his foul required hence on the
fudden.

This plainly, is *to fet our eyes on that which is not.*
Prov. xxiii. 5. For *riches make themfelves wings and*
fly away. And all worldly elements perifh in their
ufing, *Col.* ii. 22. And not only things themfelves,
but all thoughts about them, occafioned by them,
perifh in a breath, *Pfal.* cxlvi. 4. vanifh with the
owner's breath.

All thefe things are fo much *without us*, and fo
fubjeft to the power of this vain and uncertain
world, that they do not *make* us when they come,
nor *mend* us while they ftay, nor *undo* us when they
are taken away.   X 3   They

They are chiefly an exercise and proof of virtue to us, as of moderation, and reference to God's will in the *getting* of them ; of fobriety and charity in the *uſe* of them ; and of patience, and acquieſcence in the divine providence, in the *loſs* of them.

That which is in value and worth far beyond them, and which ſhould be ſo in our eſteem, is the reſolution of our minds concerning them ; the compoſure, and eſtabliſhed government of our ſpirits, a moderate indifferency as to the concernments of the world, and a ſubmiſſive contentment in whatſoever the divine diſpenſation allots, *Phil.* iv. 11, 12, 13.

'Twas judgment and noblenefs of ſpirit in the apoſtle, 1 *Cor.* vi. 12. *All things are lawful to me, but all things are not expedient. I will not be brought under the power of any thing,* &c. No worldly ſovereignty or authority ſhall be over my mind.

'Tis worthineſs of ſpirit to ſtand thus reſolved : *Be the world what it will ; let the things thereof, go or come, I will be my ſelf*; not diſturbed, not diſcompoſed, not at a loſs in reſpect of ſettlement and ſelf-enjoyment.

2. Then it is the great concernment of our ſouls, not at all to admit of any temptation or ſuggeſtion, to do any thing in this life, to the *prejudice* of our ſtate in eternity.

We are ſo wiſe and conſiderate in our worldly affairs, that we will not ſell an eſtate in reverſion, (which brings in no preſent profit, nor is ours in poſſeſſion for the time being) but at a reaſonable and valuable rate : which argues, that if we had
faith

faith of things future, and were refolved in our minds of the reality and certainty of them, we would do in *fpirituals*, proportionably to what we do in *temporals*.

This is the great point of wifdom, and fhould be the over-ruling principle of life, to fubordinate all to the end, to ferve the intereft of our fouls in eternity, of all affairs and tranfactions of time. For what exchange for the foul loft ? *Matt.* xvi. 26. And the redemption of the foul ceafeth for ever, *Pfal.* xlix. 8.

It were incredible, but that we have too great experience of it done ; that men fhould frequently force themfelves, abufe their fpirits, confound judgment of good and evil, lay wafte their confciences by departure from the modefty of human nature, and the holy rule of life, in anfwer to every call, to gratify humour, comply with fancy, fatisfy luft, to live (as licentious perfons phrafe it) *freely in the world* ; whereas there is fo great confequence of all moral motion ; and alfo men, by the ufe of themfelves, frame themfelves into a conftitution and fpirit and by their prefent determination, affectation and choice, lay foundation of a ftate to continue in another world, not confidering that an habitual difpofition is a *fettlement* not eafily altered, a fortification not fo foon demolifhed, a poffeffion of tedious and difficult recovery by way of ejectment ; which when it is done, a long courfe muft be run, of law and reafon. *Matt.* i. 2, 29. Strength, armed in poffeffion, maintains itfelf againft oppofition and attempt, and commands all within doors into obedience. Nor

is

is it eafy to fet on foot contrary practice. In fuch a cafe, when men by bias and inclination are contrary bent, and confirmed by ufe, and cuftom ; againft which a refuge of lies, (tho' too many betake themfelves to it) fudden remorfe of confcience, not ingenuoufly wrought, but enforced by the pain of a difeafe and ficknefs, a colourable repentance on a death-bed, when the pleafures of fin can be no longer purfued, may feem too weak, and not leifurely enough to prevail.

This indeed men reckon upon, to *compenfate* for their ill fpirits and lives, but it hath little fatisfaction of reafon in it ; and indeed, men in love with fin, do but dally in point of amendment, are not deliberate or ferious, and fo lay ftrefs fondly.

3. Then it is fairly knowable in *this ftate,* and by fomething thereof as a foregoing participation or fign, what our ftate and condition, for fort and kind, *will be* in the world to come.

For in this world, God doth erect a ftage, bring creatures thereon, prepare materials, lay a foundation : hereafter he will not fall on a new creation, and abolifh this ; nor do altogether a new thing in kind, when he removes his great and large family into the other world ; but will do the work of another day upon, and concerning the former fubject.

We will take the reprefentation of his work from fcripture. *He will gather his wheat into his garner, and burn up the chaff with unquenchable fire,* Matt. iii. 12. which in the fulnefs of it, is done in the upfhot of his kingdom ; however in degree, it may begin before.　　　　　　　　　　　　He

' He will fort the *good feed* and the *tares* which grew in his field, by his permiffion, and patience till harveft; receiving his grain into his barn and remitting the tares to be burnt, *Matt.* xiii. 30.

He will take cognizance of his *guefts*, rejecting thofe who truft themfelves in, not having a wedding garment; entertaining thofe that are fitted, and fuitably clothed: *Matt.* xxii. 13, 4.

He will admit the *wife virgins* with their trimmed lamps; and fhut the door againft the *foolifh*, then found unprovided, and to feek, as we have it, *Matt.* xxv. 10, 12.

He will reckon with the *truftees* of his talents, and receive *good and faithful fervants to the joy of their Lord*, but caft the *unprofitable into utter* darknefs, *Matt.* xxv. 23, 30.

He will make difference, by *everlafting punifhment and eternal life*, upon the account of neglect, and fervice, *Matt.* xxv. 46.

In all which *variety* of reprefentations, we have an uniform relation both of ground and proportion : which doth fettle, and afcertain the reference of time to eternity, and of the ftate of the one refpectively to the other. For we may obferve, that he ftill goes upon what was *before*, and according to the difference of the fubject. Which alfo in fcripture not clothed with allegory, is clearly declared. 2 *Cor.* v. 10. *We muft all appear before the judgment feat of Chrift, that every one may receive the things done in his body, according to what he hath done, whether good, or bad*, 2 Theff. i. 8. *The Lord Jefus fhall be revealed from heaven, with his mighty angels, in*
flaming

flaming fire ; *taking vengeance on them that know not
God, and that obey not the gospel of our Lord Jesus.
Christ, who shall be punished with everlasting destruction from the presence of the Lord, and from the glory
of his power* ; *when he shall come to be glorified in his
saints, and to be admired in all them that believe.* And
this to do, is said to be a *righteous thing* on God's
part, and a worthy and fitting thing to be done on
man's part, *v.* 5, 6, 11. For the state of the subject
the reason of the things, ground and proportion are
indifferently observed.   Which being so, we may
have a *fore-sight* of things future, from what we
now are, and feel ; whereas, of things perfectly new
and never before, or altogether arbitrary and subject to will, there can be no fore-knowledge arising
from ought of the things themselves.

. 4. Then let us have *faith and patience* to go
through the world withal ; for the day draws on
apace, for the stating and rectifying of things ; the
proportioning of recompence and reward to action,
and the compleating and consummating what is
weak and imperfect for the present.

He is unreasonably impatient, and hasty, who
will not stay and expect the season of the year, and
what that brings ; but mutters and complains of
injury, and hard measures, because he cannot have
harvest in seed-time.

Tho' an inheritance fall to a person not at years,
or a parent will by benevolence to his child, ante-
vert his own decease, and preposterously make him
heir *per voluntatem* before-hand, who is to be *per
naturam* in succession (as *Charles* the V. king of *Spain*
and

and the *Netherlands*, diftinguifh'd in his fpeech to his fon *Philip*, when he furrendered his kingdoms to him, having before furrendered his empire of *Germany* to his brother *Ferdinand*) yet the general law which in common looks at particulars, and only aims at minors advantage and fecurity, admits not an undoubted heir at law, the power, or liberty of difpofe in his incomplete ftate, left thro' immaturity, or inexperience, he confent to what after wifdom would choofe to have otherwife. Neither is this *remora*, or detention efteemed matter of tyranny, or a grievance, but meets with equal compliance, being a provifion of fecurity.

Scriptures and experience of ages fhew us, that *ingentia dei opera magnam patiuntur moram.* God takes a large compafs to bring about his great works. Shall not we acknowledge God's priviledge, and yield to his pleafure, by being content to ftay till the time appointed of our heavenly father, *Gal.* iv. 2.

He deals very unequally with God, from whofe goodnefs and bounty we expect all things of faith and hope, for matter and fubftance; who will not permit to his liberty, circumftances of time and place. We are wont to fay, to perfons who gratify us, *take your own time* : and we ftay with patience, and receive with kind acceptance.

I doubt not, but as God in the world of nature, hath *fitted one thing to another,* as the wife man obferves, *Eæl.* vii. 14. whereby vanity, deformity and ineptitude to the end are excluded, which might extend to the maker's reproach, as failing in skill, or goodnefs; fo will he alfo in the *intellectual world*
of

of souls and spirits, finally *proportion* capacities and states (for the other world will be admirable for congruities) and fit moral actions and dispositions with recompence and reward, that no challenge may befal his superintendency, and government.

DISCOURSE XXI.

The Necessary REPENTANCE of a SINNER.

ISAIH i. 16.

Wash ye, make ye clean, put away the evil of your doings, &c.

TWo things are necessarily to be acknowledged and supposed to encourage motion in religion, endeavours after piety, and application to God.

First, To know and be assured, that God will not be wanting to afford the assistance of his grace and spirit.

Secondly, That by this assistance of God's grace and spirit, we are enabled to do our duty. That God doth afford his aid and assistance ; and that by this we are enabled to do our duty, and that which God requires of us ; these two things are necessary for us to believe and understand, to
strengthen

strengthen our hands in our work, and so encourage us in good endeavour, and to make application to God, or else we shall fall into one of these two inconveniencies.

First, We shall be ready to say or think, that God doth *reproach* us when he doth seem to exhort us, and that he doth as it were but mock at us, in our misery and necessity, when he speaks most kindly to us ; than which, nothing is more unworthy the divine goodness. This is to do something like that which St. *James* doth reprove, *James* ii. 16. for one to say to a brother or a sister, that is naked and destitute of food, *be ye warmed and filled,* but gives them not those things that are necessary for the body. Now I ask, can we think that God will do that himself, which he finds fault with in others ? Is there not quite another representation made of God, *Psal.* ciii. 13. That God pities them that fear him, as a father doth his children : because that he knoweth their frame, and remembers that they are but flesh.

By which the prophet would teach us, that God doth make allowance for our advantage, and that he is full of compassion, and that it is far from him to make a shew of that, which he doth not mean ; this being a thing so horrid, that no person among us of any fairness, candour, or ingenuity, is guilty of ; and when any one is found out, to speak that which he did not mean, and intend to perform ; he is the more disrelished and avoided. Or else,

Secondly, That the exhortations that are in scripture are to *no purpose,* and shall take no effect ;

all

all which doth ill reflect upon God, and mifreprefents him to his creatures, and difcourages our application to him, and is apt to take us off from following after God, and laying hold of him, as the
phrafe is, *Prov.* iii. 18. of wifdom, *lay hold of her,
let her not go, for fhe is thy life.* Should we believe a-
ny thing of this nature, concerning God, it would
be fo great a difcouragement, that we fhould let all
alone, and not think ourfelves greatly concerned to
act in a way of religion.

For I remember the great *philofopher* hath obferved, * That no man, in point of wifdom, tho' he be
concerned never fo much, will take into confideration things that are impoffible.

There are two things which no wife man doth
fubmit to his own care or thought, and they are
neceffaries, and *impoffibles.* For things *neceffary,* he
needs not charge himfelf with them ; for they will
be done of courfe ; and for things *impoffible,* it is a
vain thing for him to undertake ; for they cannot
be done by him, or any power whatfoever. Wherefore we are not to conceive ourfelves to be in the
ftate of impoffibility ; therefore we muft fuppofe,
that God is with us by his grace and affiftance ;
and while God is with us, that we are able to do
thofe things that he requires of us, *to wafh and make
us clean, and to put away the evil of our doings.*
Which words are to be confidered,

Firft, According to their *form.*

* Arift. Rhet. l. 1. c. 4.

Secondly,

Secondly, According to their *matter.*

1. According to their *form,* they are an *exhortation;* and so for that purpose, I have made choice of them to set on a former argument : it having been made appear, that God is not wanting in necessaries, nor doth forsake till he be forsaken, and that it is not in vain, that we are exhorted to our duty.

2. As the words may be considered in respect of the *matter,* they afford these two observations.

First, That *sin* is, in itself, a thing of defilement and pollution.

Secondly, That *religion* is a motion of restoration, or this is religious motion, *to wash and make us clean, and to put away the evil of our doings.*

But that which I shall insist upon, is to consider these words as an *exhortation* made by an instrument of God, one that God did assume, own, and stand by ; and therefore we may imagine that God was present with this exhortation, and that those who were thus exhorted, not only ought, but *might* do something in answer to this exhortation : for no intelligent agent acting in a way of wisdom, as the all-wise God always doth, would call any one to that which he knew was not in his power to do : and therefore we must not attribute any such thing to the all-wise God. No man of wisdom and understanding, does either himself attempt, or call upon others to do that, which neither he, nor they are able to do.

We do therefore conclude, that when God calls upon persons to do any thing, he doth afford necessary

fary affiſtance, by which they are enabled to obey
and do the thing he commands. In *Ezek. chap.*
xxxvii. we find God to ask this queſtion of the prophet, *can theſe dry bones live ?* the prophet gives a
wiſe anſwer, *O God thou knoweſt*, intimating that by
the power of nature it could not be done ; but if
God would make uſe of his power (as we. read he
did) then it was poſſible ; for he calls to the wind
to blow and bring bone to his bone, and cauſed fleſh
and ſinews to cover them ; by which means, he
cauſed dead and dry bones to live.   In common
philoſophy we determine, that ſome things cannot
be done, but then we confine it to the power of
nature : but by the power of God, things that are
impoſſible to be done by the power of nature, may
be done.   The like inſtance is of *Lazarus*, he was
dead, and had been dead for ſome time ; yet our
Saviour calls to *Lazarus*, and bids him *come forth,*
John xi. 43. Now as I before hinted to you, the
way of motion in intellectual nature, is different
from the way of motion in inferior nature : In intellectual nature, the way of motion is to propoſe,
declare and ſhew, to excite by reaſon and argument,
to warn, to admoniſh, to foretell, to convince, to
promiſe, to threaten, to reward, to puniſh, to en-
lighten the underſtanding, to move the will, to affect the conſcience, and the like.   Theſe are the
ways of motion in intellectual nature ; now, he
who by his voice doth rend the rocks, and make
mountains to quake and tremble : he doth alſo,
when he pleaſeth, melt and break the ſtony heart ;
but then it is in *this* way, as it is remarkable what

we

we read, *Gen.* ix. 27. God perfuaded *Japhet to dwell in the tents of Shem.* And it is paffion in a way of perfection, thus to receive from God ; or, as we call it, to *suffer under divine motion* : and it is con-fervative of our liberty and freedom, and moft na-tural for a creature, that is made intelligent and voluntary, thus to admit the creator's touch. Eve-ry creature according to its nature, is affected, mo-ved, and fuffers under God. Now intellectual na-ture is moved in this way, in a way of illumination, perfuafion, mental conviction and fatisfaction ; for this you muft know and underftand, that intellectu-al nature, remaining fuch, cannot be divefted of in-telligence and freedom ; for thofe are its neceffary and effential perfections, and a man ceafeth to be a man, if divefted of *thefe*, and turned out of intel-lectual nature ; he ceafeth to be a man. But as long as he is a man, he cannot be without the neceffary perfections of human nature intelligence and liberty.

That which may be faid in this cafe is, that ill habits do ftrangely byafs, and incline our faculties : but tho' they do this, yet they do not abfolutely determine our faculties, or fink them : for thefe fa-culties are of the effence of our fouls. I confefs 'tis with much difficulty, they are to be overcome ; for the prophet *Jeremiah* faith, that they which are *ac-cuftomed to do evil can no more do well*, than the *black-moor can change his skin, or the leopard his fpots*, Jer. xiii. 2, 3. which reprefents the difficuty to be even morally impoffible, and not to be done without great difficulty ; but yet no habit doth abfolutely deter-mine any faculty ; but the faculty is free notwith-

ftan-

ftanding any habit acquired, or never fo long in
poffeffion : otherwife it were impoffible ever to recover any habitual finner, which, thanks be to God
through his grace, proves fometimes otherwife. And
of this we have many inftances in fcripture, of perfons that have been fhot into the world, and in very hazardous employments, as *fitting at the receipt
of cuftom*, who were odious to the *Jews* becaufe of
their very employment, perfons ranked with finners;
yet upon our Saviour's call, they left all and followed him : you have alfo an account by the divine
author to the *Hebrews*, of *Abraham*, Heb. xi. 8. That
he did leave his country and all his friends, and acquaintance and worldly intereft, and obeyed the heavenly call, *not knowing whither he went :* there is fuch
an impreffion on the mind of man, but in a way
fuitable to intellectual nature, that doth carry them
on as effectually, as the feveral creatures by an impreffion made upon them, gathered themfelves to
Noah into the ark, *Gen.* vii. 7. &c.

But now I fhall proceed to give you an account
of three things; only let me put you in mind of the
faying of an eminent perfon, and it is this, That *it
is better to have no opinion of God, than to have an unworthy opinion of him* * for if you have no opinion of
him, it is fimple unbelief, but if you have an unworthy opinion of him, it is to ufe him with con-
tumely and difhonour. When God calls upon men to
repent and turn *to him*, and thereby declares himfelf
favourable, and that he will admit men to his favour and grace; not only that they fhall meet with
entertainment

* Plutarch de fuperftitione.

entertainment if they do come, but alſo that he will afford ſuch grace and aſſiſtance that they may come. To think that God means otherwiſe than he expreſſes himſelf, is to think worſe of God, than any good-natured and ſober perſon would be thought of, or doth deſerve. Therefore if we are called upon by God, *to waſh and make ourſelves clean,* theſe words do import, that God is in readineſs, and will contribute neceſſary aſſiſtance, and thro' his grace and aſſiſtance we may do that which he requires of us.

And that I may fully ſtate this matter, I will do it in theſe *three* particulars.

Firſt, I will ſhew, that God doth primarily deſire the *good* of all his creatures.

Secondly, That he doth not deſire man's ſalvation without his *return.*

Thirdly, That he doth not deſire man's return, without his own *conſent.*

Firſt, God doth primarily *deſire* the *good* of all his creatures; elſe I pray you what can you make of theſe ſcriptures, that God *would have all men to be ſaved and to come to the knowledge of the truth,* 1 Tim. ii. 4. He ſaith, *what would I have done more for my vineyard that I have not done:* Iſa. v. 4. Can he ſay this, who doth not that which is neceſſary and requiſite on his part: *Why will ye die,* ſaith God to the houſe of *Iſrael:* Ezek. xviii. 31. The anſwer were eaſy, if God were wanting in neceſſaries to his creatures; can he be ſaid in good earneſt to deſire any thing, that doth nothing of that which is within his power to effect it.

When

When God faith that *thy deſtruction is of thy ſelf :* Hoſ. xiii. 9. If ſome doctrines be true, may not it be ſaid, *no, it is of thee,* becauſe I am under an abſolute neceſſity of being deſtroyed ? The *wiſe man* faith, That *God hateth nothing that he hath made* ; Wiſd. xi. 14. but his love is very little, if he doth nothing to ſecure his creation. To what purpoſe is that exhortation of our Saviour, *Matth.* xi. 28. *Come unto me, all ye that are weary and heavy-laden, and I will give you reſt,* if men cannot come unto him ? And alſo blame is laid upon men that *they would not come unto him, that they might have life,* John. v. 40. Could not they which were ſo perverſe, if they had imagined ſuch a thing as this, of God's being wanting to his creatures in neceſſaries, eaſily have retorted theſe words upon our Saviour ? *Prov.* i. 31. It is ſaid, *I called, but ye refuſed to come ; I cried, but ye gave me no anſwer.* But further let us conſider the *means* that God has provided for our recovery. The ſcripture expreſly faith, that Chriſt *taſted death for all men,* Heb. ii. 9. and declares that he is a *propitiation, not only for our ſins, but for the ſins of the whole world,* John. ii. 2.

Nothing more certain, than that God had no hand in making any of thoſe three things, in reſpect of which we are liable and in danger to eternity, to wit, *ſin, death* and *hell.* And this hath been acknowledged, as you read, *God made not death,* Wiſd. i. 13. And in another place, *God made not hell.* Theſe are not of God's product, they are not things of God's intention, they are not things that God decreed, deſigned, or contrived. He never laid
the

the foundation of any of thefe; but they are confequent upon degeneracy, defection and apoftacy;
as it is exprefs'd, *the backflider in heart fhall be filled
with his own ways;* Prov. xiv. 14. He fhall reap
the fruit of his own doings. But here I muft anfwer
an *objection*, and it is this:

If God were fo well-minded toward men, and fo
much defired their good and welfare, why did he
not prevent fin, and make. it impoffible that ever fin
fhould enter into the world; fince he hath wifdom
enough, and power enough. to prevent it.? To this I
will reply three things.

Firft, Can we blame God, that he doth not pervert the order of *fecond caufes*? Is this a failure in
God, that he fuffers fecond caufes to act that which
is proper to them? If God doth make a voluntary
and intelligent agent, it doth neceffarily follow, unlefs he fruftrate his own workmanfhip, that he
muft fuffer a voluntary agent to act according to his
own will.

If this do not fatisfy, I add in the *fecond* place;
can we blame God, that he did appoint a *probation-
ftate*, which could not have been, unlefs man had
been left free and voluntary; efpecially confidering
that in this probation-ftate, God was not wanting
in thofe things. that were requifite and fit for this
creature, that was put in a ftate of probation and
trial, preparation and exercife: and if this will not
fatisfy; I fhall add a

Third, And that will put all out of doubt; and
that is this; that all thofe things confidered, which
are the provifion of God; man (to fay no more) is

more

more fufficient to his effect, and the purpofes of his
creation, than any other creature whatfoever : I fay,
confidering the *provifion* of God, and the accomplifh-
ments of man in that ftate ; man is no lefs fufficient
to his effect, than any creature to the effect of his
own nature. For, as that to which man is called
and required, is of a higher nature, than any other
creature below him ; fo alfo are his faculties and
principles higher and nobler; and there is over and
above thefe, the affiftance of grace, which is fupernatural, and more than is due to him. This is fuch
an affiftance as is able to raife a man to that which
is fupernatural, and to fit him for the ftate of glory ;
and yet you fee inferior nature is fufficient to its end
and it hath not failed, and we are confident that it
will not fail. Now, why a *man* that is invefted with
nobler principles fhould not act at a higher rate, according to thefe principles and endowments, is a
thing not to be anfwered : And that he fhould fit
ftill, and ill reflect upon God in undutifulnefs and
unthankfulnefs, is without the leaft appearance of
reafon in the world. And this is enough to vindicate the honour of our maker. But then,

Secondly, We cannot fay, that God defires any
man's falvation without his *return.* For it is repugnant and impoffible, that any man fhould be happy
in a way of obftinacy and rebellion againft God,
that fhall live in contradiction to his maker. For
can any man be happy in conjunction with his enemy, in a ftate unnatural to him, where he hath no
harmony, takes no pleafure and fatisfaction ? It
cannot

cannot be that a man should be saved, unless he return; for these terms cannot stand together, to live in opposition and contradiction to God, and yet to be reconciled to him, and to be made happy by him. If we live in sin, and take delight therein; we cannot take delight in the most righteous God. You may as soon conjoin light and darkness, *Christ* and *Belial* together. So that you cannot say, that God desires a thing which is so absurd and contrary to all reason, that any should be brought to happiness without restoration, and return to God.

Thirdly, Neither can we say, that God desires man's return without his own *consent*; for if he should desire this, he should desire that which cannot be: for being intelligent and voluntary agents, we cannot truly be said to do that, which we do against our minds. For to an human act two things are necessary; that there be the *judgment of reason* in the understanding, and the *choice of the will*. If the mind do not consent, 'tis not a free act; and if not done freely and of choice, it cannot be an act of virtue; and if not an act of virtue, it cannot be of any moral consideration. That God that doth graciously allow for all our involuntary weaknesses, imperfections, and failings, being surprised and diverted from our duty; yet he will not dispense with the want of two things; sincerity, that is honest-meaning and intention; and the act of our will; without these, he will not be satisfied nor in the least dispense; and this is called in scripture, a *perfect heart*, 1 Chron. xxviii. 9. where a man doth honestly intend and mean. My *son give me thy heart*,

Prov.

Prov. xxiii. 26. *And* if there be a *willing mind;* 2 Cor. viii. 12. *'tis accepted* of God, whether the gift be more or leſs ; yea, if there be honeſt meaning and hearty intention in the perſon ; that which is not accepted in the matter, is accepted in the perſon. Thou did'ſt well *that it was in thy heart,* to build me a houſe, 1 *Kings.* viii. 18. tho' God would not ſuffer him to build it. And when the *tabernacle* was to be built, God would not receive ought from any one but thoſe that brought it with a willing mind. *Not by conſtraint, but willingly.* Exod. xxxv. 5. *And they ſhall be a willing people in the day of my power,* Pſal. cx. 3.

But that I may give ſatisfaction to ſome good minds that are full of doubtfulneſs, becauſe at firſt they are not ſo voluntary, free and willing ; and becauſe they are fain to ſtrive much with themſelves, here I ſay, *'tis no leſs an act of the will, though a man be at the firſt attempt unwilling and averſe* ; yea though he ſuffer great difficulty to bring himſelf to it ; this is no leſs a willing act, than if he were at firſt more willing. For this man hath wrought himſelf to it by reaſon, conſideration, and argument ; and ſo his conſent is the better grounded.

Therefore, if a man do find an averſation and indiſpoſition, and he doth ſuffer difficulty by that which riſeth up againſt him ; yet if he takes pains with himſelf, and begs God's aſſiſtance, and takes his duty into conſideration, and by reaſon and argument brings himſelf to conſent ; this man is rather more willing than he that did it with more eaſe, and more ſuddenly ; for here is the more deliberate

liberate confent becaufe of the former averfenefs and
indifpofition; and therefore we may encourage ourfelves, tho' at firft we find fome averfion and indifpofition and unwillingnefs; yet if we conquer and
overcome them, it is a true act of virtue, becaufe
of thefe difficulties and incumbrances.

But that cannot be imputed to us, in which we
do not confent; for if we act againft our mind, it
is not our act; for in all human actions, it is requifite that there be the judgment of reafon in the underftanding, and the choice of the will.

But to *conclude, firft*, things of *impurity*, the holinefs of God will not fuffer him to have a hand in;
as for inftance, to make a man happy that is unho-
ly and wicked: and therefore it is neceffary in the
nature of the thing, that renovation and fanctifica-
tion go before falvation.   And,

Secondly, Things *inconfiftent*, the wifdom of God
doth engage him againft; for he that is wife, will
never engage himfelf in things that cannot be done.
Now this is inconfiftent, for a man to act againft
his will.   There are two acts of a man, the exterior, and the interior: the *exterior* act of a man,
that may be forced; but this is lefs the act of a man
than that which is *interior*, and this can never be
forced by any one whatfoever; neither do the laws
of God or man charge that upon us, which we neither will nor confent unto.   If a man fall into the
hands of thieves, who force him along with them,
and make him prefent while they commit a wicked
fact; the law will not make him a partaker, becaufe his perfon was expofed to violence. Unlefs a

man

'man hath confented, he is not obnoxious, neither in the fenfe of God's law, nor the laws of men.

The *exterior* man, is fubject to exterior force, becaufe he cannot refift a power that is too ftrong for him; but the *interior* man is free againft all the world; nothing without us can force confent. A man may diffent tho' his perfon be in durance, and tho' his tongue fhould be made to fpeak, and his hand to write, and his feet to walk. Where the exterior man is under force, both God and man hold him excufed. It is the act of the interior man that God doth reckon upon, and here he expects confent. So that you fee, God doth not defire any man's return without his *confent*; for indeed, if he do not confent, he doth not return.

God, who is an infinitely wife agent, and firft mover, he doth apply himfelf to his feveral creatures proportionably to their qualities and ftate; and as I faid, when he doth apply himfelf to an intelligent agent, the way of motion is by way of reafon, as to propofe, declare, to fhew, to excite, &c. But intelligent nature, continuing fuch, cannot be divefted of freedom and liberty; and therefore the application that muft be made to it, muft be by illumination, perfuafion, mental conviction and fatisfaction; and this is as fufficient and available to intellectual nature, as any application in any other way, can be to a natural agent : and you may as well blame an intellectual agent if it be not admonifhed, perfuaded, and fatisfied, when reafon is offered; as you may blame an inferior nature, if it fhould be wanting to its proper effect.

I

I shall now for *application*, infer two things.

First, That we ought to be *thankful* to God, and to acknowledge him, for the gracious *assistance* that he doth afford unto us : for this will be argument enough against us at the day of judgment, that we were admonished, exhorted, shewn, taught ; all which would have been in vain, if we were not able to hear God's voice, and to obey him. That is therefore the first inference, that we do duly *acknowledge God*, and be thankful unto him for the gracious assistance that he doth afford us.

The *second* is this, that we do *make use of*, and employ this divine assistance ; which is in the apostle's language, 2 *Cor.* vi. 1. *Not to receive the grace of God in vain :* And this we do, when the principle is without effect.

DISCOURSE XXII.

The EXERCISE and PROGRESS of a CHRISTIAN.

PHILIPPIANS iii. 12.

Not as though I had already attained, or were already perfect ; but I follow after, if that I may apprehend that for which also I am apprehended of Christ Jesus.

I Observe out of these words three things.
　1. Where the apostle professeth his *faith*, there
he

he teſtifieth his *humility.* In the 11 verſe he did declare his *faith* and future expectation ; *If by any means I may attain to the reſurrection of the dead.* Here he declares his humility, *not as tho' I had already attained, or were perfect,* &c.

2. Where he doth teſtify his *humility,* there he doth engage himſelf to *care and diligence.* But *I follow after, if that I may apprehend that for which alſo I am apprehended.*

3. Where he doth engage himſelf to *diligence,* there he doth take notice of the *grace of God. If that I may apprehend,* &c. And ſo you ſee that his faith of the reſurrection is accompanied with an humble ſenſe of his own ſhortneſs, and purſued with great activity, induſtry, care and diligence.

In purſuit of theſe propoſitions, I ſay theſe three things.

1 The faith of God, humility of ſpirit, and active care and diligence in the affairs of our ſalvation, are things that are united in the common root of truth and goodneſs.

2. They do *comply with each other* in their nature and diſpoſition.

3. They *mutually promote* each other in their ſeveral operations.

If you ask, what are the great things in religion ? I will refer you to three texts of ſcripture : For that which is properly chriſtian, *Put on the Lord Jeſus Chriſt :* Rom. xiii. 14. For that which is a proper creature-diſpoſition, *Be cloathed with humility,* 1 Pet. v. 5. For that which is our work and buſineſs in time, *Work out your own ſalvation with fear and*

and diligence. Phil. ii. 12. *He that puts on Chrift* muft put off himfelf; for the image and form of Chrift is felf-denial; for Chrift put himfelf in the form of a fervant, and a fervant parts with his own will. He that will be like unto Chrift, muft live in entire felf-furrender; and fo faith the apoftle, *As the elect of God, holy and beloved, put on humblenefs of mind, meeknefs, long-fuffering,* &c. Col. iii. 12. *In lowlinefs of mind let each efteem other above himfelf,* Phil. ii. 3. They that are *Pharifaically conceited,* muft be unbelievers; for do any of the *Pharifees believe on him?* John. vii. 48. For, as pride and · conceit do ill affect the fubject in which it is, fo it doth alienate from God; *For God refifteth the proud, but giveth grace to the humble,* Jam. iv. 6. There is no better preparation for faith, than humility; *for the humble he will teach,* Pfal. xxv. 9. And the humble hath fubmitted himfelf to be *a fool, that he may be wife,* 1 Cor. iii. 18. But the proud is in an indifpofition, and horrid contradiction and oppofition to faith: For this is the proud man's fenfe and language, if I may allude to the tree, *Judges* ix. 9. *Shall I leave my fatnefs?* So faith the proud man, fhall I relinquifh all confidence in the good things of nature, my excellent gifts, my parts, my acquirements, improvements, my education, employment, my feveral virtues and great endowments, and various performances, my merit whereby I do tranfcend others; and fhall I come to be beholden to any one? This was the temper of the proud *Pharifee, this people that know not the law are curfed.* John vii. 49. It doth not become fuch as

we

we are, to give up our confidence, and wholly to renounce and disclaim our selves. It is the humble, and modest, and ingenuous spirit that is the ready believer; and we have many testimonies for this, *Luke* vii. saith our Saviour, *I have not found so great faith, no not in Israel.* Of whom doth our Saviour speak this? Look the beginning of the chapter, and you shall find it of the *centurion*, whom the *Jews* reported to be worthy for whom he should do courtesy; he having done gallantly for their nation, *and built them a synagogue.* But he saith, that he was *not worthy that our Saviour should come under his roof.* Of this man it is that our Saviour saith, that *he had not found so great faith, no not in Israel.* I make this further out in two particulars.

1. They that are humble and modest, are in a due *disposition* and *fitness* of mind for the belief of divine things; for *the full soul loatheth the honey-comb*, Prov. xxvii. 7. Those that are in a disposition to come to our Saviour, are those that are *weary and heavy laden*, Matth. xi. 28.

2. These have the advantage of God's promise; for it is said, That *God will look to him that is of an humble and contrite spirit*, Isa. lvii. 15. And these are the persons that God will take care of, and instruct. *The humble he will lead in judgment, the meek he will teach his way*, Psa. xxv. 9. So that these, and these only are the children of promise. But thus much for explication.

To make some improvement of this for the *justification of religion*, as the apostle saith, *Rom.* iii. 4. *Let God be true, and every man a liar.* Let not
the

the unbelief of fome, make the faith of God of none effect : fo in this cafe, let not the mifcarriage of fome who pretend to believe, tend to the difcredit of our religion; but let us refolve that the trouble-fome, proud, and felf-conceited ; that the wilful, boifterous, and tempeftuous ftorming tempers be re-puted falfe in their profeffion. For the chriftian temper and fpirit is modeft and humble, fenfible of its own fhortnefs and imperfections, and want of growth ; and knows its own dependence upon God both for the grace of favour and acceptance, as alfo for the grace of aid and affiftance. Therefore let every one that profeffeth his faith, give proof of his *humility.* By this means we fhall difcharge religi-on from all imputation : for if any one that pro-feffeth chriftianity, be of a proud, troublefome, haughty, infolent, contentious, quarrelfome and un-quiet fpirit, let him be reputed falfe to his profef-fion ; but let religion be *juftified*; for the chriftian fpirit is modeft, humble, fenfible of its own wants and imperfections ; it is a calm mind, a gentle and benign fpirit, and fo the fcripture fpeaks of it ; *A good converfation with meeknefs of wifdom.* Jam. iii. 13. and *ver.* 17. *The wifdom that is from above, is pure and peaceable, gentle, eafy to be entreated, full of righteoufnefs and good fruits. The fruit of the fpirit is love, joy, peace, long-fuffering, gentlenefs, goodnefs, meeknefs,* &c. Gal. v. 22. *With all lowlinefs and meeknefs, with long-fuffering, forbearing one another in love.* Eph. iv. 2. I do wonder how any man that profeffeth himfelf a chriftian, can read thefe plain texts offcripture, and maintain himfelfin felf-will, felf-
conceit,

conceit, or gratify his own humour, imagination and fancy, prefer himſelf before his brethren, be boiſterous, tempeſtuous and troubleſome in the place where he lives. For either this man, notwith-ſtanding his profeſſion, is not a chriſtian; or elſe theſe perſons were miſtaken that put theſe charac-ters down in holy ſcripture. No certainly, we are not to allow and eſteem him a chriſtian, that is haughty, arrogant and ſelf-conceited; for no princi-ple in the world lays ſuch ground of modeſty and ſo-berneſs of ſpirit and temper, as the chriſtian religion doth. And nothing is more unnatural to the true ſpirit of religion, than a proud and haughty mind; for this of all things is moſt ſcandalous to it. 'Tis eaſier a great deal to bear the ſcorn and contempt of the irreligious, than the inſolency, forwardneſs, and ſelf-conceitedneſs of ſelf-flattering profeſſors.

We may, and ought to prefer the modeſt, gentle, calm ſpirit, that we find in ſome ſtill and quiet be-lievers, before the arrogant, cenſorious, ſelf-aſſum-er; and have reaſon to believe, that there is more of God and of the chriſtian profeſſion in the modeſt ſtill, quiet ſpirit, who makes no noiſe in the world, who are rather to God than to men; and that they are more noble-ſpirited, and better chriſtians, than the other. I will give you a demonſtration of this, becauſe that temper I have been ſpeaking againſt, is that which brings a reproach upon chri-ſtianity. Profeſſors of religion are thought to be troubleſome to the world, and incendiaries; and where men are proud, arrogant, and ſelfiſh, and al-low themſelves in ſelf-will, they are ſo indeed:

but

but thefe are not in the higheft form of chriftianity. For divine truth, fublime reafon, and tried notions of things, are to be found as the comely ornament of an humble fpirit, and in fouls fubdued to God. *Thefe,* and thefe only, have a right fenfe of things, and are capable rightly to eftimate and judge. A generous notion will not lodge in a haughty, prefumptuous breaft : for thefe are not cool enough for wifdom to enter into their fouls ; for wifdom is the fruit of deep fearch, and ferious confideration ; and *he that knows moft, thinks he has moft ftill to learn.* They are the empty veffels that make the greateft noife. We need no other difcovery of conceitednefs than its own expreffion and behaviour ; they are always talkative, cenforious, dictating, impofing, felf-admirers. But he that is fincere in religion, can fearch and difcover them : juft as one that is a mafter of his art or fcience, can detect a pretender, difcover a bungler, and fhew his cheats : there is alfo a naufeoufnefs and fulfomnefs in the converfe with thofe that are conceited, and full of themfelves ; they being felf-flatterers, and great admirers of themfelves, and highly in love with the fpurious iffue of their own brain ; and tho' their notions are imaginary and fantaftical, and truly ridiculous to any one that is of any difcerning fpirit, yet they are importune and troublefome : whereas he that fpeaks truth in the evidence of reafon, he commands every ear ; for man's foul is a-kin to truth, and whatfoever truth doth appear, a man's foul doth greet it as its firft and neareft acquaintance. But if it be the prefumption of a conceited brain, it cannot be received ; and therefore those persons must be importune and troublesome to fasten their notions upon unwilling receivers. Take it for granted, no wise man is fond of any notion, nor given up to any persuasion, so as not willingly to hear of any thing to the contrary.   And really, it doth not become any of us to be fond of any notion that we have received, or to be under the power of any persuasion, so as not to be willing to submit it to examination, and to offer it to severe and impartial search ; for we are all finite and fallible, and we ought to think we are short and may be mistaken ; and if I receive that for truth, which is not so, I am deceived, and brought into a fool's paradise, and can lay no stress upon it ; or if I do, it will fail me.   But all truth is connatural, and of some use and advantage to the soul of man ; but if it be a lie, and false, which I took for truth though I may be saved by the substantial truths that otherwise I received ; yet so far forth as I am mistaken so far forth shall I be frustrated, and never the better. Just as in the case of which the apostle speaks, 1 *Cor.* iii. 12. They that build upon the foundation, *wood, hay, stubble,* &c. *may be saved,* because upon the foundation ; but their works shall suffer loss. But why should I not have my understanding be a receptacle for truth ? Why should I have any thing that is false there, when I shall never be the better for it ? The most I can expect is, that God will excuse me, because I am honest-minded.   But it becomes me, if I will do honour to God, and right to my own soul, impartially to examine whatsoever I receive as true in matters of

religion ;

religion ; and to commit it to ferious and impartial
judgment : And I leave it with you, That no wife
man, nor truly good man is fond of any opinion,
or addicts himfelf to any perfuafion, but hath this
in the refolution of his mind, that if any opinion be
made known to him to be a miftake, he will leave
it ; and this is inherent to all thofe that are of fober, modeft, meek, and gentle fpirits. But thofe
that are haughty and arrogant think too fondly
of themfelves, and believe that every body ought to
receive their dictates from them : they are indeed
too full of themfelves, ever to be wife ; they think
they have attained, and fo are beyond the apoftle,
who when he had profefs'd his faith of the refurrection, faith, *not that I have already attained, not that I am
already perfect, not that I have already apprehended.*

I know there is a great allowance to be given to
men's fuppofitions : that which a man hath long
thought, and imagined, and hath been brought up
in, and often put in his prayers, and often propofed to
others ; it is a hard matter for him to call this into
queftion. But if we confider that we may be miftaken, being finite and fallible ; it becomes us, at
the leaft, to be enquirers after truth, and to have
an ear open after information, and to be refolved to
follow truth whenever it may appear. But on the
other hand, there is no fuch troublefome converfe
in the world, as the company of one that bolfters
himfelf up with the opinion of his religion ; but
indeed knows not himfelf. To conclude, the
right believer, is moft modeft and humble ; lefs ri-
gid, and cenforious ; lefs captious and given to take

Z 2   exception

exception ; and fo his converfe and fociety is lefs
offenfive and burdenfome. So far is true religion
from doing any harm, or making any difturbance in
the common-wealth of mankind ; for it is indeed
the *ornament of a meek and quiet fpirit, which in the
fight of God is of great price.* 1 Pet. iii. 4. And
this for the application, where our apoftle profeffeth
in a high degree his *faith* of the refurrection, and
his refolution to fubdue and fubordinate all things
thereunto; for he faith, *If by any means I may attain the refurrection of the dead,* there he doth immediately fubjoin the expreffions of his *humility*;
the deepeft fenfe he hath of his own fhortnefs and
fallibility ; *Not as if I had already attained, or were
already perfect :* not that I think I have already apprehended. How carefully doth he avoid all commendation of himfelf; how doth he decline pride
and arrogancy, how far is he from felf-conceited-
nefs and proud reflection upon himfelf, from all
haughtinefs and felf-affuming ? *Where is the moft of
God there is leaft of felf.* This is the firft. Where
he doth profefs his *faith*, there he teftifies his *humility.* Now to the *cafe itfelf, not that I have already
attained, or that I am already perfect, or that I have apprehended.* In the fpiritual ftate there is more or lefs of
ftrength, but not more or lefs of truth ; for the truth of
things confifts in an indivifible point ; either a man
hath true grace, or he hath no grace at all ; either he
hath real goodnefs, or no goodnefs at all ; either truly
in the ftate of grace or not at all in it; either he hath a
true intention, or he doth not mean at all in religion :

on : The *profane* do not come near to religion,
they do not pretend to it, but difclaim it, and in
practice renounce it; and the *hypocrite* he doth but
pretend to it; for religion is only with the *honeft-
bearted*, with him that fincerely means and intends.
Therefore the gracious and merciful God whom we
adore and worfhip, in whom we have our confidence, his goodnefs is fo great, that he will indulge
to us human infirmities, and bear with us in our
miftakes; but he is fevere and impartial concerning our honeft meaning and true intention: *He that
doth not truly mean and intend, is nothing at all in religion.* So that though in the way of goodnefs, there
may be more or lefs ftrength, yet not more or lefs
of truth: there is perfection of parts, not of degree;
there is truth of intention, tho' not fulnefs of performance, there is intention of all duty; there is a
voidance of all known evil, and care of coming to
the knowledge of the truth. Thefe things are neceffary; for God doth give an abatement for ignorance in fome things, where we have not had opportunity to know; for furprifals now and then;
for fhortnefs and frailty; for cafes of temptations,
and fudden affaults, or indifpofitions of mind: but
if here be a failure in thefe, it is expected, that at
fome diftance of time there fhould be a recovery;
and thofe failings are matter of great grief and offence, and a provocation to after-care and diligence; and therefore thefe confift with the ftate
of grace and regeneration; and God gives an
allowance and pardons us in thefe cafes; if in fome
particulars we are ignorant, when we are defirous

ous to know, but have not had opportunity to enquire ; or where there have been fudden furprizals,
violent affaults ; for being out of frame and temper, at times : But in thefe cafes 'tis expected, that at fome diftance, we recover ourfelves, blufh before God, and be afhamed for our
former diftemper, and that it be matter of grief and
difpleafure to us, and afterwards it prove an argument to us of greater care and watchfulnefs. Thefe
things are confiftent with the regenerate ftate. But
it is unnatural to this ftate, for any one to commit
a known fin deliberately, or willingly to omit a
known duty : for we muft be honeft-hearted, and
fincerely intend to pleafe God, and do that which
is acceptable in his fight : and this is that which St.
John fpeaks of, *He that is born of God doth not commit fin ; for the feed of God abideth in him.* 1 John.
iii. 9. It is indifpenfably neceffary that we be fincere, and honeftly mean, and truly intend : but in
this ftate we are fhort, and in fome particulars fail ;
in fome things we are ignorant, incogitant, and
fometimes are furprifed ; and for thefe things the
apoftle faith, *Not that I have already attained, not
that I am already perfect ; and I account not my felf to
have apprehended.* But in refpect of fincerity, ho-
neft-heartednefs, and good intention, there is no
allowance, not the leaft difpenfation for a failure in
thofe particulars. And thus I have given you an
account of the firft thing, where the apoftle expreffeth his *faith* of the refurrection, there he tefti-
fieth his *humility.*

DIS-

DISCOURSE XXIII.

The EXERCISE and PROGRESS of a CHRISTIAN.

PHILIPIANS iii. 12.

Not as though I had already attained, or were already perfect; but I follow after, if that I may apprehend that for which also I am apprehended of Christ Jesus.

I Come now to the *second*, where he doth teſtify his *humility* there he doth engage himſelf to *care* and diligence. *But I follow after, if that by any means I may apprehend that for which I am apprehended of Christ Jesus.* And indeed we have all encouragement from the divine revelation, as to faith, ſo to patient labour, and ſerious good endeavours: and this is our great concernment. The ſober modeſt believer he is not in haſte, but he *lives by faith*; and by this, he ſtays himſelf; as the prophet ſaith, *The juſt ſhall live by faith*, Hab. ii. 4. which is thus applied by the apoſtle reſolving in himſelf, That *he which ſhall come will come and will not tarry*; Heb. x. 37. and therefore he will *ſtay himſelf upon God*, and not be in haſte. And indeed, *wherever God is, there is both help and ſtrength*; ſo that he may act, and be up and doing. Wherefore, every good

man

man applies himſelf to God, and attends upon his pleaſure, waiting for his influence in a careful and diligent uſe of all means, in the purſuit of his faith. And indeed, ſuch an one doth not tempt God, either by impatience, or diſtruſt, or by the neglect of his duty. For concerning the uſe of the means, he who looks up to God, puts himſelf in a way of ſubſerviency to his agency and providence ; and he that doth not do ſo, his faith is but in co- lour, and meer pretence ; he is not ſerious in religi- on ; he does not mean, tho' for ſome end, he may profeſs : for we expect God to come in a way of bleſſing ; and therefore we ſhould think it fit and neceſſary on our part, to be found in his way ; to wit, in the uſe of means : and for any that acknow- ledge God, ſo far as to pray to him, and to beg his preſence, influence, and bleſſing and not to ſet himſelf in in a way of obedience, and to anſwer his faith by ſubſer- viency, and acting in the due uſe of ſuch means as God hath appointed ; this is not religion, but a pro- vocation of God. 'Tis a true ſaying, *God is not moved* by men that are aſleep ; with them that are lazy and ſluggiſh ; but by thoſe that are in motion : when men are upon action, God doth acknowledge them. We muſt *pray with humility and fervency* ; *believe with expectation* ; *and do with care and diligence.* This is the true chriſtian temper, and practice. He is not re- newed, or enlivened with the noble and vigorous ſpi- rit of the goſpel, who doth not thus : but is in the dull ſpirit of the world ; and as to ſpiritual things, he re- mains ſtill as a heavy clod of ſtupid earth, not ſown at all with the ſeed of God, as the apoſtle uſeth the phraſe,

1 *John*

1. *John* iii: 9. *The seed of God doth not remain in him.* For if it did, he would not sit still, nor consent to act in the contrary nature. No one can imagine, that we are endued with power from above, or that we are made *partakers of the divine nature* by a communication of God to us, and his influence upon us, but it will shew itself in generous and noble acts towards him.

But to give you an account of this I will suggest three things.

1. That these are *principles of action.* For *faith* carries us on against despair, which doth discourage action: and then *humility,* that excludes presumption, self-opinion, and conceit that it hath already attained, and that nothing remains to be done.

2. It is the *cause of action.* For while we are in the state of *faith* and hope, there is no full possession; but we are in expectation. And then where there is *humility,* there is sense of want; nothing there is found partial, nothing fond and conceited; but the truth of things takes place.

3. There is necessity of action. For we are to be subservient to God. The work is to be done in us, and so cannot be without us, we being only passive. *Repentance* which is indispensibly necessary to the recovery of a sinner, *cannot be given to us unless we also repent.* For conversion is a mutual act, and so is faith. *We do believe to the obtaining of remission of sins, and we must work for eternal life with fear and trembling, because God works in us to will and to do of his own good pleasure.* Phil. ii. 12, 13. And the apostle conjoins these two as things are connatural:

tural : which muſt ſtand or fall together. *Work out your own ſalvation, for it is God that worketh in you.* And *awake thou that ſleepeſt, and ariſe from the dead, and Chriſt ſhall give thee life.* Eph. v. 14. They are put in conjunction, as things that are *connatural*; and the one does ſuppoſe the other. A man can neither be made holy here, or happy hereafter, by any thing that is wholly without himſelf, but he muſt have an internal temper, life and ſenſe, and feel and conceive, conſent and chuſe: for converſion and regeneration are vital acts, and do denote an internal act, life and motion. *Eph.* ii. 1. *You hath he quickened,* ſaith the apoſtle, *who were dead in treſpaſſes and ſins.* Thus much for explication, where he doth give teſtimony of his modeſty and *humility,* there he doth engage himſelf to *activity, care* and *diligence. But I follow after, but I preſs forward to the mark for the prize of the high calling of God in Chriſt Jeſus.*

Now from what I have ſaid, I *infer* two things.

1. Then, they are not in good earneſt to ſave their ſouls, who are careleſs and negligent about them. We give our minds to that, which we intend and mean ; and where we do not mean, we are nothing at all, tho' there be a ſhew and ſeeming delight. They ſpeak prophanely, who ſay, they will truſt God with their ſouls, while they themſelves are careleſs and negligent about them. There is none doth ſo depend upon God for food and cloathing, or any of the neceſſaries of this life ; but they themſelves will uſe their beſt brains, are thoughtful, are careful, and found in the uſe of ſuch means as are

. proper

proper for that end. Now in religion, effects and operations are always proportional to the principle: slight and ineffectual powers and principles are neither in nature nor in grace ; for we see *that power is altogether in vain, that never is in use, in act, nor employment.*

2. Let not shew and pretence, words and profeffion signify religion ; so shall the world be defend-ed against scandal : let not these I say, testify religion, for they are not sufficient, and by these means, the world shall be preserved from scandal. Men are not so vain, saving only in the case of religion, as to think one is *persuaded,* if he doth nothing at all ; I say, we are not so vain, saving only in religion, as to think, that any one is in good earnest satisfied and resolved, if he do no more than talk. Certainly the demonstration and proof of faith is from its effects ; and so hath St. *James* stated it ; *shew me thy faith by thy works.* Jam. ii. 18. For religion is regular, is rational, is uniform, and all its parts are proportionable and homogenial ; so that disposition and profeffion, principle and practice, they are conformable. If a man be real in religion, and the several parts of it, the operations are uniform, and proportionable ; the disposition of the mind, the profeffion such a man makes, the principles whereby he acts, and his practice, they are all of the same stamp. And thus I have given you an account in general concerning the truth of this, *that* where any man who is serious and an honest-hearted believer ; where he doth declare his faith, entertain any divine revelation, there his faith is attended with
modesty,

modefty, and humility; he thinks *foberly of himfelf according to what he ought to think* : but he doth pur-fue his faith with vigour and activity ; he does thofe things that become a man to do, that profef-fes himfelf to be fatisfied and fully perfuaded ; his profeffion and principle and practice, they are all right and uniform, all rational, and confiftent one with another, and there is no interfering.   But I have been all this while in generals, and I remem-ber in *philofophy*, we have a good rule that faith, all *fallacy lies in univerfals*.   There is no man prickt in his confcience by telling him only that he is a fin-ner at large, and in general.   Therefore this being a practical point, you fhall give me leave to inftance in certain particulars, and they fhall be but few : but main and principal, and fuch which are of that importance, and indifpenfible neceffity, that I can-not abfolve any man from the leaft of them, be he of any capacity or under any difpenfation whatfoe-ver.   I fay I cannot abate him any of them.   There-fore thefe three things I charge upon every living foul in purfuit of his faith of the refurrection ; and if he fail in thefe, he is a pretender to the faith of the future ftate, and not ferious in his religion, or really confcientious.   The firft of the three is this:

1. In the fear of God, carefully to *avoid all known evil* ; for this I find to be a character that God himfelf gave of *Job* i. 1. *That he did fear God, and efchew evil* :   And if fo be through temptation, or affault, or miftake, or through human infirmity, or occafional indifpofition, a man be difturbed ; yet then he doth after a time, when he is at leifure, recover

covet himself, and renew himself by repentance. This is the firft : it is neceffary upon account of religion and confcience, that every body that pretends to the faith of the gofpel, or makes profeffion of it, that he do live exactly according to the difference of good and evil ; that is, that which he doth know to be evil, he do carefully and confcientioufly avoid. But,

2. As he muft avoid that which is evil ; fo out of love to God, and in compliance with his nature and will, he muft *do all known good.* Out of fear of God, he muft decline evil ; and out of love to God, and defire to fulfil his will, and to comply with him, and to pleafe him, he muft charge himfelf to do all known *good,* and to perform all known *duty* : and this is, in fcripture-language, to *walk with God* : and to *live in all good confcience.* But then,

3. To *fubmit,* and refer *the ordinaries of life,* things that may lawfully be done in time and meafure, *to ferve* and advance *our future eftate,* which is our great concernment. Thefe three, are the fundamentals of religion ; and confequently, are all of them indifpenfably neceffary ; they are of univerfal concernment, and they take in all and every one ; and ought to be obferved in all times, and all places, and by all perfons : and a man that is not throughout in thefe three, that cannot acquit and approve himfelf to God in them, he is not qualified, not capable to move a queftion about uncertain and difputable matters : but he is as ridiculous as he was in the fenfe of the great philofopher, that being in a deep and deadly difeafe, came to the
phyfician

phyſician to know how he might be cured of the *reduvia* or little loofe fleſh about his nail : ſo is e-very man that troubles himſelf with queſtions, and difputes about matters of religion, that is not tho-rough-paced in theſe three : he deceives himſelf, and that which he faith is nauſeous, fulſome, and troubleſome to any ſober chriſtian. And I cannot account any man a right believer or true chriſtian, that is not found in the practice of theſe three things, *viz.* carefully to *avoid all known evil* ; and to *per-form all known good* : and a watchfulneſs over him-ſelf to *ſubordinate the lawful affairs of life*, things that may be done in meaſure and degree; to ſubor-dinate theſe to that which is main and principal, *viz.* The ſaving of the ſoul in eternity. For theſe three are the things that we underſtand when we ſpeak of religion, and conſcience in the ſubject, and without violation of the rules of charity, we may ſay, that he which fails in theſe, falls ſhort of the deſerved repute or eſteem of an honeſt and conſcien-tious believer. And thus I have brought generals to particulars, and ſhewn that it becomes every man that profeſſeth the faith of the goſpel, the faith of the reſurrection, to charge himſelf with all thoſe things that are purſuant in theſe. It becomes him to have a *modeſt ſenſe* of himſelf, but in the uſe of means to charge himſelf with great *diligence*, and to live in attendance upon God, and expectation of his influence, and aſſiſtance ; and particularly he is to charge himſelf with theſe three things, moſt re-ligiouſly and conſtantly : *to avoid all known evil*, and *perform all known duty*, and the doing of that good that

that his judgment and confcience tells him he ought
to do ; and in the ordinaries of life, things that
may lawfully be done in meafure and degree, to *fubordinate thefe to ferve and advance the intereft of his
foul in eternity*, which is his main and great concernment ; and this is unqueftionable, indubitable, and
indifpenfible in religion ; and if there be a failure
in any of thefe, a man cannot approve himfelf, for
a man of honefty and integrity to God ; a man of
good confcience ; a man that is in a temper and in
order to eternal life, nor in a true ftate of religion.
And fo I have done with the *fecond* propofition, and
come to the *third*.

III. Which was this, where he profeffeth his *humility*, there he engageth himfelf to *induftry* and *diligence :* and where he doth this, he doth acknowledge the *grace of God : that I may apprehend that for
which I am apprehended ;* which words import three
things concerning the grace of God.

Firft, They intimate the *priority* of God's grace;
that his grace doth firft lay hold of us, and prevent
us.

Secondly, They intimate the *freenefs* of God's
grace ; for he was apprehended before he did apprehend, therefore he had no antecedent merit, nothing on his part that did procure : and,

Thirdly, The *efficacy* of God's grace, that he was
apprehended. And what fhall I fay more ? if God
be firft in his grace, and do all voluntarily and freely without antecedent merit, or after recompence ;
and on purpofe for our good ; are we not then beholden to him, and may we not fay with the a-
poftle,

poftle, *By grace I am what I am,* 1 Cor. xv. 10. and that I *live, yet not I, but Chrift liveth in me?* Gal. ii. 20. I formerly fpake fomewhat to this; but now it comes more directly in my way. I fhall endeavour to fatisfy all men.

The grace and favour of God expreffeth it felf in a way of benevolence and *compaffion,* or in a way of love and *complacency.* That of benevolence and compaffion prevents all our application to God and converfion to him ; for *God fo loved the world, that he gave his only begotten fon, that whofoever believes in him, fhould not perifh, but have everlafting life,* John iii. 16. When we were in a ftate of fin and unregeneracy, God did bear us good-will, to wit he bare the affection of benevole nce, he had compaffion for us. But the love of *complacency* and delight, that is fubfequent to our regeneration ; *for it is repugnant, that God fhould take pleafure in us, till we do harmonize with him,* which is by our regeneration, and being made like him, and comfortable to him. And the grace of God is taken, both for his *favour* and good inclination towards us, and alfo for his divine affiftance ; and the former is that which is the caufe of the latter ; for out of God's benevolence and compaffion, he doth afford aid and affiftance : upon that fcore he doth awaken us, call upon us, and excite us; he doth both begin, go on, and confummate. The very firft beginning of a good mind is from the grace of God ; we are not only prevented, but promoted by him, and every good work is perfected by the continuance of divine grace. We cannot acknowledge the grace of God too much, provided we do

it

it right, and not neglect it. But this is the abuse of the grace of God, to neglect it. For his grace and favour towards us, is for our encouragement; his aid and affiftance is for our performance; and fince he doth fo declare his grace and goodnefs to us, we are obliged to obey and pleafe him. And fince he doth afford us his aid and affiftance, we are enabled to turn to him : and all men that have any experience of themfelves, or acquaintance with God, are free and ingenuous, in the *acknowledgement*, that we are beholden to the grace of God both for the ftrengthning of us, and carrying of us on; for the exciting of us and enabling of us, and profpering of us in any good work, fo that we may fay, *our fuf-ficiency is of God*, 2 Cor. iii. 5. And as this is true in it felf, fo it is the *fenfe* of every one that is partaker of God's grace; and he that hath attained to the higheft growth in religion, this man I dare fay, will make the freeft and fulleft acknowledgement of the divine grace, and he will fay fincerely and heartily, that *through the grace of God, I am what I am*, 1 Cor. xv. 10. There are two queftions which will eafily be refolved, *Who made thee to differ from a-nother ? Or what haft thou that thou haft not receiv-ed ?* 1 Cor. iv. 7. I fay thefe two queftions are readily and chearfully anfwered by every one that is the fubject of the grace of God. If he do but confult his own experience, he will fay, that he has no-thing but what he received from God, and is the fruit of his grace ; and that it is the grace of God that makes him fo differ from another. And as this is the fenfe of every good man that is beholden to the grace of God for what he is, fo it is *becoming* and *comely*, to acknowledge grace, and to look upon it as the leaft return that we can make. For on our part, there is neither antecedent merit, or after recompence ; *we live by grace, and therefore it is comely for us, to acknowledge grace,* Pfal. lxvi. 16. The gracious and ingenuous foul doth not account any thing more reafonable than to be grateful to its benefactor.

I will conclude now with this, that upon this fcore of magnifying and advancing the grace of God, two things are not to be done, which fome that are unwary do interpret as derogatory to the grace of God, and fo I hope fhall prevent all miftakes. To wit,

1. They are not to be blamed or looked upon as negleﬁers of God's grace, or undervaluers of it, or to abate it in the leaft, who vigoroufly and with all imaginable zeal, call upon men to *ufe*, employ, and improve the principles of God's creation: that charge it upon men, as a point of religion and confcience, to ufe, employ and improve the principles of God's creation. I find that fome men take offence, to hear *reafon* fpoken of out of a pulpit, or to hear thofe great words of *natural light*, of *principles of reafon, and confcience.* They are doubtlefs in a mighty miftake, for thefe two things are very confiftent, as I fhall fhew you by and by, and there is no inconfiftency between the *grace of God*, and the calling upon men carefully to ufe, improve and employ the *principles of God's creation,* and the telling men they fhall meet with no difcouragement from
God,

God, forafmuch as he will not leave them, till they
firft leave him. And indeed this is a very profitable
work to call upon men to anfwer the principles of
their creation, to fulfil natural light, to anfwer natural confcience, to be throughout rational in what
they do; for thefe things have a divine foundation.
*The fpirit in man is the candle of the Lord lighted by
God, and lighting men to God.* It is from God by
way of efficiency, and to God finally. And then

2. For the other, thofe two great places of fcripture will anfwer all that I fay, to wit, that we may
fpeak clearly and fully to any one that is in a way
of religion or in dependance upon God, or in the
ufe of means, that there is no *difcouragement* lies upon him, from any thought or purpofe of evil in God
againft him, or that God will be wanting to him,
unlefs he firft fall off from God, and leave him. *In
every nation, he that feareth God and worketh righteoufnefs; is accepted of him,* Acts. x. 15. And therefore to fpeak of natural light, of the ufe of reafon in
religion, is to do no differvice atall to grace;
for God is acknowledged in both: in the former,
as laying the ground-work of his creation: in the
latter, as reviving and reftoring it. So that thefe
do agree together, as God doth agree to himfelf;
God laying the religion of confcience, and making
man in fuch a power of judging; and God reftoring
him to the felf fame ftate again, after he had
confented to iniquity, whereby he had marred his
principles, and difabled himfelf; fo that I fay, thefe
two do as well agree together, as God doth agree

A a 2

with

with himfelf ; for God is the *author* of nature, and the *reftorer* of it. By the way I will obferve how little there is in many controverfies ; if wife and temperate men had the managing of them ; but when once there is fufpicion and jealoufy, thefe make and increafe differences. This is in fhort all that I will fay, it is not poffible for any one that is a right believer not to depend on the grace of God ; it is highly ingenuous for him to make all poffible acknowledgements, it becomes him to think that he owes all his hopes to the goodnefs of God, and that he ftood in need of a divine ftrength for every new motion ; yea to attribute every thing that is good to the grace of God.

But notwithftanding this, *firft* we are to call upon one another, every body is to engage himfelf to excite all the powers of nature, to act according to reafon and to anfwer all principles of natural light and confcience; and this we are to do in compliance with grace.

And *Secondly*, We will by no means upon any pretence difcourage any one that is in a difpofition God-ward ; for we are by fcripture warranted to tell men, that God doth not forfake men, till he be firft forfaken of men, and that God will not refufe any one that comes unto him ; but is a real friend to fouls, and doth delight in the converfion of finners, and doth his part toward the attaining of it ; and this I have added to take off offence and fcandal, that fo no one may be miftaken. *Men are not fo far to prefs the principles of God's creation, as to neglect the grace of God : nor fo far to depend on the*

grace

grace of God as to neglect the principles of God's crea-tion. I put them in conjunction, and they agree as well together, as God doth with himself.

DISCOURSE XXIV.

The PRACTICE of thofe who are improved.

PHILIPPIANS iii. 15.
Let as many of us therefore as be perfect, be thus mind-ed : and if in any thing ye, be otherwife minded, God fhall reveal even this unto you.

LEt therefore as many of us as be perfect, be thus minded. But had he not denied perfection before, ver. 12. *not as though I had already at-tained, either were already perfect* : who doth he now fpeak of ? Let as many as be perfect be thus minded, take an account of this in fix or feven particulars.

1. It is a fuppofition of *charity* ; what he had be-fore denied of himfelf he doth admit in refpect of others. And indeed we feel our own infirmities, and know our own weakneffes, fhortnefs and im-perfection ; but we obferve other men's graces. The beft of men know more by themfelves, than by others. He finds how oft he is out of frame and-temper, how oft he is indifpofed : but other per-fons are known only by their excellencies, by their

A a 3   virtues ;

virtues ; and we believe better of them, then we know by ourfelves. This is that which the apoftle faith, *charity hopeth all things, believeth all things.* Modefty becomes us in refpeft of ourfelves : but charity bids us entertain a good opinion of others. You fee he gives to others the greateft advantage, and full allowance ; but he takes no more to himfelf than is certainly due. Thus doth he praftife according to his own rule, *Rom.* xii. 10. *Be ye kindly affeftioned with brotherly love, preferring one another.* That is the *firft* thing.

2. It is a word of *encouragement* : becaufe we are wont to fay to new beginners and learners, *well done* ; when it is only well begun. Thus God himfelf, in his goodnefs, and kindnefs towards us, for our encouragement doth own *Job* as a *perfeft and upright* man, *Job* i. 8. and he faith it again, when he was traduced ; and *Satan* belied him : and yet fee what *Job* faith of himfelf, *Job* ix. 20. *If I juftify myfelf, my own mouth fhall condemn me.* That is, the *fecond.*

3. It is the force of his *argument,* and then it amounts to this ; as you would prove yourfelves good proficients, as you would make it appear that you are thofe that do grow and increafe in goodnefs, do fo and fo. And then the notion that it affords us, is this ; that the defign and intention of perfeftion fo far as it is attainable to human endeavour, is belonging to the ftate of goodnefs. The regenerate eftate doth not affign to its felf *manner* or *matter,* or fuch a growth ; but tends to perfeftion ; fo far as the principle of it doth require. And even
                                                            thofe

thofe that die in peace, if they had lived longer in
this ftate of probation and trial ; undoubtedly they
had made further improvement of that ftock of
grace that God had beftowed upon them. And upon this account, long life is a mercy ; becaufe of
greater growth, fuller improvement, and more fervice. And that is the third account.

4. It is faid *refpectively*, and in a contradiftinction.
So we find him expreffing himfelf : perfect in contradiftinction to children and weaklings, fuch as are
weak and imperfect. 1 *Cor*. iv. 10. there are
weak and ftrong ; and 1 *Cor*. iii. 1. there are thofe
fpoken of that are *fpiritual*, and thofe that are *carnal*.
Perfect are thofe that are fpiritual, that have their
fenfes fpiritually exercifed. And the *weak*, they are
called flefhly or carnal : and he gives an inftance of
thofe that are carnal ; they are thefe that are iniclin-
able to divifion, and to fay *I am of Paul, and I am of
Apollo*, &c. when thofe that are *fpiritual* are above all
thefe things, and make no head or divifion ; but look
upon all as God's inftruments, and as thofe that indifferently belong to God ; and to join a man's felf to any
one of thefe as a head, is a piece of carnality, and
not of fpirituality. And it is a notion worth our
obfervation ; that it is not all perfection that is boifterous, and that makes a noife in the church of
God ; as here *they* did, one crying, *I am of Paul* ;
and another of Apollo : I am of Cephas, &c. *are ye
not carnal ?* &c. Thefe are *weak* perfons, and fuch
who, the apoftle faith, are not to be admitted to
queftions and doubtful difputations. Thefe are to
be fed with milk, and not with ftrong meat ; they

are

are not to be admitted *to* curious enquiries. And this is the fourth thing.

5. Perfection *of the way*, or means ; and this belongs to all men.   We are *perfecting*, 2 Cor. xiii. 11. as the word is, which is the fame word which we have, *Matt.* iv. 21. where it is faid that the *fons of Zebedee* were *mending their nets* they were making up holes, and breaches that were found in their nets. And *this is our perfection* ; *to be mending our felves*, and bringing our felves out of diftemper ; to be repairing ourfelves, by renewal and mortification, by affifting and helping one another. This is the perfection *of the way*, and this it is to be in the ufe of *means*.

6. The perfection of our *rule*, and principles or ground, or end : fo we are perfect. For here we are as the apoftle, ftriving, if that by any means *we may attain unto* perfection. *This* every man fhould have in his eye, at this he fhould aim, this fhould be his end and defign, to *prefs towards the mark of the high calling of God in Chrift Jefus.* And this is perfection, becaufe we have the right end in our eye.

7. There is perfection of the *difpofition* and intention of mind, *viz. fincere and honeft meaning* ; and *this* every body muft have, or he is *no body in religion* ; and fincerity of heart, uprightnefs of foul, and true intention of mind, this is the beft of us, in this ftate.. In *this* doth religion greatly confift, that men do heartily and fincerely intend, mind, and mean God, goodnefs, righteoufnefs and truth, and are able to make it out, that their religion is not fubfervient to worldly ends and purpofes : for

this

this is foul and shameful, a great sacrilege and profana-
tion of God, and holy things ; to name God, and to
mean the world ; to pretend conscience, and to
have our designs ; to engage our selves in a way of
religion to gain credit, for worldly purposes. No,
God and religion are things too holy, and sacred, to
serve any other ends or purposes than the honour
of God, and the sanctifying of our souls here, and
saving them hereafter : and whosoever names these,
upon any other purpose, he is a sacrilegious person,
and a prophaner of things that are holy. And this is
the account that I now give you ; that though he had
denied perfection before, yet here he doth admit it.

Now for the words read unto you, I gather up
the substance of them in these four propositions.

1. There is *that* in religion, which is *necessary*
and determined, fixt and immutable, clear and
perspicuous ; about which they who are of growth,
and proficiency in religion, do not differ. *As many*
as are perfect, are thus minded.

2. There is also *that* in religion which is not so
clear, plain, and evident ; about which it may
happen that they may be otherwise minded ; that is,
otherwise one than another ; or otherwise than
they should be ; or otherwise than the truth is. If
any *be otherwise minded,* *i. e.* in other matters, they
may be otherwise one than another; otherwise than
the truth ; otherwise than they ought to be. That
is the second.

3. There is reason to think, that God will bring
out of particular mistakes, him that is right in the
main. *God shall reveal even this unto you.* For
I do not look upon this as spoken with the spirit of

prophesy ;

prophefy; but fpoken according to chriftian reafon.
God fhall reveal in his time, *i. e.* there is reafon
to think that God will bring out of particular error and miftake, him that is right in the main.

4. They which agree in the main, but differ in
fome particulars, ought neceffarily to *hold together*
as if they were in all things agreed. They ought
to *walk by the fame rule : and to mind the fame things.*
They who agree in the main, though they differ
in fome particulars, ought to own one another, and
to hold together ; and encourage one another to
growth, progrefs, a nd proficiency ; they are to u-
nite themfelves in heart, and good-will, in love and
affection, as if there were no difference between
them, but in all things agreed. For the *main and
principal* things in religion, wherein the honour of
God is concluded, *this* is fuch a ground and foundation of union, that matters of particular apprehenfion, ought not to make difference or feparation.

You fee what ufeful matter lies before us ; and
all thefe four obfervations do lie plainly in the
words. And if thefe things were well digefted and
confidered, there would be a folid foundation laid
for peace and unity in the church of God ; and
men would agree in hearty love and good-will, and
be mutually helpful one unto another ; and no fuch
thing as hatred or difpleafure found among them,
one againft another. And he that runs may read
thefe things in the words ; which being of fo great
ufe and import for the edification of the church of
Chrift, I fhall fpeak to them feverally : only the
two firft fhall run together.

I, and

I, and II. The things that are *main* and *princi-pal* in religion, in thofe things all that are of growth and proficiency in religion, *do mind the fame things :* and wherein they may be otherwife minded, *i. e.* either otherwife one than another, or than the truth is, or otherwife than they ought, and fhould be ; thefe are things of lefs moment, weight, and con-cernment.

Now that I might fhew you the great things of religion wherein there is an univerfal harmony, con-fent and agreement ; it is not neceffary for me to remove from the text : I mean from thofe things that have been fpoken to you out of this chapter. The things that the apoftle had infifted upon, are thefe.

· (1.) He had declared Chrift for juftification, from thofe words, *that I may be found in him :* for this is the chriftian foundation, that finners are accepted in and through the beloved. This is the chriftian fpirit, to hold the head, to go to God in and through Chrift ; to depend upon his mediation, re-commendation, interceffion ; and not to look for ac-ceptance for our own worthinefs ; to have no con-fidence in our felves, or in our own righteoufnefs, but in that righteoufnefs which God hath declared and eftablifhed ; even that *righteoufnefs which is of God by faith,* as the apoftle expreffeth himfelf, when he difclaims his own *righteoufnefs, that was of the law,* and flies for juftification to that righteoufnefs which God had declared ; even gofpel righteoufnefs, or the righteoufnefs which is of God by faith.

(2.) And

(2.) And then *another* thing declared by the a-
poftle in this chapter, is *Chrift Jefus* to the effects
and purpofes of mortification, regeneration, and divine and fpiritual life. *That I might know him, and
the power of his refurrection, and the fellowfhip of his
fufferings ; being made conformable to his death.* From
which words I have declared unto you, that the
death and refurrection of Chrift muft all be verified,
and made true in us, as in Chrift. We muft be
planted into the likenefs of his death, which is done by
our dying to the world, and felfifhnefs ; and by
mortifying the flefh with the affections and lufts.
And we muft have in us, the *power of his refurrection* ; which is expreffed by our nativity from above,
by fpirituality, heaven-mindednefs ; by fubordinat-
ing all things in life, to the hopes of the future ftate:
*If by any means we may attain to the refurrection of the
dead,* Thefe are great and important forms of
words, and do contain in them, the great things of
religion. And though I might refer you to thofe ;
yet, in fo weighty a matter as *this,* that I may be
exact, and fpeak diftinctly ; I will put things into
their forms and modes, that you may the better underftand them.

The great *materials of natural light,* are firft in
reafon, and then reinforced in fcripture. The articles of faith are firft in fcripture, and being there
revealed, are after juftified in reafon : there is no
true reafon againft them, but there is full fatisfaction
in them.

1. The great things in religion are thofe in the
firft place that concern God : and thofe things
which

which concern God, I refer to two heads. (For,
all things that relate to God are not equally neceffary for us to determine ; but fome things are neceffary for our happinefs ; and to found in us religion and confcience, to determine and refolve concerning God.) *viz.*

Firft, The neceffary *perfeƈtions of the divine nature* ; whereon all religion in us doth depend.

And now I will fingle out *two :* for divers of the
divine perfeƈtions are incomprehenfible, as his om-
nipotency, eternity, ubiquity, and divers other attributes which we admire and adore, but we cannot comprehend. But fome of his perfeƈtions are
fuch, that the knowledge of them is *fundamental* to religion and confcience in us. And,

I will inftance in *two,* which are neceffary for e-
very one to refolve himfelf in, or elfe his religion
will not be grounded ; and they are thefe. The
holinefs of God, or his righteoufnefs : and the *truth*
of God and his faithfulnefs. I name but two, becaufe by holinefs and righteoufnefs I mean the fame;
as alfo, by his truth and faithfulnefs I underftand
one and the fame thing. 'Tis fundamental in religion to know *thefe,* and acknowledge them, and
to be refolved in a man's mind about them : for o-
therwife we fhall have no right conceptions of God
nor make due applications to him ; nor will our
hope and confidence in God, be fufficiently encouraged, or grounded. As for any *other attribute* of God
we are not fo much concerned to underftand and
determine : but religion is without ground and foundation, if a man doth not know God to be *holy* and
righteous,

righteous, and cloath him with *truth and faithfulnefs :* if we do not give God the honour of his
truth, and veracity, who will believe him ? If any
one doubt whether God be holy and righteous, he
hath not an example for his imitation ; for we muft
imitate God in his holinefs and righteoufnefs ; in
his truth and faithfulnefs. And therefore thefe perfections are neceffary for us to know, and underftand : otherwife religion in us, hath not an original. For *it is religion to imitate God in thefe* ; in holinefs, in righteoufnefs, in truth, and faithfulnefs.
This is the firft thing concerning God, that we
are concerned throughly to underftand, and to be
well fatisfied about ; or elfe we have no copy for
our imitation, nor no encouragement to build our
faith upon him, or to depend upon what he hath
declared. But, as for the *other* attributes and perfections of God, as his eternity, his immenfity, his
omniprefence, and the like ; none can grafp them,
or comprehend them, or declare about them ; but
here we are glad rather to admire and adore. But as for
his *holinefs and righteoufnefs,* &c. what thefe are we do
know, and are concerned to know ; and there is nothing in thefe that doth confound human apprehenfions, and thefe are fundamental to our religion. But then

Secondly, Concerning God, it is neceffary that
they to whom divine *revelations* are made, do entertain them, acknowledge, and fubmit to them.
As for them to whom they are not revealed, there
can be no more than negative infidelity ; which is
not the foundation of any man's condemnation : but
to them to whom they are revealed, it is neceffary

to

to them, in point of confcience, and upon account of their future happinefs, that they to whom God doth declare himfelf, that they do entertain his revelations, acknowledge, and fubmit to them. And here comes in the *chriftian faith* ; the fum of which is this, that we owe our falvation to the grace and goodnefs of God, declared by *Jefus Chrift.* And this is the fum of the chriftian faith, and this is that which every body is concerned to know, and underftand, retain and believe : and thefe things are *neceffary and fundamental,* and in which all good men do harmonize and agree, as neceffary to be believed concerning God.

2. There are things which are according to *human nature,* which may be diftinguifhed thefe *three* ways.

1. The things that are founded in our ftate, and *relation to God,* do import,

Firft, Our *reverence* of the deity.

Secondly, Faith and *affiance* in God.

Thirdly, Obedience to him, and conformity to his will. And thefe are founded in our *relation to God,* and that capacity which we ftand in to him : for we are made *intelligent and voluntary* ; and have notions of God and apprehenfions of him ; and internal fentiments. And this fpeaks our capacity, above the creation below us; and by thefe are we able to take cognizance of God, and to make acknowledgments to him and to perform duty towards him and to make returns unto him. Thefe things are founded in our capacities, and in the relation that we ftand in to God, as his creatures. For this is fundamental in reafon, that if I be in the

ftate

ftate of a creature, according to my ability, and capacity, I am bound to do homage to my maker, as my fuperior, and to acknowledge him as my original ; and therefore ought to obferve, and obey him, to fulfil his will, and make returns unto him ; and thefe are unavoidable to intellectual nature; and infeparable from it. And if we fail in thefe, we are in a ftate of deformity, and contradiction to God, and to our own natures. But then,

2. Things that are grounded in our *conftitution of parts.* We are compounded of body, and fpirit, and fuch things are *thefe three,* that are fecured upon this account, as *modefty, fobriety,* and the *government of reafon,* above fenfe. And thefe are neceffary as being founded in our make and conftitution : and in refpect of our compofition it becomes us, to be *modeft,* becaufe of our lower and inferior part ; and to be *fober*; and it is fit that reafon fhould have predominance over fenfe ; that reafon fhould rule and govern the bodily part, becaufe that reafon is fuperior appointed of God, and thefe are founded in our very make and conftitution. And then,

3. There are things belonging to that *refpect we ftand* in toward *each other,* as fellow creatures, and that is *juft, and equal dealings* ; and not to do one another harm. No man living in the world, can leave any one of thefe things out of his religion : they are main things ; and all men that are of any confcience or fobriety, do agree in all thefe things ; and he cannot be an honeft man, and of any growth and improvement in religion, that makes any doubt of them.

Thefe

. . Thefe are all of them indifpenfibly *neceffary*, up-on the account of religion, and every good man is true to them. He is well informed concerning the holinefs of God, and his faithfulnefs : he doth en-tertain the articles of faith that are clear and plain, in the revelation of God ; the fum-of which is this, that he owes his hopes of falvation to the grace of God declared by Jefus Chrift : he knows that he ought to anfwer the *relation* he ftands in to God, and that he ought to act according to his capacity : and to have reverent thoughts of God, and to have faith, affiance and truft in him ; to obey God, and to ful-fil his will, and do his pleafure. And in refpect of *himfelf*, fince he is fpirit, as well as flefh ; he ought to maintain a government of reafon over fenfe ; and he ought to be *fober*, and not make his rational fa-culties drudges like the *Gibbeonites*, to hew wood and to draw water : but to govern his affections and paffions by his more noble part. And becaufe he is *one in the family of God*, he ought with all his fellow creatures to live according to rules of *juftice* and e-quity ; and not to beat his fellow fervants, but to do no body any harm. And thefe things are as evi-dent as the fun that fhines ; and in thefe, I cannot difpenfe with any one, nor make any allowance. If any one fail in thefe he fails in that which is neceffary and vital, to make him a good man. And this is *gene-ral and univerfal*, in refpect of the ftate of all per-fons : in all ages, and times whatfoever. In this muft he declare his religion, that he hath a true de-fire, and endeavour to know what is right and good ; and having found it out, to comply with it in heart

and life. And I do not know how any man can
fatisfy himfelf as touching his duty to God, if he
do not thus much : nor make it appear that he hath
any care of his own falvation, and future fafety, unlefs he doth fincerely fet-himfelf to know what is
pleafing to God, and what will give him an offence :
and then to be careful to avoid what will offend
him, and do what is acceptable unto him. For to
know in fome meafure, the difference between good
and evil, right and wrong, *this* is every body's *wifdom* and underftanding ; and then to do according
to this known difference, *this* is a man's *goodnefs.* If
he do not the former, he is not at all improved in his
intellectuals : if he do not the latter, he is not at all
reformed in his morals. And if neither improved in
his intellectuals, nor reformed in his morals, what
hath he to fhew upon account of religion and confcience ? What hath he to fhew that he may call
religion ?

The rule of natural knowledge is *fenfus animæ* :
the rule of revealed truth is facred fcripture. Concerning the materials of *natural knowledge,* he hath
abufed his nature, who finds not feeds of thefe
fown in it. Concerning *revealed truth,* he that is
not fatisfied in the authority of fcripture revealing to
us matters of faith, is not yet perfwaded to become
a chriftian. To make one religious in general, the
principles of God's creation may fuffice ; to make
one a chriftian, the receiving matters of faith, is neceffary : to difcerning of things of *natural knowledge,*
the true fevere impartial ufe of reafon is needful : to
the knowing the things of *revealed truth,* the fair
and

and ingenuous conftruction of words and phrafes iⁿ
fcripture, is needful. Not but that the materials of
natural knowledge, inftances of virtue, meafures of
good and evil, are *repeated,* acknowledged, and reinforced in fcripture.

This feems *general* in refpect to all times and
places ; a true defire and endeavour to know what
is right and good ; and being found out to comply
with it in heart and life: I know not any thing elfe
whereby any may approve himfelf to God, as doing
his duty to him; or teftify the care of his own foul,
as doing what is worthy of it and tending to its e-
verlafting fafety.

But thus much for *explication,* and 'tis of great *ufe*
many ways.

1. That men may *charge* themfelves not to fail
in the neceffaries of religion.

2. That men knowing what are the neceffary
things that religion requires ; and what are thofe
things wherein good men may chance to be otherwife minded, one than another ; yet they may *live
in love,* and hearty good will, and no way provoke
one another. And *this* is of mighty ufe, in the life
of man. And I have taken the more pains in it,
that I may fatisfy any perfon concerning thofe
things, which are of abfolute and indifpenfible neceffity in religion. For if a man be peremptory
and confident of a notion, and the ground of it is
but a fuppofition ; when ftrefs comes to be laid u-
pon it ; it is like a building without a foundation,
and when ftorms and tempefts arife, it will be over-
turned, and fall to the ground. For a man is fure

of

of nothing in religion unlefs he can fatisfy his mind from unqueftiohable grounds, and foundations. And therefore I have fhewn you how the *neceffaries* of religion are founded ; and how they do arife. And they that are of any growth and proficiency in religion, they do not differ in thefe : for they are either clear in reafon, or revelation, or both ; and a furer foundation there is not in the world. And fuch are thofe things that I have named, fuch as are immutably and unchangeably good ; fuch as thefe have neceffary place in the doctrine of the gofpel ; as alfo in the grounds and principles of reafon. And all elfe belong to thefe immutable and eternal rights ; thefe unchangeable principles of good and thefe have great place in the doctrine of the gofpel. For is it not faid exprefly, that *God* fent his fon into the world, to *turn us from our iniquities ; and the grace of God that bringeth falvation teacheth us to live pioufly* in refpect of God : and *foberly* in the government of our affections : and *right eoufly*, and equally one with another. This is moft certain, that all the notions of natural knowledge and inftances of moral virtues, are repeated and reinforced in fcripture. Scripture ratifies them all ; juft as it is faid, in the *regeneration* we are *created over again* in Chrift Jefus, to thofe good works whereunto we were *appointed.* So that the recovery of Chrift is a reftoration, and further confirmation of all the principles of God's creation ; of all that refult in refpect of natural light, of all principles and obfervance of God, of good government over ourfelves, and righteous dealings one with another. So that here
though

though you may diftinguifh *reafon,* and *fcripture,* yet
there is nothing in *reafon,* but it hath an acknowledgement in *fcripture* : and it is reinforced, and hath a
further eftablifhment by it. And the great things of
God's creation, are thofe which the recovery we
have by Chrift prepares us unto, and ends in. And
that which the fcripture doth *over and above* reveal,
is this ; it gives a man affurance, that God is placable and reconcileable ; and alfo declares to us, *in
what way,* and upon what *terms,* we may be confident, that God will pardon fin, and receive a finner
to mercy, *viz.* upon his repentance and faith, and
returning to his duty. And thanks be to God that
he hath given us this affurance. And to me it is
matter of the *eafieft belief,* of any thing in the world,
and that for two reafons.

1. Becaufe the matter is *worthy of God.* For it is
a matter of eafy belief to think, that the *firft* and
chiefeft goodnefs will pardon a creature, that was
never better than finite and fallible ; upon the fenfe
of his error, acknowledgement of his offence, and
return to duty. I fay, this is matter of the eafieft
belief, that the *firft* and chiefeft goodnefs will pardon fuch an one, one way or other. And then comes
in the *gofpel,* that declares, that God doth this, and
will do it, in and through *Chrift.* And the *way* he
directs us to, is the way of *repentance* and *faith,* and
this repentance and faith is made poffible to us,
through the grace and affiftance of God. And then
they are terms highly defirable and grateful to us.
For a man can have no fatisfaction if he hath done
amifs, till he doth repent, and as much as in him

lies, undo what he hath done. If a man hath any
ingenuity, if he hath done wrong, he will ask forgivenefs, and make fatisfaction. And fo it is in the
cafe of repentance, if a man be once of a good difpofition God-ward ; it is a harder matter for fuch
an one to obtain forgivenefs of himfelf, than of God.
Now, when God hath told us, that he will pardon
fin, if we ask him forgivenefs in the name of *Chrift*,
and be heartily forrowful for what we have done amifs
and return to our duty : he doth declare *that* which
a man would have defired, and upon *fuch terms*, as
it is fitting to be done. For this is *fanatory* to us,
and fatisfactory to our reafon and underftanding ;
and for the reftoration of our natures. For if a man
hath done a thing which is amifs, and endeavoured
to make fatisfaction ; though he meets with a perfon that is perverfe and implacable, yet he eafeth
his mind, becaufe he hath done the beft in the cafe.
So that, thefe terms are comfortable, becaufe we
are affured of them, by divine revelation : not difficult in themfelves to believe in the ufe of a man's
reafon, confidering that God is the *firft and chiefeft*
good ; goodnefs is his prime perfection : and the relation that we ftand in to God, confidering that we
were not made in the height of angelical perfection
but liable to temptation from our bodies, and to
mifreprefentations from our fenfes. And in this nothing elfe is propofed, but that which a man, in the
ufe of his reafon would think fit, and would do if
he be of any good difpofition, whether he were enjoined it or not. He would revoke an error, renounce what he hath done amifs, deprecate the offence

fence of his fuperior, and return to his duty. This
is *fatisfactory* to the reafon of a man's mind ; and
reftorative to us, to our natural principles. Then,

2. Thefe I fay are certain, fixt, immutable and unchangeable becaufe clear either in reafon, or revelation, or both. And then becaufe they are fuitable
and *connatural* to the regenerate ftate ; and we cannot fail in thefe, unlefs we defert our own natures.
For if we be in the regenerate ftate, there is the *feed
of God* in us, and good nature towards God, and all
in a reconciliation with God. And for thefe two reafons, they that are fincere, or any ways confiderable
in religion in thefe things, they are alike minded.

But in things of an *inferior nature*, they may per-
chance think otherwife one than another, and otherwife than the truth is, and as they ought to think.
But in *thefe* great things, *as many as be perfect are thus
minded.* And they that be fo, though in other matters they may not think alike, yet *God fhall reveal this
unto them.* Now I will fhew you, how it comes to
pafs, that they, which do agree in the main, may in
other matters think otherwife one than another, or
than the truth is.

1. From the creature's *fallibility* and liablenefs to
be miftaken. And fo I underftand that fcripture,
Rom. iii. 4. *Let God be true, and every man a liar.*
Not that every man is a liar, or tells that which is
falfe, for fuch are incapable of the kingdom of heaven ;
but thus ; God is immutable and infallible, man is not
fo, but liable to error and miftakes : not that he
actually lies, but may be miftaken. And our fallibility and liablenefs to miftake is grounded in three
things :   1, Partly

1. Partly the *fhortnefs* of our *principles.*

2. Partly alfo the *diftance* of *objeɑs.*   And

3. Partly from the *mifreprefentation* of them to our *fenfes.*

Firft, The *fhortnefs* of our *principles..* We are but of finite perfections.   Then the *diftance* of *objeɑs* from our faculties ;, and therefore from an undue diftance, we differ in many things.. And, then *mifreprefentation* to our *fenfes..* We do by our reafon rectify the errors of *fenfe,* and know things by our rational faculties otherwife than they appear to our fenfes.   But, this is the truth of the cafe ;. neither by virtue of God's creation at firft, nor the grace of regeneration by Chrift, can we fecure an abfolute certainty and exemption from all error and miftake, And the reformed church doth not pretend to any fuch perfection, and infallibility. What we fhall *be* when we come into the heavenly kingdom, we do not know now ; but this we may determine, that the nearer we approach to God, the more exempt we fhall be from error or miftake : and we do approach nearer and nearer unto God, by *imitation of him,* * and participation of his nature, and by becoming like to him in holinefs, purity and righteoufnefs.   That is the firft thing,. our *fallibility.*

2. Accidental *prejudice* againft fome truth.. There is a prejudice lies upon feveral of us againft feveral truths, upon feveral accounts.

1. By virtue of *education,* that which is wrought in us by education, is like a colour in grain, or laid in.

---

* Similitudine appropinquamus deo, diftamus diffimilitudine.

in oil, that will not wear out or change. Any truth hath great disadvantage, if the subject hath been long possest of the contrary to it. It is a harder matter to throw out than at first not to admit. This is certain, that which is fair enough to satisfy ingenuity, will not be sufficient to take any man off from an opinion. And that is the first thing, *prejudice* by virtue of *education.*

2. Prejudice from *converse,* and compliance with those that we keep company with. For it is mightily taking with men, and they are very prone to comply with those they take pleasure in. It is observed that *a man's companion finds him such as he is, or makes him such :* therefore we say, if you know not what a man is in himself, you know him by the company that he keeps, and by those whose company he takes delight in. For converse is of a moulding and transforming nature : and it will be as it were two *bodies in one soul* especially where persons are cloathed with an high credit, reputation, and esteem of religion. And it is a mighty temptation to any one to refer himself, and run blindfold into the judgment and practice of that man, whom he hath a high reverence and esteem of as to religion.

A *Third* accidental prejudice against truth is this : *a common supposition,* common sense. We take it for an *apology* for many worthy men in the former ages of the church ; who yet lived, and for ought we know died in some error ; that they *did err, by the error of the times :* they had common errors, but no proper and particular error. If a man do not take heed to himself, he will worship one idol or another ;

er ; either the idol of general imagination, or elfe he will do as fools and conceited perfons, worfhip the idol of their own particular fancy. Then the temptation to modefty, and the advantage that we give to community and common-fenfe, will oft put a good man to it ; and make him afk himfelf this queftion and thus to reafon with himfelf; *How come I to depart from the community of others ? Why do I imagine that the holy fpirit did leave the community and join it felf to me ?* So that, he will have a difadvantage from his own good difpofition. And then we fee that the reafon of many men agreeing together is one of the beft things in the world. And *vox populi,* is *vox Dei.*

A *fourth* accidental prejudice is this ; a great *conceit and fuppofition* that it is fo : this poffeffing the minds of men that *it muft needs be fo,* makes them confident, and neglective of fearch, and enquiry. And, when reafon cannot over-rule imagination, no good is to be done. For many men are fo tranfported with imagination, that no man's reafon can have admiffion. And under this, fome men have lain all their days, and by reafon thereof were never in a difpofition of enquiry.

A *fifth,* There is a mighty difadvantage to truth in fome ; from their *bodily temper. Melancholy* tempers, and difpofitions, are many times, great hindrances to the truth. And if you would relieve their minds, you muft mend their bodies by medicine. Thefe men are highly to be pitied, and to be dealt with long patience and fupplied day by day with rational fuggeftions. For it is a hard matter in this

cafe,

cafe, where the bodily temper is a rule to the fentiments of the mind to do any good by the dictates of reafon.

A *fixth* difadvantage, is *weaknefs of parts.* Thus we find, 'tis eafier to convince a man of the nobleft fpirit, of the higheft parts, and moft refined morals, and the moft perfected intellect, than one that is weak and conceited ; for *it is rare but weak and wilful is the compofition.* But he that hath any perfection, he loves to hear, and to be better inftructed, and to have things fairly propofed. The nobleft fpirits, and moft tractable and teachable, they fooneft apprehend, and moft ingenuoufly and impartially confider. The weakeft do moft hardly lay down an opinion. Wherefore the apoftle bids us, that we fhould *not admit thofe that are weak in the faith, to any doubtful difputations.*

Now all thefe are *excufable* things ; and men that do fall fhort of truth, or are in miftake upon any of thefe fix accounts, there is pity due to them, and much chriftian moderation and forbearance ; and they are to be relieved by our prayers and good fuggeftions day after day ; now a little and then a little ; now a hint, and then a hint offered to them, as they can bear it.

But I muft fuperadd *one more :* and indeed, I am afhamed to fpeak thereof ; for it is quite out of the way of ingenuity and fincerity, and doth not belong to any one that is a lover of truth ; and it is fo bad, that I cannot fo far fail in charity, as to faften it upon any particular perfon ; but yet it doth take place among men ; and that is *affectation of fingularity.*

larity, and *worldly intereft.* When a man would be
the *head of a party* ; when a man thinks if he goes
the common way, he fhall be *but one of many,* and
not regarded ; and then he is tempted to be fingular in fomething, that fo he may be look't upon as
a fingular perfon, and of greater underftanding than
the reft of men. *But this is not the fpot of God's
children.* Deut. xxxii. 5. This man truly is in a
faction : this is unduly to *practife upon truth* ; and
quite out of the way of religion and fincerity, and I
have no apology for this man : for I cannot think a-
ny man fincere in his way, or to have a good confcience to God or love of truth in his heart, unlefs he
do verily believe that to be true, that he doth pretend to ; and that he doth believe it upon a com-
petent fearch, at leaft a true endeavour to be informed in the difference between true and falfe,
right and wrong. But for a man *to practife upon
truth, or any concernment of religion, to fubject it to worldly policy and worldly ends ; this* is fo unworthy a
thing, that nothing can be more. For our religion
is too noble and worthy a thing to be a *mean* to any
other thing than the honour of God, and the falvation of our fouls, and the good of the community.

End of the Firft Volume.

Printed in the United States
88813LV00005B/62/A